Globalization and Social Policy

Globalization and Social Policy

Nicola Yeates

SAGE Publications
London • Thousand Oaks • New Delhi

First published 2001

 SAGE Publications Ltd
6 Bonhill Street
London EC2A 4PU

SAGE Publications Inc.
2455 Teller Road
Thousand Oaks, California 91320

SAGE Publications India Pvt Ltd
32, M-Block Market
Greater Kailash – I
New Delhi 110 048

British Library Cataloguing in Publication data

A catalogue record for this book is available
from the British Library

ISBN 0 7619 6801 6
ISBN 0 7619 6802 4 (pbk)

Library of Congress Control Number available

Typeset by Mayhew Typesetting, Rhayader, Powys
Printed in Great Britain by The Cromwell Press Ltd,
Trowbridge, Wiltshire

For my mother, Jean Yeates,
and
in memory of my father, Ray Yeates (1921–2000)

In the ethical progress of man,
mutual support, not mutual struggle,
has had the leading part.

Kropotkin (1902)

Contents

Tables

Acronyms and Abbreviations

ACP (states)	African, Caribbean and Pacific (states)
ANZCERTA	Australia and New Zealand Closer Economic Relations Trade Agreement
APEC	Asia-Pacific Economic Co-operation (Forum)
ASEAN	Association of South-East Asian Nations
CARICOM	Caribbean Community and Common Market
CEFTA	Central European Free Trade Agreement
COMESA	Common Market for Eastern and Southern Africa
CPF	Central Provident Fund
CUSFTA	Canadian-US Free Trade Agreement
EU	European Union
FAO	United Nations Food and Agriculture Organization
FDI	Foreign Direct Investment
GATT	General Agreement on Tariffs and Trade
GDP	Gross Domestic Product
GNP	Gross National Product
GPA	Agreement on Government Procurement
ICFTU	International Confederation of Free Trade Unions
IDA	International Development Association
IFI	International Financial Institution
IGO	International Governmental Organization
ILO	International Labour Organization
IMF	International Monetary Fund
INGO	International Non-Governmental Organization
IPPF	International Planned Parenthood Federation
MAI	Multilateral Agreement on Investment
MERCOSUR	Mercado Común del Sur (Southern Core Common Market)
NAFTA	North American Free Trade Agreement
NGO	Non-Governmental Organization
NIC	Newly Industrialized Country
NSM	New Social Movement
OECD	Organization for Economic Co-operation and Development
PAYG	Pay-as-you-go
PWC	Post-Washington Consensus
RTA	Regional Trade Agreement
SADC	Southern African Development Community
SAP	Structural Adjustment Programme

SAPTA	South Asian Association for Regional Cooperation-Preferential Trade Agreement
TREMs	Trade-related Environmental Measures
TRIPs	Trade-related Intellectual Property Rights
TRIMs	Trade-related Investment Measures
TNC	Transnational Corporation
UNCTAD	United Nations Conference on Trade and Development
UNDP	United Nations Development Programme
UNESCAP	United Nations Economic and Social Committee for Asia Pacific
UNESCO	United Nations Educational, Social and Cultural Organization
UNFPA	United Nations Population Fund
UNHCR	United Nations High Commission for Refugees
UNICEF	United Nations Children's Fund
UNRISD	United Nations Research Institute on Social Development
USAID	United States Agency for International Development
WB	World Bank
WHO	World Health Organization
WTO	World Trade Organization

Web-Site Addresses

Centre for Research on Globalization and Labour Markets	www.nottingham.ac.uk/ economics/leverhulme
Council of Europe	www.coe.int
Corporate Watch	www.corporatewatch.org.uk
Direct Action Network Against Corporate Globalization	www.agitprop/artandrevolution/ fullstory.html
ESRC Centre for the study of Globalization and Regionalization	www.warwick.ac.uk/csgr
Global Exchange	www.globalexchange.org
Globalism and Social Policy Programme	www.stakes.fi/gaspp/
Group of 8 Information Centre (with University of Toronto)	www.g7.utoronto.ca
International Confederation of Free Trade Unions	www.icftu.org
International Council for Social Welfare	www.icsw.org
International Labour Organization	www.ilo.org/public/english/
IMF	www.imf.org/
Labour Solidarity Network	www.labournet.org
OECD	www.oecd.org
Public Citizen – Global Trade Watch	www.citizen.org/pctrade/ tradehome.html
Reclaim the Streets	www.reclaimthestreets.net
Transnational Institute	www.tni.org
World Bank	www.worldbank.org
WTO	www.wto.org

Acknowledgements

This book is the culmination of nearly a decade's work which began with my doctoral thesis on the social dimension of European integration. The following chapters now bear little resemblance to that work, but develop many of the ideas contained within it, principally the importance of an international political economy perspective and a multi-disciplinary approach to social policy. My treatment of globalization and social policy has inevitably had to be as broad-ranging as the topic itself and I have been acutely aware that one book cannot do justice to the full complexities of the subject. One of my principal objectives is to reassert the continuing importance of political struggle in shaping social development. In this spirit, it offers an important counterweight to a growing acceptance in many quarters of the inevitability of globalization and the irrelevance and futility of politics.

I would like to thank first and foremost Peter Townsend, who played a formative role in shaping my early ideas and who encouraged me to look at 'the bigger picture'. I also appreciate Bob Deacon, Paul Teague and Tomás Mac Sheoin for their interest in, advice and comments on this book, or various parts of it, at different stages – particularly to Bob for his persistent reminders that I 'need to get on with it as quickly as possible'! A number of the ideas presented here have benefited from attending the various Globalism and Social Policy Programme (GASPP) seminars (STAKES/University of Sheffield) since 1997. I would also like to acknowledge John Brewer, Madeleine Leonard, Marysia Zalewski and Mary Daly, in the School of Sociology and Social Policy at Queen's University, Belfast, who offered encouragement at crucial times during the writing of this book.

I also extend my thanks to Sage, particularly to Rosie Maynard, Karen Phillips, Louise Wise and Lauren McAllister and to various publishers for their permission to reproduce various tables used in this work. Some of the material appeared in 'Social politics and policy in an era of globalization: critical reflections', *Social Policy and Administration* 33(4) in 1999 and was reprinted in *Revue Belge de Sécurité Sociale* in 2000.

Nicola Yeates
Belfast.

Introduction

'Globalization' has become an established, if contested, term in academic and political debate. For some, the prevailing image of globalization as flows of capital, people and information is a welcome, even exciting, development which presents new opportunities; for others it casts a 'sinister shadow', an unfolding tyrannical rule of peoples by a totalitarian global economic regime (Hay and Watson, 1999; Teeple, 1995). Whatever one's position on globalization – enthusiastic, revisionist or sceptical – the reality of what may now be called 'globalization studies' is undeniable. Globalization is said to herald profound changes to the objective reality of the world, our perceptions of the world and our lived experience; it pertains to global economic and political structures, but it also touches all our lives in multiple ways and in a range of spheres: in work, education, politics, family and leisure (Giddens, 1999). The far-reaching nature of the transformations that globalization is said to bring, or to have brought about, attributes to it an almost 'revolutionary' quality.

Social policy is a key arena in which the politics of globalization are fought out. Debates about the appropriate model of social development have risen in prominence on the agendas of supra-national and international institutions, while national social policies are (said to be) increasingly framed – if not steered – by 'globalization'. Central to globalization studies have been questions such as, how does global capitalism currently differ from previous periods? If it does differ, in what way? What are the implications for governments, employers, workers, communities, families, households and individuals? Regrettably, many of those who view globalization primarily as a matter of political economy have tended to read off its implications for welfare states from analyses of the changing status and power of the state; otherwise, the welfare functions and activities of states have been ignored altogether.

Academic social policy for its part has been traditionally oriented to the national sphere and, with the exception of the field of European social policy, has only relatively recently – since the mid 1990s – examined the global context of social policy development. Even so, an intellectual project around globalization and social policy among scholars in the 'core' countries has already spawned a great deal of work: Alber and Standing, 2000; Baldwin, 1997; Bonoli et al., 2000; Burden, 1998; Clarke, 2000; Deacon and Hulse, 1996; Deacon et al., 1997; Deacon, 1995, 1998, 1999a, 1999b, 2000a, 2000b; Esping-Andersen, 1996, 2000; George, 1998; Gough, 2000a, 2000b, 2000c; Jordan, 1998; Leibfried, 2000; Midgley, 1997; Mishra, 1996, 1999; Moran and Wood, 1996;

Navarro, 1982, 1998; Pierson, 1998; Rieger and Leibfried, 1998; Rhodes, 1996, 1997; Room, 1999; Scharpf, 2000; Standing, 1999; Stryker, 1998; Wilding, 1997 and Yeates, 1999. This project will undoubtedly continue to rapidly gather pace as the transnational sphere becomes more integrated into academic thought and parlance. This will require, *inter alia*, that social policy draws on a wider range of fields (e.g. international relations, development studies) and a wider range of countries (e.g. NICs and developing countries) than has traditionally been the case. The global political economy of welfare has been under discussion in development studies for far longer than in academic social policy in the West, and the integration of social policy analysis from the perspective of developing countries into analytical frameworks relating to advanced industrialized countries should prove fruitful (Deacon et al., 1997; Gough, 2000a; MacPherson and Midgley, 1987; Morales-Gómez, 1999).

This book is situated at the interface of 'globalization studies' and social policy. It aims to bring globalization into the study of social policy and social policy into the study of globalization. It is premised on the idea that only a global perspective can reflect the complicated 'geography of community' (Scholte, 2000) that shapes social policy. Central to this study is a critical reading of 'strong' globalization theory because of its influence within globalization studies. Briefly, 'strong' versions of globalization portray it as a techno-economic, naturalistic and inevitable force which erodes states' political powers, policy autonomy and their public policy role. Governments are depicted as coming 'under siege' from global capital and its institutional allies and as having no choice but to pursue social and economic policies that are compatible with the 'realities' of globalization and the 'needs' of the international business classes. Globalization is said to undermine 'mature' welfare states, particularly those with comprehensive state provision, and stall their development elsewhere.

My critique of this deterministic, reductionist narrative attempts to rescue questions of political agency and social conflict which, I contend, are crucial to any analysis of globalization and social policy. The basic approach of this book, then, views the relationship between social policy and globalization as a 'dialectical', or reciprocal, one. I show that far from states, welfare states and populations passively 'receiving', and adapting to, globalization, as portrayed by 'strong' globalization theory, they are active participants in its development. The discussion accordingly focuses on the ways in which social policies and politics contribute to, place limitations upon, and generally shape globalizing strategies, processes and outcomes. In this respect, I contend that globalization is best viewed as a process ultimately steered by a range of forces within and between countries.

The chapters are primarily organized around a critical examination of the claims of 'strong' globalization theory as they bear on social policy. Chapter 1 begins the study by outlining the different dimensions of globalization and highlighting some general issues raised within globalization studies. It considers what globalization potentially means for social policy and reviews various approaches to the study of globalization in relation to social policy. Chapter 2 examines in more detail empirical trends associated with, or commonly attributed to, economic globalization. Here, I demonstrate that although there are clearly changes in the structure of international trade, production and finance, the global economy is far less developed and more uneven than 'strong' globalization theory claims it to be. The emphasis in the following three chapters shifts to the political regulation of globalization, and the structures and processes of 'global governance'. Chapter 3 is concerned with the relationship between capital and national states, and it critically examines claims that the role and the power of the state have been substantially diminished by globalization. Here, it is shown that although states may have been 'decentred' they remain remarkably resilient and powerful actors, both globally and nationally. Chapter 4 examines international regimes governing capital, people and development, the involvement of international governmental organizations in social policy and the ways in, and the extent to which they steer the social policy process. Chapter 5 attends to issues of social conflict and political struggle and the importance of 'local' or 'internal' factors, including protest and opposition movements, in shaping the globalizing strategies of both states and capital. I show that these local factors play a decisive role in determining the timing, pace and effects of globalization. The study concludes with a summary of the principal arguments as they relate to the overall theme of the book.

On a final note, any analysis of the relationship between globalization and social policy necessarily has to be international in scope because the ways in which states engage with and 'receive' globalization differ according to their rank within the global political economy and according to their individual national histories, institutions and political power structures. Not all states have historically achieved the same levels of sovereignty, autonomy or regulatory capacities, produced the same strengths of civil society (Pérez Baltodano, 1999), or exhibited the same types of welfare provisions. Consequently, the ways in which they experience globalization, and their responses to it, can be expected to differ quite significantly. The discussion attempts to reflect and illustrate this by drawing on the different positions and experiences of countries in regions around the world – Western Europe, Central and Eastern Europe, East and South-East Asia, Latin America, North America and Africa.

1 Globalization and Social Policy: Mapping the Territory

Globalization is a central concept in this book, but my use of it is far from uncritical. It is important to recognize from the outset that globalization is a highly contested term, the frequent usage of which has tended to obscure a lack of consensus with regard to what it entails, explanations of how it operates and the directions in which it is heading (Gordon, 1987; Mittelman, 1996). As one observer has noted, 'the more we read about globalization from the mounting volume of literature on the topic, the less clear we seem to be about what it means and what it implies' (A. Amin, 1997: 123). Yet it could be argued that even to ask whether 'globalization' corresponds with a social reality, let alone analyse its implications for social policy, is to participate in sustaining a myth. It seems necessary therefore to begin by examining competing views of what globalization is and its analytical pitfalls and possibilities, both in its own right and as applied to social policy.

Spheres and dimensions of globalization

At its most basic, globalization refers to an extensive network of economic, cultural, social and political interconnections and processes which routinely transcend national boundaries. Petrella (1996) has usefully isolated seven types of globalization, along with their main elements and processes (Table 1.1). No doubt further 'globalizations' will appear in future.

Various approaches to globalization are visible in the literature. One distinction is between qualitative accounts that emphasize lived experience and identity, and quantitative accounts that stress the reality of the structures of the world polity and economy (Wolff, 1991). Another distinction is between macro and micro perspectives on globalization (Hout, 1996). The macro perspective locates the underlying forces driving globalization at the level of intersecting economic, technological and political forces. The micro-perspective emphasizes changes taking place at the level of firms and their business environments and notably moves towards the post-Fordist, 'flexible' system of corporate and inter-firm organization. The macro-perspective can be found in the work of sociologists, economists and political scientists; the micro-perspective is more often found in the work of those with backgrounds in business

Table 1.1   *Globalizations*

Category	Main elements/processes
1 Globalization of finances and capital ownership	Deregulation of financial markets, international mobility of capital, rise of mergers and acquisitions. The globalization of shareholding is at its initial stage.
2 Globalization of markets and strategies, in particular competition	Integration of business activities on a worldwide scale, establishment of integrated operations abroad (including R&D and financing), global sourcing of components, strategic alliances.
3 Globalization of technology and linked R&D and knowledge	Technology is the primary catalyst: the rise of information technology and telecommunications enables the rise of global networks within the same firm, and between different firms. Globalization as the process of universalization of Toyotism/lean production.
4 Globalization of modes of life and consumption patterns; globalization of culture	Transfer and transplantation of predominant modes of life. Equalization of consumption patterns. The role of the media. Transformation of culture in 'cultural food', 'cultural products'. GATT rules applied to cultural flows.
5 Globalization of regulatory capabilities and governance	The diminished role of national governments and parliaments. Attempts to design a new generation of rules and institutions for global governance.
6 Globalization as the political unification of the world	State-centred analysis of the integration of world societies into a global political and economic system led by a core power.
7 Globalization of perception and consciousness	Socio-cultural processes as centred on 'One Earth'. The 'globalist' movement. Planetary citizens.

Source: Petrella, 1996.

administration and managerial economics, although it also features in work by geographers and other social scientists tracing the expansion of contracting networks (Gereffi and Wyman, 1990).

Economic globalization entails the 'emergence of new patterns in the international transfer of products and knowledge' (OECD, 1996a: 19), and refers to changes in capital and labour flows, production systems and trade in goods and services. Commonly used indicators of economic globalization are trends in international trade (imports and exports), foreign direct investment (FDI), international finance and corporate alliances and networks. International trade and investment is not only said to have become a structural feature of national economies (albeit to different degrees across economic sectors and countries), but the territorial basis and structure of capitalist production and accumulation is considered to have spread throughout the world via the development of global capitalist structures and activities. Transnational corporations (TNCs) are held to be driving agents in this 'globalization' of production and finance, operating on a transnational or global basis in terms of product design, sourcing, production, marketing and sales. They are believed to operate within a global economy in which all aspects of the economy – from raw materials extraction to distribution – are integrated and interdependent, and the dynamics of which are separate from the interaction of separate national economies (Bretherton, 1996).

Cars are an example of a global product. These are no longer produced in, or identified with, any single country, and their components are produced in factories across the world and imported for assembly. Credit cards are an example of a 'global service', serving specialized and high-value world markets, based on clusters of advanced technologies (data processing, advanced materials, telecommunications) and managed by globalized organizations (Petrella, 1996). The example of credit cards illustrates the central role that technology is deemed to play in enabling globalization. The spread of information and communications technologies and networks, notable examples of which are the internet and satellite broadcasting, is viewed as a primary catalyst of globalization, since they have been central to the operations of transnational capital. Electronic technology has transformed the quantitative possibilities of transferring cash and money capital into qualitatively new forms of corporate and personal financing, entrepreneurship and credit systems (Sklair, 1998a: 8).

These new technologies have produced communications systems which are 'instantaneous in effect and global in scope' (Bretherton, 1996: 4). They not only link national markets and systems, but are also thought to have contributed to (a perception of) the 'compression' of time and space and the 'shrinking of the world' into a 'global village' (Giddens, 1990; Harvey, 1989; Robertson, 1992). Thus, communications networks mean that 'local happenings are shaped by events occurring many miles away' (Giddens, 1990: 64). New technologies also enable migrant workers, refugees and displaced people, to maintain social relationships across the globe, while problematizing the maintenance of national boundaries and loyalties (Albrow et al., 1997; Verhulst, 1999). Here, technology is seen to be transformative of identity. Ethnographic studies have emphasized the transformation of the notion of community, from one which privileges the local to one which includes virtual communities or neighbourhoods (Elkins, 1999), and have described migrant communities whose cultural identity is constructed and maintained by transnational sources and technologies (Albrow et al., 1997). Smith effectively sums up the consequences of these developments:

The blurring of previously accepted boundaries differentiating states, ethnicities and civil societies is producing new spaces of daily life, new sources of cultural meaning, and new forms of social and political agency that flow across national borders. (1995: 250)

The issue of identity has been a prominent theme in globalization because cultural studies was one of the earliest fields to embrace the globalization thesis. The *cultural* 'take' on globalization generally emphasizes the subjective side, or lived experience, of globalization. For Robertson, one of the first cultural theorists to analyse globalization, in the words of Wolff, 'it is primarily consciousness *of* and response *to* globalization which affects and permeates the lives of people and societies'. Basic to this version of globalization is a sense of global awareness – 'the scope and depth of consciousness of the world as a single place' (Wolff, 1991: 162, emphasis in original) – the idea that we are all 'planetary citizens' without distinction of nationality (or indeed, class, sex, gender, 'race'/ethnicity, (dis)ability or sexuality) and the growing discourses of globality that arise from this consciousness. Cultural studies also analyses globalization in terms of the cultural effects of the increased flow of peoples (migrant workers, refugees and tourists), ideas, information and images on a global scale. It is associated with commercial culture (film, popular music, TV) through flows of media and communications. Some have questioned whether a 'global culture' is being formed, as the transmission of Western (US) culture through commercial channels is seen to dilute or eliminate local cultural forms. Thus, the same technology that has been instrumental in the globalization process is also accused of facilitating global cultural imperialism through the centralization of control of the mass media in the hands of Western media conglomerates and the transmission of Western values throughout the world. However, despite claims that we are heading towards global cultural uniformity, there is a growing emphasis on how local cultures adapt and respond to globalizing influences, and how cultural difference and distinction is reasserted through, for example, ethno-nationalism and religious fundamentalism – cultural practices which also have strong political expressions.

Political globalization refers to the changing global context of political awareness, processes and activity (Holton, 1998: 109). At one level, claims are made that economic globalization leads to political freedom. As *The Economist* editorialized: 'Affluence, it seems, breeds democrats; just another benefit, as it happens, of rampaging global capitalism' (18/1/97: 14). More realistically, the development of the 'free market' leads to the development of the middle class globally, a class that proceeds to make democratic demands of previously authoritarian governments. Here, the democratization of previously national security states such as South Korea and Taiwan is cited as resulting from economic liberalization in those countries caused by their continuing engagement with, and integration into, the global economy.

At another level, globalization is said to have intensified transnational political interactions. In the same way that the global sphere is constituted by profound power transformations or differentiations of economic structures and processes (Kayatekin and Ruccion, 1998), so it is also said to be constituted by the differentiation of political-institutional structures and processes (Cerny, 1995, 1996). Bretherton defines political globalization as 'a growing tendency for issues to be perceived as global in scope, and hence requiring global solutions', as well as 'the development of international organizations and global institutions which attempt to address such issues' (1996: 8). Political globalization as 'globalism' thus refers to the growing awareness that social, economic and environmental problems are essentially transnational and global-systemic in their nature and that the resolution of these problems requires concerted, joint action by states and non-state agencies at the level of supranational and international institutions, organizations and agencies (Deacon et al., 1997).

Governments, TNCs, NGOs, social movements, trade unions, professional associations and trade associations are increasingly directing political action towards global arenas as well as national arenas in an attempt to influence how global capitalism and national territories are governed. The globalization of political action by NGOs, for instance, can be linked to social movements against globalization, while communities of interest are actively encouraged by supra-national agencies to consider themselves part of an international community of transnational politics and policy. As Meehan argues in the context of the EU, political action is

> now having to be carried out through a web of common institutions, states, regional and local authorities and voluntary associations on the domestic front and simultaneously, in national and/or transnational alliances at the common level. (1992: 159)

Such alliances may consist of domestic interests, that may be antagonistic at times, against another state, or they may be based on a 'shared interest among civil associations in promoting a common policy against the wishes of their respective governments' (Meehan, 1992: 159). Thus, social politics and policies are no longer confined to the domestic sphere, or to the governmental sphere – if they ever were – and greater account must be taken of the transnational realm in charting the development of social policy, since social politics are fought out concurrently locally, nationally and internationally by state and non-state actors (Owoh, 1996).

A further theme of political globalization is the growing interest in understanding how states interact with the global political economy and the consequences of this for statehood itself (Buelens, 1999; Cerny, 1996, 1997, 1999; Green, 1997; Holton, 1998; May, 1998). Indeed, much of 'globalization theory hinges on the present and future role of the nation state as a political entity' (Green, 1997: 165). This debate has focused on the constraints imposed on sovereign states by international economic forces and agents (notably TNCs and IGOs) and the extent to which states are emasculated, fragmented, or restructured by them. Thus, globalization is considered to have weakened states due to the growth of alternative frameworks of community, compromising the state's previous capacity to monopolize the construction of nations or 'control many of the circumstances that spawn collective tendencies' (Scholte, 2000, 165–6). There is also thought to have been a qualitative shift of power away from governments towards non-state actors – notably business and industry, but also IGOs and NGOs – and some accounts present this as having occurred to the extent that the possibility of using state power as an instrument for promoting social justice is now far more limited (Pérez Baltodano, 1999).

This emphasis on the *loss* of state sovereignty and autonomy is not without its problems: it can be argued that constraints on state auto-nomy are hardly new – state managers have historically been con-strained in their freedom to decide, for example, what development strategies to pursue and how resources should be allocated (Weiss, 1997, 1999), while it can be asked how far the social policy of a country or locality was ever wholly shaped by national government policy (Deacon, 1999b). Moreover, any significant weakening of state autonomy and capacity may owe as much to 'domestic' institutions and pressures as to global ones (Pierson, 1994, 1998). Finally, the framing of statehood under globalization in terms of loss of autonomy tends to present any restric-tion on state power, be it from internal or from external sources, as undesirable, whereas it may be necessary to prevent, for example, human rights abuses or hold governments to account for such abuses.

One's views about the consequences of globalization(s) for states, welfare states and for the welfare of populations basically hinge on whether or not one accepts that a qualitative shift has taken place from the 'old' international order based on international relations primarily between nation states and separate national economies, to a 'new' order characterized by a unified global economy and by 'global relations between organized capitals' under which relations between national states are subsumed (Teeple, 1995: 74; Bretherton, 1996). It is specifically to the claims of 'strong' globalization theory that the discussion now turns.

'Strong' globalization: beyond the state

At its crudest, 'strong' globalization theory presents the global economy as dominated by uncontrollable global forces in which the principal actors are TNCs. States are structurally dependent on global capital while TNCs have unlimited freedom in choosing the most conducive, or profitable, terms and conditions for their investment and production operations. Since TNCs owe no allegiance to any state, they (re)locate wherever market advantage exists. It is important to note that 'strong' globalization theorists come from both the right and left, politically; the former celebrate what the latter condemn.

'Strong' globalization theory is highly economistic. The major advantages and disadvantages of globalization are expressed in economic terms, and global economic forces are assigned a determinant role in social change. Liberal theory presents globalization as the welcome loosening of political constraints upon economic production and exchange and as a force leading to greater political and economic integration worldwide. Globalization creates consumer choice and prosperity for all, but most especially for the consumer of commodities or services in the new global economy. Thus, the wonders of Disney, Coke and McDonald's are brought to those previously ignorant or deprived of them. Other benefits of globalization include greater ease of travel and communication, as well as an increased choice of lifestyle and consumption habits. The expansion of production and consumption on a global level can only lead to the greatest happiness, with all for the best in the best of all possible worlds. Moreover, free markets destabilize economically oppressive conditions and institutionalize more impersonal and efficient resource allocation processes. Improved competitiveness reduces the risks of an open economy and expands opportunities for material progress, regardless of initial inequalities (Ratinoff, 1999). Critical theory is also prone to economistic accounts of globalization, but regards it less as an integrative force than as a polarizing one with undesirable social, economic and political consequences locally and globally. Critical theory highlights global structures of power and inequality and in particular focuses on how globalization has created and/or underwritten the accumulation of wealth by the few and the impoverishment of the many, both between and within countries. As Hout, for example, argues, 'globalization involves an increasingly sharp division between "core" states who share in the values and benefits of a global world economy and polity, and "marginalized" states, some of which are already branded "failed" states' (1996: 168).

A major claim of 'strong' globalization theory is that globalization amounts not merely to the extension of capitalism on a global scale, but to the emergence of an integrated, or unified world economy which has a separate dynamic to that of national economies and which is not fully under the control of political institutions. Sklair, for example, depicts globalization as 'the emergence of truly global processes and a global system of social relations not founded on national characteristics or nation-states' (1998a: 1). Similarly, Meiksins Wood characterizes globalization as 'another step in the geographical extension of economic rationality and its emancipation from political jurisdiction' (1997: 553). Thus, globalization is portrayed as a qualitative shift in the development of capitalism:

> The history of capitalism has ceased to be defined by and limited to national boundaries. It would be wrong to draw the conclusion that the world has entered a post-capitalist era. The ownership of capital still matters and it still remains the dominant factor of economic and socio-political power in the world. The great change that is occurring is not between a capitalist and post-capitalist society, nor between a 'good' capitalism (the social market economy) and a 'bad capitalism' (the jungle, or 'casino' market economy). Rather, it is between a weakening of all aspects of a society founded on national capitalism and the growing power and dynamic of global capitalism. (Petrella, 1996: 68)

In short, 'strong' globalization theory holds that there has been a dramatic shift in structural power and authority away from states towards non-state agencies and from national political systems to global economic systems (Strange, 1996). A broad distinction can be made within 'strong' globalization theory between those who frame this shift primarily in terms of the transformation of the state and those who frame it primarily in terms of class struggle.

The transformation of the state

For many analysts, the transformation of the role and structures of the state lies at the heart of the globalization process (Cerny, 1996; May, 1998). However, the nature of this transformation is disputed. For economic globalists, such as Ohmae (1995a, 1995b), the 'problem' of the state in the global economy is that it is an encumbrance: states distort global capital flows, get in the way of trading and are too small to manage the global economy. Since the territoriality of states presents obstacles to efficiency in a common, global market, they will eventually be superseded by political institutions more suited to today's 'borderless' economic geography, it is claimed. In contrast, for economic nationalists and the political left the 'problem' of the state in a global economy is primarily one of its emasculation: its political authority, sovereignty and policy autonomy have been supplanted by transnational structures and processes over which it has little, if any, control.

Certainly these analysts are correct in pointing to the emergence of a more complex, and less state-centred global political order. First, states' traditional functions and policy competences have been redistributed 'up' to the supranational level, 'down' to lower- or upper-level state institutions and 'across' to the market (Keil, 1998; May, 1998; Strange, 1996). Second, compared with the 'old' internationalized order, the national state has 'retreated' from a position of being the principal actor to being just one among many other non-state actors which include the following: TNCs, international bureaucracies, outlaw business organizations (drug cartels, the mafia); professional associations; media and communications organizations; transnational authorities in the fields of sports, art, music, and transnational social, political and religious movements. Like the state, these compete to set norms, values and customary procedures and influence the distribution of resources globally and subglobally (Strange, 1996: 32). Thus, states are no longer the highest level of political authority, the exclusive subject of international law, sole mediators of domestic politics, nor are they necessarily the principal representative of their populations (Sassen, 1998).

The nature of these institutional and organizational changes in the way that territories, populations and trade are governed has been taken as evidence by 'strong' globalization theory that states have not merely been *accompanied* by other actors, but that they have been *overshadowed* by them, particularly by capital. This is a crucial distinction. Many scholars of globalization would accept that politics is no longer confined to the national sphere and that the political order has become more 'polycentric'; states are 'merely one level in a complex system of overlapping and often competing levels of governance' which link the local and global spheres (Hirst and Thompson, 1996: 183; see also Cerny, 1999). However, strong globalization theory contends that this polycentrism has *significantly* eroded the power of states and governments to shape domestic affairs. As one commentator insists, 'state policy *is* becoming more driven by external forces' (A. Amin, 1997: 129, emphasis in original). External forces are increasingly shaping state policy as a result of growing interdependence and competitiveness; governments are required to be 'other-regarding' of each other's decisions, policies and actions, and must yield to the sheer economic and political power of global actors (notably, TNCs and IGOs). Indeed, globalization is deemed to have 'penetrated the walls of sovereign states, linking national histories with world history', the result of which is 'the end of national politics as a domestic activity capable of determining a society's future' (Pérez Baltodano, 1999: 40). Thus, states are not only more permeable to the influence of 'external' forces, but these forces are increasingly determining the course of national development, irrespective of the needs or wishes of electorates. States' powers are further diminished by attempts to promote coordination among them (in order to regain some modicum of control) because transnational regimes have increasingly developed the capacity to operate autonomously of the states that founded them.

This 'crisis' of the state is often presented as a democratic crisis (Martin and Schumann, 1997). 'Strong' globalization theory is in no doubt about the extent to which globalization represents an attack on democratic institutions:

> corporations . . . have gained additional scope for action and power *beyond* the political system. Over the heads of government and parliament, public

opinion and the courts, the balance-of-power contract that characterized the first modernity of industrial society is now being terminated and transferred to the *independent realm* of economic action. (Beck, 2000: 4, emphasis in original)

International trade and investment bear a disproportionate amount of influence over the direction and content of national policy, so much so that governments are as, if not more, sensitive or 'accountable' to the requirements of international capital as to their electorates. Not only have corporations and international institutions escaped the clutches of democratic political systems, but the deregulatory 'logic' of globalization leads to the dismantlement of social and labour regulations – regulations which are the outcome of centuries-old democratic struggle – and the erosion of democracy itself:

> the attempt on the part of capital to undo these gains of democratic struggle by denationalizing the economy and thus moving economic policy beyond the pale of democratic decision-making appears as a major, if covert and indirect, assault on democracy. (Mishra, 1999: 108)

Class struggle

Those who characterize globalization as the supersession of national capitalism by globalized capitalism tend to frame their arguments primarily in terms of class struggle between capital and labour (Fox Piven, 1997; Navarro, 1982). Thus, for Robinson, capitalist globalization not only represents the 'liberation' of private capital from political regulation as 'the old nation state phase of capitalism is superseded by the transnational phase of capitalism' (1996: 18), but it also denotes a new stage in the class war:

> It was incubated with the development of new technologies and the changing face of production and of labour in the capitalist world, and the hatching of transnational capital out of former national capitals in the North . . . This war has proceeded with transnational capital being *liberated from any constraint on its global activity.* (Robinson, 1996: 13–14, emphasis added)

It is important to note this emphasis on globalization as a *new stage* in class conflict, rather than as the end of class conflict and its replacement by concerns about economic efficiency and enlarged consumption. Sklair (1997) argues that globalization is the result of a social movement *for* globalization by the global ruling class – the 'transnational capitalist class' (TCC). The TCC sponsors transnational practices in the economic sphere through corporate executives of multi-nationals and their local affiliates; in the political sphere through globalizing state bureaucrats, capitalist-inspired politicians and professionals; and in the cultural-ideological sphere through consumerist élites such as merchants and the media. The emergence of the TCC is said to have rearticulated class relations at the national level, and in two key respects. First, capital's freedom to roam the world in search of the most favourable production and accumulation conditions has greatly enhanced its power over standards of living of 'immobile' workers, particularly the working classes, in the core countries. Second, globalization has entailed 'the integration of Southern capitalists into the emergent system of trans-national capital' (Robinson, 1996: 28). Thus, it is primarily the urban rich in both the rich and poor countries alike who are the primary bene-ficiaries of globalization, and the working classes, especially in rural areas, who are its losers (Korten, 1995). These accounts are correct in emphasizing the continuing importance of political, indeed class struggle, but are fundamentally mistaken in their apparent insistence that transnational capital has been liberated from all socio-political restraints.

In summary, 'strong' globalization theory stresses the primacy of global, 'external' forces over national or 'internal' ones, and, relatedly, the primacy of economic forces over political ones. It stresses the exist-ence of a unified, 'borderless' economy in which deterritorialized capital flows freely between countries. Although it is generally accepted that capitalism has always been a global system (Moran, 1998) and that states' policies have historically been bound by parameters acceptable to it, 'strong' globalization depicts a qualitative erosion of states' political power and policy autonomy by the growing power of 'external', and largely economic, forces.

A range of counter-arguments can be made against 'strong' global-ization theory which cast serious doubt on claims about the diminished capacities of the state, the defeat of oppositional or regulatory political struggles, and the retrenchment of social policy as 'logical', inevitable outcomes of globalization. These criticisms are discussed throughout the different chapters of the book. The next section of this chapter highlights some *general* problems with the concept of 'globalization', while the subsequent sections examine the relevance and use of a global(ization) perspective in social policy analysis.

The use and misuse of globalization

'Globalization' comes with a number of reservations and limitations of which it is important to be aware. One problem with globalization is the wide diversity of its definition and use — including its use without definition – and the large number of disciplines in which the concept is being explored. Globalization seems to offer strong explanatory powers for analysts in a wide range of disciplines, judging by the enormous literature which now exists on the subject within the disciplines of political science, economics, geography and sociology and within the fields of business administration, managerial economics, urban studies, cultural and media studies, international relations, development studies and, most recently, social policy. The definition of globalization may vary subtly (or not) between disciplines and fields of study, and the intellectual traditions using the concepts have different histories and inherited structures of thought and analysis, so the possibilities for misunderstanding multiply. Even among those writing on economic globalization, 'it is far from evident that [they] are referring to the same sets of events and issues . . . different referents have been drawn upon to pin down the meaning of "globalization"' (Allen and Thompson, 1997: 213).

A second problem is that globalization is one of a range of competing terms to describe the current state of the world political economy. Alongside 'globalization' sit, with varying degrees of comfort, the following terms: 'transnationalization' (national boundaries no longer define the limits of economic exchange or political activity); 'multinationalization' (the transfer of capital through the setting up of production abroad); 'internationalization' (exchanges of capital, people, ideas between two or more states); 'universalization' (the spread of people and cultural phenomena around the planet); 'liberalization' (the removal of regulatory barriers to international exchanges or transfers); 'Triadization' (the concentration of economic, political and technological development in the most 'advanced' regions of the world – the US, Western Europe and Japan and, to a lesser extent, East Asia); 'Westernization' (the homogenization of the world along particularly American lines); and 'regionalization' (the development of world-regional trading blocs involving significant internal divisions of labour, such as EU and NAFTA) (Hout, 1996; Petrella, 1996; Scholte, 2000). It is often unclear whether these terms are used as synonyms for 'globalization'; whether they are meant to indicate something quite distinctive from globalization; or whether they are invoked to describe components of an overarching process called globalization.

Third, globalization is invoked both *descriptively*, to depict existing trends, processes and phenomena, and *prescriptively*, to advocate how the world should be developing (Wilding, 1997). For example, globalization is invoked by representatives and apologists of business interests as clear evidence of the need to remove trading restrictions in order to facilitate further transnational economic activity (Ohmae, 1995a, 1995b; OECD, 1996a). Such is the degree of conflation between description and prescription that 'globalization can be used to serve rhetorical objectives' and may be 'advocated or rejected merely to justify a particular strategy' (Ruigrok and van Tulder, 1995: 139).

A fourth problem with globalization studies is that the empirical basis of the discussion is often less than prominent or even convincing. As a consequence of the debate being pitched at a highly rhetorical, even ideological level, it is difficult to ascertain to what extent the world economy is actually globalized, or to what extent it merely exhibits globalizing tendencies (Hirst and Thompson, 1996). A particular problem is that globalization is often discussed exclusively from the position of the advanced industrialized countries and/or from the perspective of economic, political and intellectual élites who are likely to have benefited from this 'shrinking world'. Thus, globalization usually tends to refer to the economic, political and institutional changes within and between the countries of the Triad where capital flows have been most intensive, to the neglect of countries situated outside the 'core'. Yet the relationship between the US and globalization differs from that of a European country, or from that of, say, an African or a Latin American country. Moreover, globalization may not mean the same thing to a city planner as it does to a production analyst, to a media studies specialist as it does to an international relations expert – and this is without even considering what the term may mean to a striking dock worker, state bureaucrat or entrepreneur.

Fifth, the application of globalization to explain a wide range of causes and effects has detracted from its potential as a useful explanatory factor of social change. While the political right prescribe 'more' globalization as the solution to many, if not most, social problems, the political left blame globalization as the primary cause of many, if not most, social problems – unemployment, poverty, rural depopulation, urban over-crowding, drug use and abuse, family change, ill health, crime, sex and labour trafficking. The analytical task of more clearly specifying global-ization as a project or a process, as well as its impact, is complicated by the problem of how to disentangle globalization from other social processes, such as modernization or industrialization (Crow, 1997), or how to distinguish the effects of 'globalization' from the effects of other trends, such as demographic and social change, the decline of Fordism or the collapse of the long-term boom (Wilding, 1997: 411). Furthermore, if a causal link between globalization and social policy is difficult to establish, so the effects of globalization are also difficult to identify because the full impact of globalization may be yet to come, while the wider environment and other factors may counteract any globalization influences that are at work (Gough, 2000b: 3–4). As Hay and Watson argue, 'it is possible to accept that the structures of the international political economy are in the process of being reconstituted without necessarily attributing causal influence in such a process exclusively to globalization' (1999: 418). In the social policy context, Pierson argues that 'to focus on globalization is to mistake the essential nature of the problem' (Pierson, 1998: 540). Although he acknowledges that globaliza-tion 'has undoubtedly accentuated and modified the pressures on welfare states in important respects', the real source of the problem lies at the national level – in the slowdown in the growth of productivity associated with the shift from manufacturing to services employment, coupled with the expansion and maturation of governmental commitments and a demographic shift to an older population (1998: 541). By this account, globalization may well be *associated* with welfare state change, but it cannot be attributed a causal, or determinant, factor in this change. It is to the relationship between globalization and social policy that the discussion now turns.

Globalization and the study of social policy

Notwithstanding the reservations and limitations of globalization that have just been outlined, used carefully, a globalization perspective offers fruitful avenues for social policy analysis as it does for the social sciences generally:

> The inspiring capacity of globalization is precisely that it forces social scientists to critically reflect upon how they construct their objects and to search for more appropriate fields of investigation which take into account people's actual entanglement in wider processes. (Geschiere and Meyer, 1998: 603)

Globalization implies that social policy has to be studied from both a national and a transnational perspective (Ratinoff, 1999). The core emphasis of social policy as a field of academic study has traditionally been concerned with the organization, delivery and consumption of welfare services at the national level. Globalization 'disrupts the "national" focus of attention' (Clarke, 2000: 201) and forces us to 'think globally'. This has a number of consequences.

It focuses attention on the ways in which individuals, families, communities, regions and countries are embroiled in international and transnational structures and processes. It requires us to consider that the causes of social problems – and their solutions – are not necessarily confined to national institutions and structures (Pérez Baltodano, 1999). The global structure of production and trade, for example, bears on national systems of economic security and inequality through its effects on the structure of employment, the distribution of unemployment, family structures, the gender division of labour, and the degree of income inequality. The global causes of increasing mobility of people internationally, which may be manifested in the North as 'social problems' of migrants, refugees and asylum-seekers, can be seen to lie in uneven development and geo-economic inequality.

Thinking globally also requires us to think much more *comparatively* to reveal the national particularities that mediate the relationship between national (and sub-national) and global structures. This in turn requires a recognition that social policy, as expressed in the advanced industrialized countries, is not universally applicable. Comparative social policy has tended to focus on social policies in the advanced industrialized countries, and latterly the newly industrializing countries, to the neglect of the much wider variety of arrangements, formal and informal, in place around the world for securing human health and welfare. Extending the remit of social policy analysis to the developing countries would, in addition to recognizing this diversity: facilitate a better comprehension of the political, economic, demographic and cultural factors in social policy development; highlight the marginalization of welfare considerations in developing countries by governments of industrialized countries; heighten awareness of the global political and economic forces to which all countries are subject; and draw attention to the variety of ways in which states receive and respond to these forces (MacPherson and Midgley, 1987).

In one sense, of course, there is no great originality in suggesting that we have to 'think globally' to understand social policy development. Welfare state-building in the advanced industrialized countries throughout the nineteenth and twentieth centuries occurred within an internationalized economic and political order, which was characterized by a high volume of international trade and economic interdependence and developed international monetary and exchange rate regimes. During this time there was also a substantial international transfer of policies. The economic and political relationship between colonial powers (e.g. Britain) and their colonies (e.g. Ireland, Australia, Canada, India, Hong Kong) is central to understanding the historical development of social policy in the latter, with the colonial power 'exporting' welfare ideologies and systems to the colonies (which still bear the legacy of that particular international order today). Japan imported Western models of welfare as early as the 1870s (Goodman, 1992), and Western thinking has also influenced the development of welfare in Taiwan and Korea (Goodman and Peng, 1996). Moreover, the 'golden era' of welfare state-building – 1950s to 1970s – in Western Europe took place within a context of post-war economic aid and development sponsored by the US through the Marshall plan, an early example of a structural adjustment programme (Milward, 1994). Development studies, for its part, has highlighted how the welfare of populations in developing countries has long had an explicit relationship with the global political economy insofar as they have been 'ignored' by globalizing capital (e.g. much of Africa), the object of globalizing strategies by Western transnational corporations in search of cheap, 'flexible' labour, or the objects of 'development' strategies by the IMF, World Bank and UN. Indeed, globalization theory's concerns with the relatively recent erosion of the policy autonomy of states in the advanced industrialized countries by external forces, is predated some 20-odd years by dependency theory, which attributes a pivotal role to international actors and institutions in shaping national policy strategies in developing countries.

However important and fruitful comparative analysis is, it is also crucial to recognize the influence of international institutions over social policy and welfare: in the words of UNRISD while 'many of the most serious social and economic problems certainly remain at the local or national level . . . people's life chances are also being fundamentally affected by decisions taken in international forums' (UNRISD, 1995: 168). The integration of a global perspective in social policy requires it 'to change gear from a focus solely on national and comparative social policy to a focus that gives equal weight to supranational and global social policy' (Deacon et al., 1997: 8). Globalization emphasizes both the international dimension of human welfare and focuses attention on international institutions as social policy actors in their own right. International institutions such as the WTO, IMF, World Bank and UN system, and regional formations such as the EU and NAFTA, not only shape the parameters of domestic economic and social policy, albeit to different degrees across countries and regions, but actively engage in 'transnational *redistribution*, supranational *regulation* and supranational and global *provision*' (Deacon et al., 1997: 22, my italics). However, with the partial exception of the EU, which is still regarded somewhat as a specialist area of study within social policy, the role of supranational and international organizations in social policy development has, on the whole, been accorded negligible attention by Western social policy analysts. These institutions are regarded within academic social policy as part of the general 'background' rather than as actively shaping the conditions of economic and social development. However limited the social policies of international institutions may be, they are indicative of the ways and areas in which governments have agreed to cooperate and be bound, in principle at least, by international rule of law, be it in relation to trade or social protection or human rights. This focus on transnational policy formulation and implementation also draws attention to the new forms of collective action that are required to secure 'global public goods' – international financial stability, health, global distributive justice – and maximize human welfare around the world (Kaul et al., 1999; Scholte, 2000).

The merits of a globalization perspective aside, its integration into the field of social policy poses questions about many of the assumptions, concepts and theories that have been integral to social policy analysis. Social policy as a field of academic study is ill-suited to thinking beyond the nation state as its theories and concepts were developed in a national context. If we accept Eade's contention that globalization entails 'the deterritorialization of traditional concepts, their diasaggregation and resynthesis' (1997: 5), then concepts such as class, community, identity, territory, justice, rights and citizenship may have to be fundamentally rethought in a global context:

> The classical concerns of social policy analysts with social needs and social
> citizenship rights becomes [sic] in a globalized context the quest for supra-
> national citizenship. The classical concern with equality, rights and justice
> between individuals becomes the quest for justice between states. The
> dilemma about efficiency, effectiveness and choice becomes a discussion
> about how far to socially regulate free trade. The social policy preoccupation
> with altruism, reciprocity and the extent of social obligations are put to the
> test in the global context. To what extent are social obligations to the other
> transnational? (Deacon et al., 1997: 195)

Even in the national context, globalization does not mean abandoning
traditional concerns and questions, but it does mean rethinking them.
For example, the mobility of peoples and cultures 'makes more visible
the tensions around the relationship between categories of nation,
"race", people and culture' (Clarke, 2000: 208). Formerly, these were
assumed to be more or less equivalent, but social and cultural mobility
has made the 'lack of fit' between these categories more evident and, as
Clarke notes, the 'realignment of people, cultures and identities within
and beyond nation-states have underlined the constructed and
contingent nature of "citizenship"' (Clarke, 2000: 209), and of the trinity
of nation, state and welfare more broadly.

Finally, one of the problems of 'globalizing' social policy analysis is
that it has developed in the North and is ill-suited in many ways to the
situation in developing countries. This is because 'welfare regimes in
[developing countries] are not the same game with different actors;
usually a different game is being played' (Gough, 2000a: 15). Thus
Gough argues that compared with OECD countries a 'wider range of
historical and institutional variables impinge on the welfare regime[s]' of
developing countries and neither a stable institutional framework, nor
the state as an autonomous site of strategic action, can be assumed.
Similarly a focus on traditional Western social programmes will miss
other policies, such as land (re)distribution, micro-credit schemes, agricultural and consumption subsidies and food security programmes, all
of which impact on the level and distribution of welfare (2000a: 14). This
is not to suggest that these definitional and conceptual issues constitute
insurmountable obstacles to comparing social policies globally, but it
does highlight that such comparisons require the reworking of frameworks developed in the context of Northern countries.

Approaches to the study of globalization and social policy

Three main approaches have been used to study globalization and social
policy. The first approach broadly entails examining the *impact* of
globalization on welfare states and social policies. It has received most

attention because it is of immediate public interest and because the national welfare arena is one where the politics of globalization are most publicly fought out. The second approach consists of examining the *contribution* that welfare states and policies have made to the current phase of globalization. The third approach examines the globalization of the social policy *process*. This section outlines the key tenets, merits and pitfalls of these approaches.

The impact of globalization on welfare states

The focus of this approach lies with the extent to and the ways in which globalization is implicated in systemic changes to the funding and structure of welfare states, particularly in the advanced industrialized countries. Globalization is said to have eroded the political, economic and social foundations of the Keynesian welfare state, altered the dynamics of welfare state development and severely curtailed the range of political strategies and policy options that can be pursued (Beck, 2000; Mishra, 1999; Perraton et al., 1997; Rhodes, 1996, 1997; Scharpf, 2000; Strange, 1996; Stryker, 1998).

Contemporary welfare state development is compared to the 'golden age' of welfare state-building which took place within an international regime of international supervisory institutions where states actively intervened to stimulate demand, growth and full employment through the controlled increase of the money supply, public expenditure and investment. This 'compromise of embedded liberalism' (Ruggie, 1983) allowed states to pursue domestic economic and social priorities, including international trade, albeit within parameters acceptable to international monetary (and trade) institutions. The nature of the contemporary global political economy renders the regulation and taxation of corporations and the provision of comprehensive social protection much more difficult for governments than was previously the case. Capital mobility increases the perceived risk, or the credibility of the threat, of flight abroad, while TNCs' strategies of tax avoidance, be it transfer pricing or the use of tax havens, reduce tax revenue available to fund public services; states themselves may forfeit potential tax revenue by lowering their corporate tax rates in order to attract investment. TNCs are able to play governments and immobile labour forces off against one another to negotiate the most favourable conditions for investment, production and taxation, 'punishing' countries and labour forces if they are deemed too 'expensive' or 'investment-unfriendly' (Beck, 2000). Indeed, the major casualties of capital mobility have been primarily male unskilled and low-skilled workers in labour-intensive manufacturing in the West, while the changing balance of power nationally between capital and labour manifests itself in the casualization of employment and declining wage levels and, by some accounts, the feminization of the labour force.

Issues of trade and international competitiveness have increasingly come to dominate both economic and social policy (Jordan, 1998; Mishra, 1996, 1999; Wilding, 1997). Social policy-making is framed by the *perception* of the logics and realities of the global economy and by *beliefs, values and assumptions* about national competitiveness in the global economy (Moran and Wood, 1996). If policy-makers believe, as many do, that there are real external constraints on public policy, that particular interventions will prompt speculation on the national currency, mass capital flight abroad, or a downturn in investment by foreign firms (FDI), then they will refrain from such interventions. As Jordan states,

> The idea of a global market is probably even more powerful than global forces themselves; governments believe that they are competing for prizes in budgetary rectitude before a panel of international financial institutions, and this affects their actions. (1998: 9)

Finally, the shift in power away from states (and labour) towards capital exacerbates the structural dependence of the state on all forms of capital, both domestic and (especially) foreign. This, it is said, is unravelling political support for governments' redistributive role (Rhodes, 1996) and 'prising open' national welfare states and the social pacts underpinning them:

> The premises of the welfare state and pension system, of income support, local government and infrastructural policies, the power of organized labour, industry-wide collective bargaining, state expenditure, the fiscal system and 'fair' taxation – all this melts under the withering sun of globalization and becomes susceptible to (demands for) political moulding. (Beck, 2000: 1)

Overall, the range of 'structurally-viable' strategic policy options available to governments is narrowed and individual governments are unable to affect the socio-economic outcomes they may desire or resist pressure to curtail activities that markets may not support (May, 1998). Two main scenarios for welfare states have been the focus of debate: welfare convergence and a 'race to the bottom'.

The *welfare convergence thesis* holds that as states become powerless to make 'real' policy choices, governments will be forced to adopt similar economic, fiscal and social policies. This is expected to entail the abandonment of comprehensive state welfare and redistributive policies and their replacement by deregulation, privatization and welfare residualization worldwide, leading to some form of convergence (Weiss, 1997). Geyer summarizes the convergence thesis well:

> Despite varying national contexts and the policies of differing political parties, the welfare states of the advanced industrial countries should become increasingly similar as the forces of globalization squeeze them into a market-

oriented welfare-state model. In essence it does not matter whether the national institutional contexts are conservative or social democratic, if the welfare state is conservative, liberal or social democratic, or if a leftist or rightist party is in power, the constraints have become so extreme that only market-conforming welfare-state structures will be allowed. (1998: 77)

Taylor-Gooby's summary of the 'new welfarism' similarly puts globalization in the driving seat of welfare state convergence:

Economic globalization, labour market flexibility, more complex patterns of family life and the dissolution of traditional class structures require a new welfare settlement. Since full employment, redistribution and expensive universal services are no longer seen as feasible, the new welfare can only justify social spending as investment in human capital and the enhancement of individual opportunities. *Welfare states are all driven in the same direction by the imperatives of international competition.* (1997: 171, emphasis added)

Thus, the corollary of the enhanced bargaining power of capital is that states are locked in competition with one another to offer incentives to the next corporate factory or call/service centre looking to locate or relocate its operations. Comprehensive welfare is said to be economically unviable in a competitive international economy where capital can pick and choose its location sites at will. Buffeted by the winds of global competition, states are expected to adopt social and economic policies which are most attractive to transnational capital and foreign investors. Governments will increasingly steer towards the political middle ground and stay clear of programmes of redistribution, renationalization or other forms of intervention of which capital and markets do not 'approve'. Defending the balance of payments, maintaining low inflation and stable exchange rates and pursuing fiscal austerity restrict the pursuit of expansionary economic and social policies, while state policy is more sensitive to the requirements and interests of international markets, potential foreign investors, the business agenda generally, and to the demands of international financial, trade and development agencies for 'credible' economic and social policies. It is more supportive of market forces generally, and more oriented to the promotion of entrepreneurship and innovation through education, training, support for R&D, assistance for small businesses and infrastructural improvements. Social security, taxation, employment and education policies are more oriented to improving the quality, supply, cost and docility of labour than with redistributing resources (S. Amin, 1997; Cerny, 1995, 1997; McMichael and Myhre, 1991; Mishra, 1999; Ratinoff, 1999; Reich, 1992; Shiva, 1997; Stryker, 1998). Governments which stray too far outside these parameters will be punished, electorally and economically, due to loss of investment and employment and will encounter lower credit ratings, higher interest rates on borrowing and currency speculation by international financial markets (Andrews, 1994; Goodman and Pauly, 1993; Stewart, 1994).

This, it is argued, essentially heralds the decline of social democratic reformist politics and projects upon which the welfare state was built (Teeple, 1995), and the convergence of social policy 'on a right-of-centre position with global capitalism driving policy rightwards' (Mishra, 1999: 55). As Ratinoff argues,

> social policy interventions are justified only under exceptional conditions, especially when human capital stock is inadequate to sustain economic growth or when the depth of inequities and discrimination prevent good governance. Both are broad enough to include most social programmes, but their exceptional nature opens the way for a more restricted and ideological view of public responsibility. (Ratinoff, 1999: 45)

Overall, national differences in welfare states are expected to become less marked as market-oriented, 'post-Fordist' welfare states become the dominant model. In some accounts the drive towards international competitiveness is leading states to adopt a more authoritarian role. Cerny (1996, 1997), for example, argues that we are witnessing the transmutation of the state from a 'civil association' into a more limited form of 'enterprise association' or 'competition state', the main task or function of which is the promotion of economic activities, whether at home or abroad. As the competition state focuses on one public role (economic) it downgrades or sheds many of its other public roles (welfare provision). However, states are required to be as, if not more, interventionist in regulating private providers as well as enforcing decisions or outcomes emerging from world markets and international agreements. As such, Cerny argues, the state is taking on 'a new and potentially undemocratic role' (1997: 258). Evans (1997) also foresees a 'leaner and meaner' kind of stateness. States will no longer deliver services that the affluent can buy privately although they will retain the more restricted institutional capacity necessary to deliver essential business services and security (domestic and global). Delivering security means devoting more resources to the repression of the more desperate among the excluded, both domestic and international.

The *race to the bottom* thesis was originally developed in the context of US federalism, and specifically in the context of environmental protection standards, in the mid 1970s (Cary, 1974). This holds that, in response to a perceived threat to their industrial competitiveness, states are likely to engage in behaviour which results in the lowering of their own standards. As each state responds and introduces sub-optimal policies in order to maintain competitiveness, so the overall level of welfare and protection is reduced (Esty and Geradin, 1998). In the welfare context, a race to the bottom occurs via competitive devaluation of social protection standards to make a country and its workers more attractive to investors (Alber and Standing, 2000). 'Social dumping', as it is also known, incorporates both the erosion of established levels of social protection as well as the arrested development of social protection and regulation. It is practised in markets and by governments. In the market sphere it involves the displacement of high-cost producers by low-cost producers and the relocation of firms to low-cost countries. In the governmental sphere it involves the displacement of the cost of social protection from the state and employers onto workers, households and their communities via social security and labour cost dumping. 'Social security dumping' refers to the restructuring of provisions – from universalism and social insurance to selectivism and social safety-nets – by shifting the burden of financing, while labour cost dumping entails government policies, legislation or actions which enable firms to reduce their non-wage labour costs. These can include reducing obligations on employers, making it easier to allow firms to by-pass obligations, or imposing costs on import-substituting industries to encourage a shift to export-oriented industries and firms (Alber and Standing, 2000: 99–100).

Fears of social dumping have regularly surfaced in transnational fora, particularly at regional level. In the EU, during the 1980s, political debate focused on the greater ability of producers to relocate within the EU and, coupled with greater price competition, it was argued that this would exert pressure on governments in high-cost countries to dismantle their labour and social rights in order to attract investment (Mosely, 1990). This gave rise to a protracted debate and a range of proposals to regulate social dumping at EU level, the outcome of which was the non-binding Charter of the Fundamental Social Rights of Workers (1989). Canadian workers expressed similar fears in relation to the impact of CUSFTA on their social standards, believing that their higher level of social protection would render them less 'attractive' to investors and employers than workers in America, particularly those in the Southern states. Similarly, opposition to NAFTA on the part of US trade unions was based on the fear that wages and working conditions would be 'competitively devalued' as a result of extending the common market in labour, goods and services to include Mexico with its low wages, poor working conditions and absence of trade union rights (Mishra, 1999). 'Social dumping' has also been among the anticipated effects of global, not just regional, economic competition on welfare provisions. Competition between the 'core' countries and the NICs of East and South-East Asia and the countries of Central and Eastern Europe is said to be used to justify the dismantlement of social welfare programmes in Western European countries (Matzner, 1998). Of note is that far less attention has been paid to the effects of international trade law on national welfare systems, although recent work in this area suggests it may have far-reaching effects on national social, health and environmental standards (see Chapter 4).

Overall, this account of the relationship between globalization and social policy stresses downward pressures on welfare states and the 'prising open' of social pacts underpinning them. The influence of 'strong' globalization theory's precepts and predictions is clearly evident in the way that the content of social policy is presented as being determined by 'external' – mainly economic – constraints, largely beyond the control of governments; that national political, cultural and social-institutional differences will simply be 'flattened' and social standards will plummet by the sheer 'weight' and 'force' of global economic forces. This presentation of globalization as pretty much single-handedly driving welfare state change is also problematic for the way in which it privileges capital and states and neglects the strategies of households, workers and communities as actors in the political process.

Social policy as a contributory factor of globalization

Whereas the first approach emphasizes how welfare states receive globalization, the second emphasizes the contribution of social policies to the globalization process. If globalization makes states (and social policies), then it is equally clear that states (and social policies) make globalization (Keil, 1998). Thus, for Rieger and Leibfried, the key questions are not so much how globalization undermines the autonomy of the state, unleashes a 'race to the bottom' or leads to welfare convergence, but instead 'what is the welfare state's contribution to the most recent wave of globalization', and 'what role does the internal transformation of developed welfare states play in the internationalization of trade, production, and investment' (1998: 365). This formulation of the relationship between social politics and globalization strikes a chord elsewhere in globalization studies. Herod (1997), for example, has argued in the case of the US, that far from workers being 'structurally defenseless' in the face of the global restructuring of capital, they have played a central role in the genesis and integration of the global economy: in essence, 'labor's structural position is not always and necessarily that of the passive victim of globalization' (1997: 169).

Rieger and Leibfried (1998) argue that social policy is a key factor which determines political action, affecting the degree of closure or openness of the national economy. In other words, social policy influences the circumstances under which open markets and economic change are perceived as opportunities to be broadly welcomed rather than unacceptably high risks to be resisted. By mitigating the economic and social impact of restructuring on the welfare of individuals, social policies provide the necessary 'political space' to relax closure vis-à-vis foreign markets and make a major contribution to social and political stability.

This approach starts from an historically grounded analysis of the relationship between national welfare states and the international economy. Rieger and Leibfried argue that social policy has been a contributory factor in economic globalization in the sense that it has assisted the integration of national economies into the world market in the 'developed' Western industrial societies during the post World War II period. By providing economic security outside the labour market for those affected by economic restructuring, welfare states have historically facilitated a shift in economic and industrial policy from closure (protectionism) to openness (free trade). They contend that 'the transformation of industrial societies to welfare states . . . became a foundation and guarantee of [economic] openness' (Rieger and Leibfried, 1998: 375), and that 'it was the institutionalization of income maintenance programs after World War II that enabled governments to switch to free trade policies' (1998: 365).

What distinguishes the current period from previous periods is that the *perceptions* of the consequences of the international economy for employment and income security have changed. International economic openness has come to be perceived as a risk by provider and claimant classes who depend on welfare states: global markets are perceived to 'dictate to national budget and finance policy' and place pressure on governments to cut public (welfare) expenditure and reduce the cost of labour. Insofar as a connection is made by groups dependent on welfare between further internationalization and further welfare cuts then this 'expresses itself as resistance to the open economy' and to policies that appear to further extend the 'open economy' into the national sphere. Thus, Rieger and Leibfried attribute to social policy a decisive role in determining the pace, timing and extent of globalization:

> The movement toward and the trends in a globalized economy have been triggered, contained, differentiated or modified, weakened or strengthened, and slowed down or speeded up through *national structures of social policy and their developments*, to the degree that these could replace protectionism (1998: 366, original italics)

The strengths of this approach are that it recognizes both the centrality of the state as a key creator, shaper and mediator of globalization as well as the historically recurrent moves towards the internationalization of the economy that more sophisticated accounts of globalization would also accept. In this respect, the emphasis rests on how states 'deploy' social policy as part of a broader strategy of economic and industrial development. It also emphasizes the role of social policies in the management of the social and political effects of this economic restructuring nationally. In addition, the strategic importance of social policy in facilitating (or impeding) globalizing strategies highlights the differential effect of 'globalization' on national welfare states, and indicates that a *variety* of strategies are likely to be adopted. Notably, it draws attention to the importance of values, beliefs, perceptions and political action in determining the extent to which states (and other actors) are able to adopt, formulate and successfully implement, globalizing strategies.

The globalization of the social policy process

Although social policy is still predominantly a national affair, cognizance is increasingly being taken of its transnational dimension: national social policy is influenced by the social politics and policies of state and non-state agencies at supranational and international levels. This has given rise to a new field of study – 'global social policy':

> Global social policy as a practice of supranational actors embodies global social redistribution, global social regulation, and global social provision and/ or empowerment, and includes the ways in which supranational organizations shape national social policy. (Deacon et al., 1997: 195)

The globalization of social policy is expressed in general agreements reached by participants (states and non-state actors) in international fora, such as the UN or G7 summits, as well as in the policy prescriptions of international institutions. This focus on the international institutional sphere and the policy process privileges the political rather than economic dimension of globalization. It emphasizes political-institutional *processes* linking the global, national and local levels as well as the consequences for the *content* of policy and the *structure* of provision. Within this approach, three 'streams' can be discerned: global social politics and policy prescriptions; global social regulation and provision; and transnational policy innovation and transfer.

Global social politics and policy prescriptions

A 'new' global political agenda with a substantial social content has emerged – global politics and policy have been 'socialized' while social politics and policy have been 'globalized' (Deacon, 1995; Deacon and Hulse, 1996; Deacon et al., 1997). The social politics of globalization are now fought out in the international political-institutional arena in addition to the national arena. The global arena is a strategically important sphere through which to advance particular interests, create public awareness of, and concern about, particular issues and influence how national territories are governed. Here, in addition to governments we find representatives of capital, labour and NGOs. NGOs, for example, have directed their actions at this sphere to shape the conditions which influence how their causes are addressed as well as international responses to global social and environmental problems. They are a significant force in constructing an alternative politics both at national and international institutional levels (Goodman, 1998):

> Non-governmental organizations (NGOs) have in increasing numbers injected unexpected voices into international discourse about numerous problems of global scope. Especially during the last 20 years, human rights advocates, gender activists, developmentalists, groups of indigenous peoples and representatives of other defined interests have become active in political work once reserved for representatives of states. Their numbers have enlarged the venerable, but hardly numerous ranks of transnational organizations, built around churches, labour unions and humanitarian aims. (Gordenker and Weiss, 1996a: 17)

Deacon et al. (1997) argue that the socialization of global politics reflects the growing preoccupation of governments and international bureaucracies with the best way of regulating global capitalism. The global arena has become a crucial battleground over which ideological and political struggles about the desirable model of welfare and the respective roles of the public, commercial and voluntary sectors are fought out. The work of Deacon and his colleagues has been pioneering in mapping the social policies of international institutions, and they have argued that:

> the social policy of a country or locality . . . is increasingly shaped . . . by the implicit and explicit social policies of numerous supranational agencies, ranging from global institutions like the World Bank and the International Monetary Fund, through supranational bodies such as the OECD and the European Commission, to supranational non-government agencies like OXFAM. (Deacon et al., 1997: 10)

Their work has proved invaluable in mapping the dominant discourses and policy positions of international institutions in relation to welfare states and in demonstrating the influence of these over national social policy. They show the apparent 'socialization of global politics' has not signalled the emergence of a unitary view or ideology either within or between international institutions about the role and future of welfare states (Table 1.2). This diversity in part reflects fractions of global capitalism, while the continued expression of varieties of capitalisms at the 'global level' warns us against apocalyptic interpretations of globalization as the end of history (Fukuyama, 1992), or as a unifying, hegemonic force rendering politics irrelevant and flattening national differences. On the other hand, what this work also confirms is that the range of welfare alternatives backed by these institutions is currently confined to variants of liberalism, and there is a marked absence of any international institution advancing a social democratic or redistributive agenda.

Table 1.2 *Global social policy discourse*

Orientation	Welfare World	Agency Promulgating
Existing welfare as:		
Burden	Liberalism (e.g. US, UK)	IMF, OECD
Social cohesion	Conservative, Corporatist (e.g. France, Germany)	EU, ILO, WB
Investment	(S.E. Asia)	OECD, WB
Redistributive commitment	Social Democracy (e.g. Nordic)	–
Emerging welfare as:		
Safety net	Social Liberalism	WB, EU
Work-fare	Social Liberalism	IMF
Citizenship entitlement	Futuristic	ILO, COE
Redistribution	–	–

Source: Deacon and Hulse, 1996.

Note: WB: World Bank; EU: European Union; ILO: International Labour Organization; OECD: Organization for Economic Cooperation and Development; IMF: International Monetary Fund; COE: Council of Europe.

Global social regulation and provision

International governmental organizations such as the World Bank, the IMF, OECD, UN and EU have done more than contribute to discussions about social policy; they have played an active role in social regulation and provision both directly and indirectly. Of all such institutions, including other regional formations, the European Union has the most extensive involvement both in relation to regulation and provision – through labour and social law, the structural funds and various social programmes. However, there have been important attempts at standard-setting at the international level in the UN and its satellite agencies, such as the ILO, while IGOs are also tangibly engaged in social provision through development assistance programmes of aid and relief and through health and population policies which are often delivered in 'partnership' with national and international NGOs. Finally, the WTO has emerged as a key actor in global social policy and debate in the 1990s as governments negotiated an extension of international trade and investment law to a wider range of sectors of the economy, including in the areas of public procurement and the provision of social subsidies in health, social and education services (see Chapter 4). In contrast to the attention on declining social standards caused by the effects of capital mobility on governments (the 'race to the bottom'), relatively little attention has focused on the impact of this international 'free trade' regulatory framework on national health, social and environmental standards and provision.

Policy implementation and enforcement is a weak area for international institutions because they do not have a local presence; indeed, they depend on the cooperation of national and local officials and politicians to implement policies and agreements. Unlike the EU, international institutions cannot enforce social rights in member states and individuals do not have rights of petition (Bandarage, 1997; Deacon and Hulse, 1996; Deacon et al., 1997; Koivusalo and Ollila, 1997; Midgley, 1997). IGOs are dependent on states to implement agreements and on NGOs to monitor and supply information on, for example, human rights abuses as well as to deliver aid and emergency relief and development assistance locally (Gordenker and Weiss, 1996a: 42; Holton, 1998). This structural dependence of IGOs on states and non-state agencies inevitably leaves a great deal of room for manoeuvre for national politics to mediate global policy objectives. The EU, even with its powers of enforcement, has found it necessary to take further measures to close the 'implementation gap'. It has done so by including a wider range of representatives (trade unions, regional government and NGOs) in policy-making in order to secure greater consensus on the objectives of action and a greater level of commitment to implementing the measures in such a way as to achieve these objectives (Wincott, 1994). Nonetheless, a good deal of diversity remains in the interpretation and realization of policy objectives.

Transnational policy innovation, learning and transfer

One of the key effects of the mobility of people and ideas is that there is greater interest and opportunity to compare how other countries 'do' social policy and also to 'borrow' their policies: 'an important element of transnational effects on national welfare states is the way in which social policies have migrated across the world' (Manning and Shaw, 1999: 120). Policy diffusion and learning is said to be associated with the transnational diffusion of culture and ideas: 'cultural diffusion and policy learning are spreading through personal contact and growing shared knowledge', social policy 'communities' are emerging 'through which policies are developed, refined and borrowed' (ibid.: 121), and policy-makers are policy-shopping abroad:

> The NHS internal market, private prisons, the movement of housing subsidies from property to people, higher education funding, private pensions, welfare to work schemes, are all areas in which policy innovation in the UK can be traced abroad. (Manning and Shaw, 1999: 120)

Like economic globalization itself (see Chapter 2), policy learning tends, however, to be mainly confined to the advanced industrialized countries and omits experiences of 'developing' countries (MacPherson and Midgley, 1987). Moreover, although transnational policy diffusion and mobility is nothing new in the history of welfare states it has been enhanced by supranational and international institutions. These institutions promote policy mobility and diffusion by encouraging inter-country cooperation, comparison and learning. Governments and policy makers are encouraged to examine what works elsewhere and to consider how it might be applied in their own territories. EU-funded social programmes and social policy research, for example, explicitly promote comparisons of national welfare systems and social policies by highlighting 'best practice' and funding cross-national exchanges of project staff as well as cross-national research networks.

International institutions have also played a direct role in policy diffusion through their working relationships with national governments. Policy dialogues between international institutions and sympathetic political and economic élites have been a key medium through which the views and policy preferences of international institutions have been disseminated nationally. These dialogues forge economic, political and ideological 'linkage' between the interests, ties and outlooks of domestic actors (businesspeople, technocrats, the military and middle classes) and international actors, and are premised on the belief that internationally-oriented domestic groups are more likely to accept the need for, advocate, and expect to benefit from policies of liberalization, privatization, monetary stability, budgetary and wage restraints than nationally-oriented groups such as labour, peasants and domestic capital (Stallings, 1992).

To conclude, while all of the approaches characterized here accept that globalization potentially entails significant implications for social policies, they are underpinned by quite different understandings of what globalization entails and its origins and dynamics; consequently they draw quite different conclusions about the prospects for social policy. The first approach draws on 'strong' globalization and conceives of globalization as an economic, external phenomenon which is largely passively received by states, welfare states and populations. The emphasis here is on the erosion of state sovereignty, autonomy and capacity and the deleterious effects of this on social standards. The second approach presents globalization more as a creation of states and as such still largely under their control. It emphasizes the adaptive and proactive capacities of states, the centrality of social politics in determining the timing, course and pace of globalization and the diversity of political responses and outcomes. The third approach also accords greater weight to political agency in its emphasis on transnational political processes and institutional structures and their implications for social policy formation, implementation, service delivery and provision. While it sees the dangers of globalization for social standards, it also maintains a belief in the continued possibility of political institutions to regulate the global economy in the interests of social protection.

2 Global Economic Structures and Processes

This chapter examines a central tenet of 'strong' globalization theory: the existence of a unified global economy. It shows that while systemic tendencies within the global economy *can* be discerned in respect of international trade, finance and production, the trend is neither necessarily towards greater global economic integration nor towards the subjugation of national economies under a globalized economy. Rather, global economic integration is characterized by sharpening inequalities at the world, regional and national levels. While it is not the intention here to deny the existence of globalization, by looking at the fit between globalization theory and the evidence I aim to provide a more nuanced and subtle, and therefore more believable, account of economic globalization and its socio-political consequences.

The chapter begins by examining international capital flows, originally expressed through trade and then supplemented by FDI. These forms of global commerce have recently been joined by a new form of international financial flow, that prompted by the deregulation of international financial markets. While these flows in international financial capital are of more recent vintage, trade and FDI are hardy veterans and the discussion looks at changes in these three areas which have been attributed to globalization. It then turns to the changes in production globally in the last few decades, interrogating the ways in which these changes have been explained by the 'globalization of production' (GOP) and 'new international division of labour' (NIDL) theses. It also examines the various positions grouped around the issues of 'flexibility' and the growth of new forms of investment and organization involved with international business networks, international sourcing and subcontracting. This examination of corporate globalization is continued through a focus on transnational corporations in the commercial and voluntary sectors, as TNCs are regarded as key agents in the globalization process. Finally, the discussion focuses on neglected aspects of business globalization – the growth of organized crime on a global level, and international migration and trade in human beings.

Global trade

Advocates of globalization often claim that the current volume and scale of international trade are both unprecedented and of a qualitatively different nature than earlier periods. One of the key defects of such claims is that they tend to be ahistorical, focusing on cyclical changes or conjunctural situations in particular periods to the neglect of long-term structural changes in the world system (Chase-Dunn, 1989; Green, 1997; Hirst and Thompson, 1996). Although international trade may be a dominant form of international capital flow, it 'is at least as old as human civilization' (Axford, 1995: 75), while most accounts of the history of international trade are problematically Western in focus and neglect non-Western global societies, such as China or Russia. Western accounts of international trade tend to begin only with the fifteenth century, when cross-border trading became more systematic within Europe and was carried out by private corporations trading in goods and finance (Hirst and Thompson, 1996). However, ancient state systems dating back thousands of years had extensive systems and routes for merchant trade between regional cities (Watson, 1992).

Indeed, much of the evidence for economic globalization is restricted to certain regions of the world and to the latter part of the twentieth century. Even within these parameters, one of the central problems with the empirical evidence in relation to exports, imports and investment flows is their interpretation. Bairoch, for example, argues that the growth rate of exports of goods from Western developed countries during the post World War II period 'surely reveals a trend to globalization rather than a minor structural change in international trade' (1996: 174). However, he ignores his own data: it was only in the 1990s that, for example, merchandise export rates in Western developed countries as a whole overtook those in the 1890s (Table 2.1). By taking as his base a trough period in international trade, subsequent growth is over-emphasized and its significance distorted. In fact, this data would seem to suggest that 'an extraordinarily developed, open and integrated international economy [existed] at the beginning of this century' (Hirst and Thompson, 1996: 31). Furthermore, and contrary to the expectations of 'strong' globalization, the trend is less towards homogenization and more towards the entrenchment of divergence. This fact tends to be obscured by statistics which subsume international differences under international similarities. Thus, while Bairoch concentrates on similarities, his data also show significant differences in export rates (Table 2.1): the majority of the growth of merchandise exporting is accounted for by Western Europe, while export rates in the case of Japan were actually about one third lower in 1992 than in 1913.

In fact, indicators of international economic exchange, like the growth in imports and exports of goods and services, *in themselves* do not signify that a transition from an international to a globalized economy has taken place (Hirst and Thompson, 1996; Wade, 1996). Quantitative measures underplay qualitative changes in the ways that states, the national, and international economy, are interlinked, obscuring the difference between

Table 2.1   *Exports of merchandise as a percentage of GDP (3 year average, except for 1950)*

	Western developed countries	US	Western Europe	EEC (12 members)	Japan
1890	11.7	6.7	14.9	–	5.1
1913	12.9	6.4	18.3	–	12.6
1929	9.8	5.0	14.5	–	13.6
1938	6.2	3.7	7.1	–	13.0
1950	7.8	3.8	13.4	12.9	6.8
1970	10.2	4.0	17.4	16.7	9.7
1992	14.3	7.5	21.7	21.1	8.8

Source: Bairoch, 1996

. . . on the one hand, the development of particular trade routes, or select military and naval operations or even the global reach of nineteenth-century empires, and, on the other hand, an international order involving the conjuncture of: dense networks of regional and global economic relations . . . extensive webs of transnational relations and instantaneous electronic communications . . . a vast array of international regimes and organizations which can limit the scope for action of the most powerful states; and the development of a global military order. (Held, 1995: 20)

Although conventional indicators of the international economy have largely failed to capture these types of changes, other measures provide a better indication of the globalization of the economy. Three notable measures in this respect are the proportion of intra-firm trade (IFT), intra-industry trade (IIT) and international sourcing to international trade and investment. These indicate that international trading patterns have changed over the course of the century in ways that reflect the globalization of industry (see also later sections in this chapter) as well as the interdependence of sectors and firms, and thus of economies, transnationally.

Intra-firm trade (IFT) refers to international trade in products between branches of multinational corporations and can be used as a measure of the international reach of corporations or as an indicator of global production systems (OECD, 1996a). IFT comprises 25 per cent of all international trade (UNCTAD, 1994), 43 per cent of all US-European merchandise trade, and 71 per cent of all US-Japan merchandise trade (OECD, 1996a). IFT is associated with the international sourcing of intermediate inputs – parts and materials produced or assembled abroad, often by foreign branches of the same firm, and imported to use in the final assembly of goods. Thus, international sourcing is a second key measure of the internationalization of businesses and firms. At the beginning of the century international sourcing involved commodities

Table 2.2   *Intra-industry trade as a proportion of total trade (%), 1970 and 1990*

Country	1970	1990
UK	53.2	84.6
France	67.3	77.2
Germany	55.8	72.2
Italy	48.7	57.4
US	44.4	71.8
Japan	21.4	32.4
Australia	20.7	30.5

Source: Adapted from OECD, 1996a

Note: % denotes extent to which industries are reliant on industries abroad for supply of goods.

such as food, metals, minerals, textiles, while now it also consists of trade in intermediate inputs for the assembly of manufactured products. Since 1980, absolute levels of direct imports of manufactured inputs have increased and have risen faster than domestic sourcing (Wyckoff, 1993). Firms source internationally because the parts needed for final assembly can be produced abroad and imported more cheaply than they can be produced domestically, either by themselves or by other firms. International sourcing in manufacturing is at its greatest in high-value, R&D-intensive products – such as computer parts, electronic components and aerospace inputs – and in mass-produced goods – such as metals, textiles and apparel and footwear. These industries are ones in which domestic firms are more reliant on links with foreign firms than on other domestic firms (OECD, 1996a). The growth of IFT and international sourcing by domestic firms in a range of sectors means that an expansion in production is as, if not more, likely to generate employment abroad than in the domestic economy (OECD, 1996a). Again, though, this varies across countries as there are strong national differences in the ratio of international to domestic sourcing: 50 per cent in Canada, 35 to 40 per cent in France, Germany and the UK, 13 per cent in the US and 7 per cent in Japan. Japan sources mainly from the US, as well as from Asia, due to its geographical proximity; EU countries tend to source from each other, while the US sources from Japan and Canada (Wyckoff, 1993).

International sourcing is also related to the growth of intra-industry trade (IIT) – trade within the same industry or product group but between countries. Intra-industry transactions as a proportion of total trade have also increased over the past 20 years (Table 2.2). IIT is associated with growing product differentiation and with the internationalization of competition between firms in the same industry. IIT is particularly strong in manufactured products, notably chemicals, machinery and transport, but less so in primary commodities (OECD,

1996a). High levels of IIT can be found in countries which are members of regional groupings. In the UK and France, for example, over three quarters of total trade is accounted for by intra-industry transactions.

Foreign Direct Investment

Foreign Direct Investment is one of the key measures of international capital flows and is commonly regarded as the driving force of the global economy. It consists of financial capital transfers from one country to another for the purpose of investing in the production of goods and services. In recent decades FDI flows have increased twice as fast as international trade (Evans, 1997; OECD, 1992, 1996a), and most of this increase is attributed to services, followed by manufactured goods (Hirst and Thompson, 1996). Nonetheless, it is not clear that the increase in FDI is a significant development for all Western developed countries: first, the stock of FDI as a proportion of GDP in 1913 (14 per cent) was greater than in 1993 (11 per cent); second, the proportion of outward FDI to GDP in 1960 was higher than in 1990 in the UK, the Netherlands and the US; only in Germany and Japan has the volume of outward FDI stocks increased significantly (Table 2.3).

Notwithstanding these doubts as to the significance of increased levels of FDI, FDI flows express and reinforce inequalities in the global distribution of trade, production and investment (Dicken, 1992). Thus, 80 per cent of FDI is concentrated within the 'Triad' – Western Europe, the US, Japan and the 'dragon economies' of Asia. Three out of the four principal source nations of transnational investment are also principal hosts of FDI (the US, UK, Germany, but not Japan) (Dicken, 1992). The investment-rich countries of the Triad contain just 14 per cent of the world population, but attract 70 per cent of FDI flows. When the nine most important developing countries and the coastal provinces of China are added, 28 per cent of the world's population was in receipt of 91 per cent of FDI flows (Hirst and Thompson, 1996). This concentration of FDI is in no small way related to the location of the largest companies: 86 per cent of the world's 200 largest companies are located in the US, Japan, France, Germany and the UK. These companies trade with other companies in these countries and invest in each others' countries, because 'the advanced nations contain the most lucrative markets, advanced technologies, skilled labour and superior infrastructure' (Moran, 1998: 64).

A corollary of this 'virtuous' cycle of investment in the Triad countries is the marginalization, even exclusion, of many other countries from investment. Table 2.4 shows the distribution of world stocks of inward direct investment over three decades. It shows that not only was the greatest increase by far to East Asia, the US, UK, France and Germany, but also that the share of foreign investment in developing countries

Table 2.3   *Outward foreign direct investments stocks (as % of GDP)*

Country	1960	1971	1980	1990
UK	18.2	15.2	15.9	15.4
France	6.0	4.8	2.4	6.9
Germany	1.2	4.7	8.5	9.5
The Netherlands	10.3	2.6	8.3	6.8
Italy	1.6	1.9	1.4	3.6
US	46.9	53.1	43.3	26.5
Japan	0.7	2.8	3.9	12.7

Source: Adapted from Bairoch, 1996

Table 2.4   *Distribution of world stocks of inward direct investment 1967, 1980, 1991 (%)*

Country	1967	1980	1991
US	9.4	16.4	22.0
Canada	18.2	10.2	6.0
Japan	0.6	0.7	0.7
EU *of which*	23.5	37.0	37.9
UK	7.5	12.5	12.5
France	2.8	4.2	4.7
Germany	3.4	9.5	6.5
Netherlands	4.6	3.8	4.2
Italy	2.5	1.8	3.3
Developing countries *of which*	30.6	22.0	23.4
Latin America	17.5	12.3	7.0
Africa	5.3	2.6	2.1
Middle East	3.0	0.9	0.7
East Asia	4.8	6.2	13.6

Source: adapted from OECD, 1996a

(excluding East Asia) fell from around 26 per cent in 1967 to around 10 per cent in 1991. It is because of these inequalities that FDI patterns have come to symbolize the 'financial delinking of much of the world from the new economic order' (Petrella, 1996: 71). Entire continents, notably Africa, have been abandoned as destinations for investment and no longer attract foreign capital outside of public donations and multilateral humanitarian aid.

Global financial markets

The major characteristics of globalization pertain not only to greater capital mobility, but also to the dominance of financial ('floating') capital over productive ('fixed') capital. The international financial sector has also undergone phenomenal growth and change in recent decades. The volume of borrowing on international capital markets increased ninefold since the late 1970s from US$95.6 billion to US$818.6 billion (1993) (Hirst and Thompson, 1996). Nearly US$2 trillion is traded *daily* on the world's principal foreign exchange markets; this is 40 times the daily value of international trade in goods and primary products (Helleiner, 1996; Roberts, 1995). This growth also entailed the territorial expansion of market activity, much of which occurred in the early 1970s, and by the 1990s 'an almost fully liberal regime of international financial movements had emerged within the OECD region, granting financial operators more freedom to act internationally than they had experienced since before the First World War' (Helleiner, 1996: 193).

Financial markets have not only expanded (in volume and territorially) but have undergone structural change. Financial conglomerates have emerged, particularly within the highly capitalized securities and banking houses, as have new types of financial trading instruments, such as derivatives and securities (Hirst and Thompson, 1996). Financial conglomerates are an outcome of intensified global competition between rival financial and banking empires and of mergers between European and US investment houses, particularly those heavily involved in fund management and pension provision (Blackburn, 1999: 20). Derivatives are the more potent symbol of the international financial market. The volume of trade within the derivatives' market more than tripled within the space of 24 months from US$4,000 billion (1992) to US$14,000 billion (1994) (Warde, 1994). These instruments are associated with the growth of 'securitization', entailing a structural shift away from conventional loan businesses (banks) towards trade in marketable bonds and other securities so that an increasing share of financial business is contracted through capital markets rather than through traditional bank lending (Hirst and Thompson, 1996). As Lütz argues, 'the nature of the securities business in particular has turned from a highly regulated activity, somewhat on the fringe of most financial systems, into the primary force changing the financial landscape of the OECD countries' (1998: 157). The growth in these types of products and the territorial extension of these markets are a result both of deregulation and of volatile exchange and interest rates. Floating exchange rates create the conditions for speculative trade to flourish because, unlike productive capital which requires reliable sources of investment funds at stable exchange and interest rates, currency speculators thrive on unstable or fluctuating exchange rates (Hallwood and MacDonald, 1994). As Korten notes, 'the greater the volatility of financial markets, the greater the opportunity for these forms of extraction' (1995: 198).

The growth in international financial markets is in many ways regarded as a far more important signifier of globalization than trade and production. For a start, international finance tends to be more global in scope than FDI or trade, especially short-term trading in new kinds of financial products, although the use of financial trading instruments tends to be confined to the Triad countries. Mainly, though, international finance is deemed to be qualitatively different from international trade and production, and to this extent, the international financial services sector is said to constitute a separate global economy (Kennedy, 1993). Compared with the global economy of the nineteenth century, when lending was mainly to finance productive investment, lending today is comprised largely of financial assets used for speculative investment. In 1986, at a time when the volume of international financial trading was half the level of that today, Susan Strange (1986) likened the international financial sector to a 'casino' in which assets are traded increasingly by non-bank, private financial institutions, entirely for speculative profit. This kind of trade brings no tangible benefits to the 'real' economy because it decouples investment from production. Financial rivalry entails scouring the earth in search of speculative gain, which 'has only the most accidental relationship with the local and regional complexes of productive and cultural activity which might form the basis of sustainable development' (Blackburn, 1999: 21). For example, financial assets are used in corporate raiding, whereby control over resources (land, corporations) are acquired – often from groups maintaining its productive value – and then liquidated or broken up and its parts sold off for profit. There has been no added (productive) value to this type of 'trading'; value and wealth have been extracted from the 'real' economy and transferred to the 'virtual', financial system (Korten, 1995, 1996). Financial trading is therefore different from production in respect of the nature of economic ties that it establishes: whereas trade, investment and multinational production contribute to longer term cross-border linkages, global finance is far more mobile and fleeting, and does little if anything to promote interconnectedness in the real economy. Thus although the most genuinely global networks are finance-based they are also the most impermanent in terms of locational commitment (Weiss, 1999).

Pension funds are a key protagonist of financial globalization and have been at the forefront of securitization. There has been a worldwide increase in pension assets and in the value of pension funds (Table 2.5). As Blackburn (1999: 5) points out, pension funds 'control assets equivalent to the total value of shares on the world's three leading exchanges'. The volume of assets held by pension institutions in the EU was equivalent to 17 per cent of the GDP of EU12 in 1992 (Mortensen, 1992). Such is the magnitude of pension funds' resources that they have given rise to what is termed 'grey capitalism', or 'pension fund capitalism' – 'the new financial complex and regime of accumulation based on the salience of pension funds in Britain and the US', but also in South America, Netherlands and Japan (Blackburn, 1999: 5). Like other forms of global capitalism, pension fund management is highly concentrated. In

Table 2.5   *Pension-fund assets (as a percentage of GDP)*

Country	1970	1980	1990
UK	17	23	55
US	17	24	43
Germany	2	2	3
Japan	0	2	5
Canada	13	17	28
Netherlands	29	46	77
Sweden	22	30	28
Switzerland	38	51	69
Denmark	5	7	15
Australia	10	9	19

Source: National flow-of-funds data, in Philip Davis, 1995

the UK, for example, five fund-managing concerns control over two-thirds of all pension assets, and just four consultants accounted for 65 per cent of fund transfers (Blackburn, 1999: 6). The relationship between the privatization of pensions and financial globalization is striking. The shift from publicly-funded and -provided pay-as-you-go pensions towards reliance on private (personal and occupational) pensions has contributed to the expansion of financial markets. The personal pensions market in particular has been nurtured through measures that erode the value of public pensions, improve tax incentives to increase the level of domestic savings (thereby furnishing funds for capital markets), fill gaps in existing provision, top-up the value of occupational schemes, and encourage the emergence of institutional pension fund investors (Amparo Cruz-Saco Oyague and Mesa-Lago, 1998; Barrientos, 1998; Blackburn, 1999; Philip Davis, 1995).

Since pension funds control significant proportions of industry, they are a factor in the corporate and employment restructuring that is associated with globalization. First, pension funds are often used for speculative gain (as described above) with the result that 'in a new layer of alienation, workers now frequently find that their own savings are being used in speculation hostile to the livelihood of their own communities' (Blackburn, 1999: 21). Second, pension fund managers are

notorious for 'short-termism', for shunning wider social objectives or more generous definitions of what is in the interest of policyholders, and for a herd instinct that makes each fund wary of behaving differently from its competitors. (Blackburn, 1999: 7)

Institutional investors insist on the performance criteria used by financial markets, compel firms to maximize their equity value, and are obsessed with cutting wage costs and shedding jobs to boost share prices (Aglietta in Blackburn, 1999).

The speculative trade of 'virtual' money within 'global cyberspace' has attracted attention because it has transformed the nature of capital flows and made them more difficult to regulate (Helleiner, 1996; Hirst and Thompson, 1996; Strange, 1986). Yet global financial markets not only thrive on volatility and instability, they have the ability to create major disturbances in world – and national – economies. Folkerts-Landau and Ito (1995) attribute the international diversification of institutional portfolios (led by pension funds, mutual funds and insurance) a key role – along with structural reform and the cyclical position of industrial economies – in the surge of capital to developing countries in the early 1990s. The deregulation of capital controls renders national economies vulnerable to currency speculators, while 'local' crises are felt globally. The crash of the Mexican peso in January 1995 and the South-East Asian currency crisis in August 1997 are prominent examples where the effects of deregulation reverberated across the world. The crash of the peso, for example, created turbulence across Latin American stockmarkets and made its effects felt on the Japanese yen, American dollar and Russian rouble (Folkerts-Landau and Ito, 1995; Korten, 1995).

The operations of global financial markets thus impinge on the ability of individual governments to effectively manage their economies. The harmful effects of financial short-term flows in contributing to disruptive market fluctuations, investment misallocation, exchange rate volatility and growth-retarding outcomes have all been highlighted (Weiss, 1999). In foreign exchange markets, greater capital mobility has resulted in large misalignments in the value of currencies, interest rates and other economic prices (Helleiner, 1996). Countries which rely on imports and exports of goods and services rather than domestic production are particularly vulnerable because they are affected to a greater extent by exchange rates. Volatility can lead to macro-economic disorders, such as the destruction of the productive base where currencies are overvalued and the development of export activities that are unsustainable in the long term where currencies are undervalued. Volatility also creates micro-economic inefficiencies since economic planning becomes no more than 'speculative' in a situation where the value of the home currency fluctuates widely. The effectiveness of tariffs to protect national economies may be undermined by price variations resulting from exchange rate fluctuations (S. Amin, 1997).

Global financial markets also restrict states' capacity to pursue macro-economic policies and other public policy objectives appropriate to their circumstances. Financial deregulation makes it easier for capital to quickly exit from domestic financial systems if financial markets 'disapprove' of certain national tax, expenditure and regulatory policies (Axford, 1995). The price governments pay for 'breaking the rules' is often exacted by financial markets which can either withdraw capital funds from a country at a second's notice and prompt financial or currency crisis, and/or downgrade the credit-rating of a country, leading to higher interest rates on bonds or money borrowed to be paid by the government (Mishra, 1999). As Korten argues:

> if the speculators . . . decide that the policies of a government give preference to 'special interests' – by which they mean groups such as environmentalists, working people, or the poor – over the interests of financial speculators, they take their money elsewhere. (1995: 203)

Consequently, governments may become more sensitive to the (perceived) 'views' of international capital markets than to the democratically-expressed opinions of their citizens (S. Amin, 1997; Held, 1995; Korten, 1995).

Global welfare markets

The integration of the world economy through private markets is seen as the most powerful dimension of globalization. Globalization has also facilitated the entry of private markets and commercial businesses in health and welfare systems around the world, and there exists a modest international market in the production and consumption of many welfare goods and services (Deacon, 2000a; Jordan, 1998; Midgley, 1997; Moran and Wood, 1996; WTO, 1998a, 1998b).

International trade in welfare services takes four forms. First, is the *consumption of services abroad* by, for example, students in secondary education (private schools) and higher education (student exchanges); patients seeking access to higher-quality medical and health services; or less expensive services not covered by health insurers, as well as people using income-maintenance services. The second form of international trade in services is the *movement of natural persons*, consisting mainly of professionals, such as scholars, consultants, doctors, nurses and midwives, providing their services in health and welfare institutions and agencies abroad. The third form of international trade in welfare services entails *commercial presence abroad* – a form of foreign investment and illustrative of corporate globalization, discussed later on in this chapter – through the setting up of services abroad by providers. In higher education, examples include: the establishment of 'local branch campuses' or subsidiaries (often locally-financed); partnership arrangements between education institutions in two countries; and the franchising of courses to institutions abroad where the local partners validate instructional methods and examination standards. In the health and medical field, this type of international trade includes sales of products and services either by foreign-based affiliates of national majority-owned health care providers or by foreign-owned organizations, such as pharmaceutical, health insurance and health management (consultancy) companies. Other examples can be found in other areas of financial services – notably in the life insurance and pensions industries, and in social research, evaluation and auditing (e.g. KPMG, Price-Waterhouse), many of which compete with local companies. Finally, the *cross-border supply of services* consists of an international component of trade in distance learning and health and medical services, such as telemedicine and telediagnosis, hospital management functions, data collection for statistical or educational purposes, and back-up advisory facilities for local staff abroad (WTO, 1998a, 1998b).

The volume of international trade in education, medical, health and social services is relatively modest, although still significant. In health, the WTO points out that:

> US 'exports' of health care services, covering the activities of US-majority-owned suppliers abroad and the services provided to foreigners in the United States, are estimated to amount to less than two per thousand of total domestic health care spending. (1998b: 5)

Nonetheless, the market is substantial, and it is estimated that US exports of health care services amounted to US$872 million, while imports of such services amounted to US$550 million. Much of this is accounted for by foreign tourists falling sick and obtaining treatment during stays in the US, although leading US medical institutions reportedly attract patients travelling specifically for their services (WTO, 1998b: 6). Such is the potential of this market that

> the US Department of Commerce sees an increasingly promising market potential in Latin America, noting that Argentinians are estimated to spend US$60 million annually on medical treatment abroad, and that more than 400,000 Mexicans could afford treatment in the United States. (WTO, 1998b: 6)

In tertiary education, the global market has undergone significant expansion in recent years, as judged by: the expansion of student exchange programmes and the growing number of students studying abroad (over 1.5 million in the early 1990s); exchanges and linkages between faculties and researchers (foreign scholars lecturing in the US numbered more than 60,000 in 1996/7 – an increase of 5 per cent from 1995/6); international marketing of curricula and academic programmes; the establishment of 'local branch campuses' and the development of educational cooperation between academic institutions in different countries. This cooperation has been underpinned by bilateral educational agreements to foster student exchanges and scientific and technological cooperation, and by international initiatives relating to the recognition of courses, programmes, diplomas and degrees in tertiary education. The global market in higher education was estimated to be worth US$27 billion in 1995 (WTO, 1998a). The leading exporter, or supplier, of students consuming education services abroad is the US (exporting around 450,000 students annually), followed by France, Germany and the UK (exporting between them about 445,000 students). Here, the US enjoys a significant trade surplus: education imports were worth US$1 billion annually, while education exports were estimated to be worth US$7 billion in 1996, making this sector the country's fifth largest service sector export (WTO, 1998a). The regulation of inter-national trade in welfare services is discussed in Chapter 3.

Global production

Central to the globalization thesis is the claim that there has been a major change in the global, productive, economy over the last three decades. The global production and service operations of businesses are often regarded as an expression of the underlying forces and changes occurring in international capitalism (Korten, 1995; Nazir, 1990). Earlier in this chapter three measures of the globalization of industry and business were highlighted – IFT, IIT and international sourcing. In this section the discussion focuses on various explanations for the global-ization of production. Grouped around the concept of 'flexibility', some have attempted to explain these changes in terms of the globalization of production (GOP) and the new international division of labour (NIDL); others regard recent industrial restructuring as evidence of a paradigm shift from Fordism to post-Fordism, or towards 'flexible specialization', while still others have claimed that changes in the organizational form of business, in particular, the development of inter-firm networks and alliances, are the causative factor. This recognition of the wide variety of relationships between different economic actors is complemented by the study of global commodity chains. Although none of these theories sufficiently explain the changes in the global system of production, a combination of insights from them can provide a useful guide to this complex area.

The globalization of production and new international division of labour

The globalization of production (GOP) thesis provided an early account of the characteristics of corporate globalization. The GOP thesis high-lighted how industrial restructuring was an increasingly internationa-lized process: production was being relocated away from 'core' urban areas by companies in certain sectors in European countries towards 'peripheral' rural communities in developing countries. At the time, this global relocation occurred mostly in labour-intensive industries such as textiles and electronics assembly, and the most favoured destinations were South-East Asia and Latin America. Since this also represented a shift in production away from strong, unionized, protected labour forces towards weakly organized and cheaper labour forces, GOP was seen to be motivated primarily by a concern to reduce labour costs. However, this relocation did not entail the relocation of entire companies. Instead, low-skilled manufacturing work, such as assembly-line work, was transferred to the low-cost countries, while high-skilled marketing, research and development, finance and administration were retained in the high-cost countries. As such, global corporate restructuring of production was seen to have enabled the establishment of a 'new division of labour' between North and South – a new international division of labour (Fröbel et al., 1980; Hymer, 1972; Massey, 1984; Schoenberger, 1988).

The NIDL thesis has strongly resonated with work on women workers internationally. Indeed, one of the strengths of the NIDL theory is its pinpointing of the importance of female labour in the international restructuring of production. There is now a rich literature on the position of women in global production systems and on the links between industrialization and the large-scale employment of women (e.g. Barry, 1995; Cleves Mosse, 1993; Halliday, 1991; McDowell, 1992; Stitcher and Parpart, 1990; Ward, 1990; Williams, 1994). Sassen (1984, 1986) argues that globalization has been premised on the feminization of wage labour, while Standing (1989) argues that the move to global flexibilization by firms has occurred through the 'feminization' of the labour force, both in advanced industrialized countries and developing countries. Indeed, the emergence of the 'global assembly line', or 'global factory' is a strongly gendered phenomenon: 'Southern countries become the global production lines and women operate the machinery' (Cleves Mosse, 1993: 68). The NIDL thesis also resonates with the escalating impact of corporate relocation on middle-class workers, such as professionals and technicians who 'are forced to compete with their counterparts in newly industrializing or post-communist countries' (Jordan, 1996: 244). Thus, as Jordan notes, 'a computer software programmer in Hungary earns around one third of what is paid for comparable work in Britain, and many international companies are relocating their production sites in Central Europe (Barket, 1985)' (ibid.).

The NIDL involved the establishment of export processing zones (EPZs) set up by governments whose borders are close to advanced industrialized economies. The Republic of Ireland 'pioneered' EPZs in the 1960s, but the most infamous of EPZs is that of the *maquiladoras* on the Mexico/US border, also set up in the 1960s (Payne, 1996). EPZs are designated areas for foreign business to manufacture goods and commodities destined for export; their activities and products are not subject to the same tariffs or taxes levied on those in the rest of the economy. Thus, EPZs link national economies through financial investment and trade but they are not integrated into the national economy in which they are located. In EPZs, labour and tax restrictions are limited and companies are offered tax incentives that permit low-cost production, no import tariffs, and, crucially, promises of a cheap, docile, unorganized workforce. Conditions of work are characterized by minimal rates of pay and insecure, temporary employment, mostly of women:

> Total employment in Mexico's maquiladoras, for example, has gone from 100,000 in 1980 to 500,000 in 1992, while in Asia about 700,000 workers are employed in the free-export zones. What is significant is the proportion of female workers involved. In Asia these are mostly unmarried women aged between 17 and 23, with the highest densities being 88% in Sri Lanka, Taiwan and Malaysia, and around 75% in South Korea and the Philippines. (De Angelis, 1997: 49)

This industrialization by supposed 'modern' methods has benefited from state and local patriarchal structures, and is dependent on pre-modern labour relations – hardly the shining light of modernization presented by some authors on the issue. Standing notes the growth of informal out-contracting of work associated with this export-oriented industrialization:

> much of the employment connected with export industries, as well as with others, is indirect if not concealed entirely. A very good example comes from a study in Mexico . . . This study showed that production was organized through a complex process of sub-contracting, with the labour-intensive, lower paid, more informal activities being put out to women workers, many of whom were not recorded in the workforce. This is a classic instance of 'modern' production relying on what is depicted as 'pre-modern' or informal labour relations. (1989: 1080)

However superficially attractive these accounts of how changes in global production affect the social geography of capitalism and the 'de-nationalization' of economies may be, the GOP and NIDL theses have been criticized on a number of counts. Fröbel et al. (1980) based their evidence on European companies, and in particular on German companies, although they later widened the scope to examine large American firms. However, one should be wary about generalizing from the strategies of a small number of firms in a limited number of countries. Their account could not explain variation in the internationalization strategies of other European, Japanese or Asian corporations. In fact, not all European companies relocated their production in low-cost countries; UK companies, for example, aimed at high-income markets.

Similar empirical problems with evidence for the GOP thesis have been raised by Gordon (1987). While he agrees that 'there have been striking changes in the dynamics of the world economy over the last 15 years', his comparison of global production from 1970 to 1984 shows

Table 2.6   *Composition of global production (%)*

Year(s)	DMEs (excl Japan)	Japan and CPEs	LDCs
1870	93	4	3
1896–1900	91	6	3
1913	91	5	4
1926–1929	89	7	3
1938	76.7	12.9	10.4
1948	76.0	10.0	14.0
1966	65.8	22.0	12.2
1973	58.7	27.3	14.0
1979	54.5	30.9	14.6
1984	52.8	33.6	13.9

Source: Gordon, 1987

Note: DME: Developing Market Economy; CPE: Centrally-Planned Economy; LDC: Less Developed Country.

that the evidence did not support many of the major claims of GOP and NIDL theorists (Table 2.6). What is striking, he argues, is not the increase in production in the less developed countries (LDCs) which the NIDL theory claims, but the increase in production by Japan and the Centrally-Planned Economies since the 1950s (Gordon, 1987: 34). The sharp decline in developing market economies' (DMEs) share of production since World War II cannot be attributed to an expansion in the relative importance of the LDCs, as the latter's share was, in 1984, equal to 1948 levels; indeed, LDCs have simply recouped the losses in production shares from 1948 to 1966. Moreover, any such growth of manufacturing capacity in LDCs has become increasingly concentrated, with a rising share of LDC production concentrated in a relatively small number of countries. Noting that the Asian NICs are the exception rather than the rule, Dicken argues that 'a mere 25 countries produce 93% of world output; as few as seven countries produce three-quarters of the world total' (1993: 24).

A further problem with the GOP thesis is that the common picture of footloose multinationals scouring the earth for the cheapest supplies of labour turns out in reality to be some way off the mark: 'About three-quarters of the value added by MNCs is still produced in their home countries' (*Financial Times*, 13/2/96: 22). This does not deny that certain parts of production processes have been relocated internationally, it only puts this relocation in perspective. Both the GOP and NIDL theses problematically assume that the sole motivation for relocation is to reduce labour costs (wages). Yet relocation to low-cost, developing countries may be prompted more by the need to secure access to final markets – one quarter of US foreign investment in developing countries is related to access to markets that are closed to foreign imports

(Gordon, 1987). Another major motivation for relocation may relate to the control, rather than the cost, of labour (see also Chapter 5). Where labour costs are cited as the reason for relocation, the value of the products is often low (e.g. plastic products, toys, textiles, shoes, garments). Some production processes require skilled labour and often these are at the cutting edge (i.e. most profitable) of technology and production. Corporations in these high-tech sectors, such as pharmaceuticals and communications technology, tend to remain within advanced industrialized countries, which are able to supply the skilled, educated labour forces they require.

In fact, low wages are only one factor among many in a more complex equation, which includes the costs of relocation and the merits of remaining in 'high-cost' countries. Corporations face restrictions on the extent and manner in which they can relocate abroad from domestic industrial relations systems, and can incur substantial costs when they exit or relocate even part of their operations. Corporations must also balance the relative merits of remaining in countries with extensive infrastructure, a relatively strong regulatory framework and strong social protection compared with relocating to countries which can supply cheap labour but which have limited infrastructure and higher transportation costs. Corporate requirements will vary depending on the conditions and methods of production involved, so these costs and benefits will vary across sectors, but it is clear that relocation is highly contingent on a *range* of factors (Cox, 1997). Indeed, wage levels were clearly not the deciding factor in cases where firms have decided to locate in Germany, or Singapore, where wage levels are higher than those of their neighbouring competitors.

Barff and Austen's (1993) study of the athletic footwear industry underlines the importance of placing TNCs' location decisions in this context. Athletic footwear production, which remained in the US in the face of relocation by 'first tier' companies such as Nike to Asia, managed to maintain competitiveness despite higher wage costs through higher productivity, enhanced training and reduced labour turnover. However, of note here is that production in the US has tended to gravitate towards the 'periphery' of the US where wages are lower – to North Carolina, for example, and where it tends to use a marginalized black female workforce.

A final problem with the NIDL thesis is that it is unclear about the extent to which the 'old' international division of labour has been replaced by a 'new' one. The use of female labour within this process certainly does not indicate that a 'new' sexual division of labour – either national or international – has emerged from the ashes of the old one; rather, it has built on the existing one. Furthermore, although companies have attempted to become 'insiders' in other countries' economies, they could not be said to have established a division of labour between foreign locations in the sense that was being claimed (Ruigrok and van

Tulder, 1995). Indeed, the evidence seems to indicate a regional, rather than a global, division of labour, or at best a coexistence between regional and global divisions of labour (Mittelman, 1995). Most restructuring has taken place between and within regions – hence the focus on the 'fracturing' or segmentation of labour markets within Western European countries and in the US. This acceptance of complexity and diversity in the production sphere requires the replacement of the crude dichotomies of the NIDL theory by a more subtle analysis:

> There is no single wave of globalization washing over or flattening diverse divisions of labour both in regions and industry branches. Varied regional divisions of labour are emerging, tethered in different ways to global structures, each one engaged in unequal transactions with world centres of production and finance and presented with distinctive development possibilities. Within each region, sub-global hierarchies have formed, with poles of economic growth, managerial and technical centres and security systems. (Mittelman, 1995: 279)

Post-Fordism and all that

A competing explanation for the changes in the economic system is provided by a cluster of theories invoking post-Fordism, flexible specialization and regulation theory. These provide a useful corrective to the GOP/NIDL theses by drawing attention to restructuring and relocation of production not only in the periphery but also in the core. Thus, while some US TNCs relocated to South-East Asia, others headed for the southern states and the sunbelt, while others stayed in New York or Los Angeles, introducing increased flexibilization and taking advantage of migrant labour forces. The principal strength of these theories is that they draw attention to the importance of flexibility, a major theme in industrial and employment restructuring. The problem with all these approaches is that, while it can be accepted that they are attempts at explaining changes in capitalism, their lack of specificity and questionable empirical referents limit their utility. As one writer contends, '"post-Fordism" has come to signal less a clear phenomenon than the subject of an amorphous debate about the changing nature of capitalism' (Sayer, 1996: 151), while another observes that:

> there is little agreement about the nature of Fordism and post-Fordism in general or the trajectories which might link them, let alone about the post-Fordist state in particular or the transitional regimes which might connect it to its putative Fordist precursor. (Jessop, 1994: 13)

Pointing to the deficiencies of empirical evidence, post-Fordism is damned for postulating no coherent relationships between its different elements, while there is no empirical evidence for the claimed break-up of mass markets, or for the supposed inability of mass production to respond to changing economic conditions, or for the claimed correlation between new technology and the scale and social forms of production. (Williams et al., in Clarke, 1990: 132)

Thus, although there have been widespread changes in the organization of work, wage bargaining and payments systems, 'these changes reflect the growing strength of management and the weakening of labour, rather than having any determinate relationship to technological change' (Clarke, 1990: 132). The following treatment focuses on flexible special-ization as it is most amenable to empirical analysis.

The 'emerging new economic order' of flexible specialization is char-acterized by industrial districts and regional conglomerations, consisting of smaller manufacturing firms (and more of them) (Curry, 1993: 99). These firms deploy 'flexible specialist' production methods to 'combine new technologies, new patterns of demand, and new forms of the social organization of production' (Clarke, 1990: 131). If the empirical basis of the GOP/NIDL model is confined to a few industries, then that of flexible specialization is more meagre yet, based as it is on the discovery of industrial districts. The Emilia-Romagna, the Marches, Umbria and Tuscany regions in Italy, the Salzburg region in Austria, and the Baden-Württemberg region in Germany are among the industrial districts cited, while territorial production complexes have been identified in Silicon Valley in California, Route 128 near Boston, Massachusetts, and in film-making in the LA basin (Curry, 1993: 103–4). Amin has criticized flexible specialization theory as

a totalizing vision in which [its proponents] see flexible specialization and locational agglomeration wherever they look . . . collaps[ing] together such heterogeneous developments as Italian industrial districts, high technology growth centres, and metropolitan business agglomerations, into one master paradigm. (cited in Curry, 1993: 116)

Not content with the discovery of an interesting production agglomera-tion, these theorists have prophesied flexible specialization as the inevitable successor to mass production. Critics have emphasized strong doubts as to whether craft production – flexible specialization – is an adequate description of what is going on in all, or indeed any, of these places. The mention of craft production in relation to Silicon Valley, for example, gives rise only to cynical laughter:

The brutal reality of the allegedly flexibly specialized Silicon Valley, the cheapened, de-skilled labour, the anti-union pogroms, the tolerance by management of drug use by employees if it helps them meet quotas, the endless traffic jams, the lack of housing and public transportation, the 14-hour days, etc., belie the pretty picture painted by the high tech firms and their enthusiastic academic supporters. (Curry, 1993: 112)

Overall, the theory is useful for drawing attention to employment flexibility and new forms of employment – homeworking, tele-commuting, part-time work, temporary work, and employment subcontracting – and for recognizing that flexible specialization 'is apparently not limited to particular products, types of production, level of technology, nor size of firm' (Curry, 1993:101). Indeed, there is much evidence to support the claim that there has been flexibilization of work; however, this has tended not to be of the Volvo quality type hymned by flexible specialization advocates but more of the McDonalds or Nike subcontracting type (Standing, 1989).

The emphasis on the spread of production through networks is perhaps the more grounded aspect within the flexible specialization literature, which draws on the example of Japan, where subcontracting networks are of immense importance and associational networks among companies are basic to the production system. The development of new forms of industrial links, notably inter-firm collaborative networks, has been highlighted as a feature of the contemporary global economy more generally (OECD, 1992, 1996a). Entire firms very rarely relocate, or even need to relocate, because internationalization strategies can be accomplished through the extension of subcontracting internationally to local businesses in developing countries. Thus, firms tend to engage in collaboration with other firms abroad in development, production and marketing through joint ventures, subcontracting, licensing and inter-firm agreements (OECD, 1992) (Table 2.7). Firms may collaborate transnationally for the purposes of development, production or marketing, or a mix of these, depending on the particular sector (OECD, 1996a; Ruigrok and van Tulder, 1995). 'Networks' of production comprise several firms, with each firm bringing its comparative advantage – be it cheap labour, innovative technology or capital goods. The main industries in which such collaboration exists are automobiles, electronics and aerospace, as well as areas in which technology is rapidly developing, such as information technology (telecommunications and computers), biotechnology and new materials. Evidence from micro-studies of corporate globalization shows that such networks tend to consolidate rather than diminish inequalities between 'core' and 'marginalized' states. These studies also dispel claims that the 'flexible' firm heralds greater equalization between firms in the production process: the formation of production networks by Japanese companies in East and South-East Asia, for example, has perpetuated the dependency of producers in the latter on technology and capital from the 'core' company in Japan (Ruigrok and van Tulder, 1995).

Another way of looking at the relationships in global inter-firm networks is provided by the 'global commodity chain' (GCC) concept. The

Table 2.7   *Corporate internationalization: forms, purposes and sector examples*

Form	Purpose	Sector examples
International trade	To expand markets and increase returns on investment	Many sectors
Foreign investment	To increase access to markets and localize production	Food products, chemicals, automobiles
International subcontracting	To allow specialization in core components and increase flexibility	Aerospace, construction, automobiles
International licensing	To broaden markets and increase returns from R&D expenditures	Pharmaceuticals, semiconductors
Cross border mergers and acquisitions	To increase scale economies and localize production	Electronics, financial services
International joint ventures	To increase market access and pool resources	Minerals, machine tools
International inter-firm agreements	To share costs and risks of internationalization	Aerospace, electronics

Source: OECD, 1992

GCC has been defined as 'sets of interorganizational networks clustered around one commodity or product' (Gereffi et al., 1994: 2; see also Gereffi, 1996), or 'a network of labour and production processes whose end-result is a finished commodity' (Hopkins and Wallerstein in Snyder, 1999: 337). 'Global' products, such as cars, very often involve commodity chains. Commodity chain analysis focuses on the transnational process of production, and the trade linkages – the goods and services that they export – which tie economies, firms, workers and households into the global economy. Each commodity chain has three main dimensions: the *structure of inputs and outputs of products and services*, linked together in a sequence in which each activity adds value to its predecessor; *territoriality*, whereby networks of enterprises are spatially dispersed or concentrated; and the stucture of *governance*, the relationships of power and authority which determine the flow and allocation of resources, financial, material and human, within the chain (Snyder, 1999: 337–8). This emphasis on structures of power and authority within GCCs not only highlights that inter-firm networks are hierarchically organized but also draws attention to a form of global economic governance other than international bureaucracies. Indeed, the particular strength of the GCC approach is that it demonstrates 'how production, distribution, and consumption are shaped by the social relations (including organizations) that characterize the sequential stages of input acquisition, manufacturing, distributions, marketing, and consumption' (Gereffi et al., 1994: 2).

Two distinct types of commodity chain are commonly distinguished – 'producer-driven' and 'buyer-driven' chains – each involving their own structures of governance and power (Snyder, 1999). Producer-driven chains refer to industries in which large, transnational manufacturers in capital- and technology-intensive industries control production networks (Gereffi, 1996: 81). The automobile industry is an example of a producer-driven chain with its multi-layered production systems, involving thousands of firms (parents, subsidiaries and subcontractors). Buyer-driven commodity chains refer to industries in which large companies 'play the pivotal role in setting up decentralized production networks in a variety of exporting countries . . . production is generally carried out by tiered networks of developing world contractors that make finished goods for foreign buyers' (Gereffi, 1996: 82). In buyer-driven commodity chains power rests with large retailers, brand-name merchandisers and trading companies; these have become common in labour-intensive, consumer goods industries such as garments, footwear, toys and houseware.

Corporate globalization: TNCs and INGOs

Global corporations are accorded a dominant role in the global economy by 'strong' globalization theory, so much so that images of their 'all-pervasive global spread' have prevailed (Gibson-Graham, 1996: 127). Certainly, TNCs – which have received most attention – illustrate the growing concentration of wealth and resources globally: 37,000 TNCs account for up to one third of world output, four-fifths of global investment and two-thirds of world trade (A. Amin, 1997; Madeley, 1999; UNCTAD, 1994). They directly employ around 73 million people, which is equivalent to about 20 per cent of employment in the industrialized countries. They indirectly control the working conditions of as many workers in their 200,000 affiliates or subsidiaries (Dicken, 1992; UNCTAD, 1994). Indeed, TNCs symbolize the structural changes that 'strong' globalization theory points to – both the 'deterritorialization' of capital and its enhanced structural power relative to states and governments. The relationship between 'global' corporations and states is the subject of Chapter 3, while the focus of this section is the composition and reach of these 'global' corporations, both in the commercial and voluntary sectors.

Earlier in this chapter it was shown that capital and trade flows are much less 'global' in their reach than has been commonly depicted. By the same token, only a very small proportion (4 to 5 per cent) of corporations can be regarded as 'authentically global'. First, most 'global' or 'multinational' corporations are spread across between just two to four countries (Dicken, 1992). Second, the functional areas of 'global' corporations are much less internationalized than advertised. A study by Ruigrok and van Tulder (1995) of the functional areas of management (sales, production, finance, R&D, personnel) of 100 TNCs on the *Fortune* list concluded that not one of the largest core firms examined was truly global or borderless in all of these respects. Some areas were more internationalized than others: sales and production were more 'internationalized' than executive boards and management styles, which were found to be more solidly national in composition and character. On this basis, Ruigrok and van Tulder (1995) conclude that many so-called 'multinational' or 'global corporations' are merely national entities with foreign operations. Sklair's study of 19 California-based corporations listed in the *Fortune* Global 500 similarly concludes that although 'the idea of globalization has strong resonances for most of the California Global 500 corporations', few of these major corporations can be considered, or considered themselves, to be entirely globalized (1998b: 213). Sklair himself points out that the sample is small, but it is also highly specific and skewed in a way that one would expect to find evidence of globalization here if it is to be found anywhere, as this is big capital (all the firms had annual revenues of over US$8 billion a year). The corporations, however, showed a strong failure to globalize. Only two corporations earned over half their revenues from outside the US (Intel with 82 per cent and Hewlett Packard with 55 per cent). The others varied from a low of 3 per cent to a high of 45 per cent. Evidence that TNCs are profoundly 'national' entities is also provided by Pauly and Reich (1997) who found considerable divergence between Germany, Japan and the US in the patterns of internal governance and long-term financing of TNCs.

While the introduction and internationalization of new technologies have been crucial to globalization, there have been disputes over how much of the knowledge embedded in these technological systems has been transferred along with the technology. In addition to the structure of TNCs, Pauly and Reich (1997) found 'stark national differences' in the degree to which TNCs exported new technology from their home base. If there has been a 'globalization of knowledge' it has at best been inherently hierarchical, although some argue that it provides an important example of 'non-globalization' (Patel and Pavitt, 1991). The greatest competitive advantage that capital has – its technological edge and the knowledge that is the basis of current wealth-creating sectors such as pharmaceuticals, biotechnology, robotics and electronics – is still concentrated in the core industrial countries. It is important to note that R&D often includes heavy state involvement and investment, particularly in the case of arms (Fransman, 1997). Due to its strategic importance both for capital and states, an overwhelming share of R&D spending and activity has also stayed defiantly within the core countries (see Chiesa, 1995; Howells, 1990; Pearce and Pooni, 1996):

> Most R&D activities of TNCs are still overwhelmingly conducted in the domestic base of the company and are heavily influenced by the local national system of innovation. Moreover, ownership and control still remain overwhelmingly based on the domestic platform. . . . Only a small part of world R&D is conducted outside the leading industrial countries and only a very small part of this is financed by TNCs. (Freeman, 1997: 39–40)

Even this foreign R&D is not up to much, argues Freeman, as

> most of it is either local design modification to meet national specifications and regulations or research to facilitate monitoring of local science and technology. The more original research, design and development work is still overwhelmingly concentrated in the domestic base, although there are important exceptions in the drug industry and electronics industry where specialized pools of scientific ability play an important role. (Freeman, 1997: 40)

While some of the more extreme claims about the global reach of TNCs appear to be exaggerated, there can be no doubt that businesses have developed forms and structures of transnational cooperation between branches or affiliates of the company to 'mix and match' supply and labour, marketing outlets, pricing and profit margins (Spybey, 1996). The growing importance of intra-firm trade and inter-firm *collaborative* networks in international trade more generally was demonstrated earlier in this chapter. Corporations internationalize their operations in order to, *inter alia*, access foreign markets and increase their market share. Alliances are one way of gaining a strategic foothold in another country's market; mergers and acquisitions are another.

All of these have both increased in number and become increasingly international in character. Again, alliances, mergers and acquisitions are mostly confined to firms located in the Triad. In the 1980s, over 90 per cent of inter-firm alliances in the field of technology in the world were signed by firms in the Triad, while just 1.5 per cent were signed by firms in Triad countries with firms in developing countries (Freeman and Hagedorn in Petrella, 1996: 78). The recent spate of mergers can be traced to deregulatory policies aiming to 'open up' domestic markets and producers to international competitors. However, deregulation, and mergers and alliances specifically, has effectively meant that the domestic market is 'shared' between a smaller number of larger producers, or carved up into cartels (Hughes, 1991), as the number of competitors within a given sector is reduced and as financial and industrial structures – and wealth and power – are concentrated at world level (Boyer, 1996; Korten, 1995; Petrella, 1996; Townsend, 1993).

Mergers and acquisitions do not necessarily increase domestic production and employment, and often result in the replacement of one national monopoly, controlled by local élites, by another, controlled by foreign élites. The extension of production by Nestlé into Poland in 1993, for example, was achieved through buying the two largest indigenous chocolate manufacturers rather than setting up new plants in competition with them. In the area of telecommunications the number of global players is expected to shrink from around 15 in the early 1990s to just six or seven by 2010; in the field of software and electrical equipment five companies share more than 50 per cent of production (Boyer, 1996; Hirst and Thompson, 1996).

It is worth noting that corporate globalization has also occurred in the voluntary sector. International coalition-building on the part of NGOs dates back to the mid-nineteenth century (Burden, 1998; Ritchie, 1996), although local and national NGOs are now complemented by a discernible international voluntary sector (Burden, 1998) comprised of international non-governmental organizations (INGOs) (Deacon et al., 1997). In terms of their location and operation INGOs are usually based in one country (often in the US and Western Europe) and may form transnational partnerships – corporate collaborative alliances – with established national and local NGOs in their countries of operation to undertake general aid work or send aid to individual people or areas (Burden, 1998; Deacon et al., 1997). Some INGOs may subsequently become major players in the 'host' countries, competing with national NGOs for contracts from international agencies (Deacon et al., 1997).

A key characteristic of the development of the international voluntary sector is the emergence of 'super' NGOs, such as Oxfam, CARE (Cooperative for American Relief Everywhere) and Save the Children, particularly in the fields of emergency aid and population and fertility. Although these super NGOs are relatively small in number, they are a growing phenomenon and are significant for two reasons. First, their internationalized organizational and strategic operations have been compared with those of the commercial sector. Smillie (1995) makes a distinction between 'small' international NGOs and large 'transnational' or conglomerate NGOs which operate like TNCs. He argues that some of these NGO conglomerates,

> have traded long-term development impact for growth, short-term child sponsorship and emergency donors . . . At corporate level many actually do bear an uncanny resemblance to transnational corporations in their opportunistic behaviour. Like many transnationals, they have maximized growth through the successful international manipulation of pricing, marketing and product. (Smillie, 1995: 212)

Second, these super NGOs are significant because a large proportion of international financial assistance to developing countries is channelled through them. In the arena of humanitarian assistance, 'eight to ten large conglomerates of international NGOs account for what may be 80% of the financial value of assistance in complex emergencies' (Gordenker and Weiss, 1996b: 218). In the field of population and fertility, five

INGOs account for nearly three quarters of assistance: International Planned Parenthood Federation, the Population Council, the Association of Voluntary Surgical Sterilization, the Program for Appropriate Technology for Health, and Pathfinder International (World Bank in Koivusalo and Ollila, 1997: 102).

The globalization of organized crime

The globalization of economic activity of a legal nature has been mirrored by a less-mentioned economic development – the globalization of organized crime (OC) groups and 'parallel' or 'grey' economies, both of which '[form] part of the transregional, even transcontinental, grey trading networks' (The CornerHouse, 1999: 5). In 1995, the UN estimated the global revenues of transnational crime organizations (TCOs) at US$1 trillion, resulting from the drug trade, arms sales, prostitution, gambling and banking (Chossudovsky, 1996). The annual turnover of the illegal drug trade alone was estimated at US$400 billion, or 8 per cent of world trade (The CornerHouse, 1999: 5).

Mittelman and Johnston (1999: 111) note that TCOs resemble TNCs in that they enthusiastically embrace the logic of the market, show great flexibility and are hierarchically structured. While they differ from TNCs in that they typically draw on a loose network of family and ethnic relationships for their cadre, TCOs resemble TNCs in that they embrace newer forms of economic activity, such as subcontracting and franchising, while being ready to invest in and benefit from new technologies and media such as the internet. They also benefit from the same international banking system: secrecy to hide and transfer their financial assets away from the taxing eyes of the state. Also, like TNCs, TCOs organize locally, nationally and globally – competing for markets and organizing global production and distribution systems, often exhibiting a regional division of labour, as in the heroin and cocaine trades, in the latter of which global commodity chains have been identified.

OC groups are being transformed by globalization. With globalization, 'there are whole new types of crime, some of them taking place in electronic space, where, with instantaneous transaction speeds, state institutions with territorial scope, such as central banks are perforce unable to exercise extraterritorial control' (Mittelman and Johnston, 1999: 107–8). Further, OC groups are driven by 'attempts to exploit the growth mechanisms of globalization' (ibid.: 109). Thus, OC groups grasp the market opportunities that globalization presents. When global regulation of trade in exotic animals was introduced, OC moved in on a market estimated in 1994 to be worth US$6 billion annually (*Time*, 14/11/94: 60). Similarly, more traditional activities, such as smuggling migrants and sex workers, have become increasingly globalized in scope (see below), while OC groups also benefited from globalization when changes in national and international agromarkets as a result of deregulation led farmers to change production crop sources to heroin and cocaine.

The globalization of crime is associated with the blurring of the line between legal and illegal economic transactions, in particular given the connections TCOs have had with what Robert W. Cox calls the 'covert world'. The globalization of crime is also associated with the criminalization of politics (Chossudovsky, 1996). TCOs, like TNCs, benefit from friends in high places. Citing the example of Italy, where, in the Tangentopoli scandal, some 3,000 state and corporate officials were investigated or indicted on corruption charges, Chossudovsky argues that:

> In the new global financial environment, powerful undercover political lobbies connected to organized crime cultivate links to prominent political figures and senior government officials. This phenomenon is common not only in the emerging market economies, but also in the EU, the US and in Japan, where corruption has become rampant. (1996: 26)

Insofar as the increase in corruption is linked to the growing internationalization of trade and finance, then corruption is no longer limited to the national system but is more and more internationalized, and 'all too often, corruption is practiced within a complex network in which the corrupt transaction is multidirectional and systematic' (Many, 1996: 317).

The globalization of labour and households

The globalizing strategies of workers and households are a relatively neglected aspect of globalization, but they link the developed and developing countries as much as orthodox indicators of trade and production. Some consideration has already been accorded to labour as a factor of production earlier in this chapter, and Chapter 5 examines the globalizing strategies of labour in some detail; so this section focuses on migration, particularly tourism, care-labour, and the skin trade. These are examples of transnational economic activity supported by global informal and commercial networks, and they illustrate the gendered nature of globalization and the commodification of culture and reproduction entailed by the spread of global capital.

Samers (1999) emphasizes the importance of placing international migration in historical context. Indeed, no novelty can be claimed for international migration, a transnational economic process as old as human history itself. Furthermore, the current phase of migration is not the phase in which international migration has been highest, and Samers notes that 'migration has now reached the level of the 1920s but far below that recorded before the First World War' (1999: 170). Despite this, the figures are impressive. To consider just one continent, by the mid-1990s some 3 million Asians were employed outside their own country but within the Asian region; a further 3 million were working outside the Asian continent, while around 9 million of the world's 'refugees and other persons of concern' to the UNHCR had their origin in Asia (Castles, 1998: 216, 220). Many EU countries, with histories of recruiting labour from foreign countries have substantial populations of foreign residents. In 1990 14.25 million foreign nationals were residents of EU member states, some two-thirds of whom were nationals of non-member states (Morris, 1997: 195).

It is also important also to note that internal migration, consisting mainly of populations moving to the city from the countryside, remains much more numerically significant than international migration, and that it is linked to the development of another effect of globalization, the growth of world cities:

> In 1950, only 29% of the total world population, and 16% of the Third World population lived in urban areas. By the year 2000 nearly half of the world population and 41% of the Third World population will live in urban areas. In Latin America and the Middle East approximately 70% of the population is already urbanized. (Araghi, 1995: 338)

Araghi has shown that this process of global 'depeasantization' accelerated during the period 1973–1990, which he links to the ongoing transformation of the world economy since the early 1970s (Araghi, 1995: 359). Globalization is certainly one of the 'push' factors impelling migration from rural to urban areas, as depeasantization results from global restructuring of agribusiness and the concentration of land ownership and massification of agricultural production. Indeed, the greatest population movement currently underway is happening within the borders of one country, China, where approximately 100 million people are on the move, driven from the land by the market system and drawn to the cities by the prospect of work in world factories.

Notwithstanding the continuing importance of internal migration, international migration is an important contributor to global financial flows. Of the estimated 100 million migrants, legal and illegal, between 25 to 30 million are foreign workers sending US$67 billion to their homeland per year (Castles and Miller, 1993). These remittances form a significant part of national GNP as well as of household economies. To give one example, the remittances of 3.5 million Filipinos who live and work abroad, either temporarily or permanently, amount to as much as 10 per cent of Filipino GNP, if unrecorded cash and goods brought home are included (ILO in Gough, 2000b), while remittances sent to Jamaica accounted for 9.8 per cent of GDP in 1997 (Stalker, 2000). Cultural tourism and 'prostitution tourism' (Farley in Jeffreys, 1999: 180) also constitute an important source of foreign exchange for governments and income for businesses and households. Producing half a billion temporary cross-border visitors worldwide annually (Petrella, 1996), the tourist industry entails 'the largest scale movement of goods, services and peoples that humanity has perhaps ever seen' (Greenwood cited in Srebeny-Mohammadi, 1997: 63) and was expected by some to have become the world's largest industry by the millennium. In smaller countries of the EU, such as Austria and Portugal, tourism receipts can be as high as 7 per cent of GNP (Hoggart et al., 1995). Revenue generated from prostitution accounts for between 2 and 14 per cent of the economy in Thailand, Indonesia, Malaysia and the Philippines (Lim in Jeffreys, 1999: 185).

Tourism is a vehicle for the commodification of culture and sex. The global tourist trade commodifies local culture by selling it as an 'exotic' product to be consumed, and indigenous culture 'becomes a commodity over which tourists have rights' (Srebeny-Mohammadi, 1997: 64). The involvement of tourist conglomerates means that a sizeable amount of tourist revenue is invariably repatriated back to 'core' countries where tourism TNCs tend to be located. In a study of the 'pleasure periphery' in Southern Africa (Botswana, Lesotho, Swaziland) Lea (1988) found that 60 per cent of tourist revenue was repatriated to South Africa by the TNCs involved. Like cultural tourism, prostitution tourism is also industrialized and internationalized (Barry, 1995) and transnational business networks are involved in the international trafficking of women in a host of ways and various shades of il/legality – from illegal 'recruitment' into sex slavery to the legal trade in wives:

> There is now a significant international traffic in wives, another part of the international traffic of women, captured in the phrase 'mail-order bride' . . . We find the international, too, in the ways that some countries become acquirers of brides and others supply them, roughly reflecting their reactive positioning in the international political economy. (Pettman, 1996: 198)

The supply of women's labour for sex-work is conditioned by uneven development worldwide (Jeffreys, 1999). In developing countries, notably the Philippines and Thailand, sex tourism has been a central component of state industrialization strategies, and for women marginalized from the formal economy, sex work is often more lucrative than work in the informal economy where most women in developing countries work, as vendors or servants, in the household or in family production (Rose, 1986; Tadiar, 1993). Another notable example of how female labour links developed and developing countries is the provision of care-labour. Global migration creates global networks of family relations, or 'globalized families' (Olwig, 1999) and sustains the 'international transfer of caretaking' (Salazar Parreñas, 2000) or 'global care chains' (Hochschild, 2000). Global care chains are similar in concept to global commodity chains discussed earlier, except that the commodity being traded is maternal care rather than some other resource. Global care chains are structured in the following way: 'migrant Filipina domestic workers hire poorer women from the Philippines to perform the reproductive labor that they are performing for wealthier women in receiving nations' (Salazar Parreñas, 2000: 561). It is important to stress that international migration, globalized families and global care chains should be seen in the context of greater population movement which is in part a response to globalization and the problems of uneven development – global capitalism helps create a particular type of international transfer as a result of a developing-world supply of mothering and a developed-world demand for it (Hochschild, 2000).

Global sexual services are just one element of what has become known as the 'skin trade', which also includes the global trade in bodies and body parts. The most well-documented part of this skin trade is the trade in kidneys, although the white baby adoption trade is also well established. The production of babies for sale to foreigners is possibly the most 'extreme form of labor alienation for women' (Bandarage, 1997: 220), which is made possible by communications and reproductive technologies and by the search for new 'markets' in which to sell their 'products' (Bandarage, 1997). These human 'products' flow from the South to the North, from the poor to the rich, assisted by cooperation between local and foreign capital (Bandarage, 1997; Kimbrell, 1996; Sachs, 1994).

Reproductive technologies illustrate particularly well how capital has succeeded in turning processes that were previously seen as private, 'natural' or biological into possibilities for the accumulation of wealth. Every stage in the production of human life has been turned into a profit-bearing operation: according to the biologist Ruth Hubbard, 'recent medical and social practices have made it possible to commodify our reproduction all down the line, making available for purchase eggs, sperm, embryros, surrogate mothers and babies'. This search for new markets and commodities has led TNCs into new sectors, such as genetics and biotechnology. Genetic engineering alters the genetic base of plants, animals and humans and is seen as an area of technological and economic growth and 'progress'. The human genome project, which involves mapping the genetic structure of humans, is an example of transnational economic activity on the part of large corporations and one where the very essence of life – genetic material – has been colonized by capital.

Conclusions

This chapter has highlighted major trends in, and issues arising from, economic 'globalization'. There has been a great deal of emphasis in globalization studies on the structural dependence on international trade and production, the vulnerability of national economies to political and economic events elsewhere in the world, and the partial de-linking of employment from production and of production from investment. Many analyses have indicated that these trends have consequences for our understanding of the global causes of (and solutions to) social problems such as migration, unemployment and poverty, and for the ability of states to manage their economies and set and realize public policy objectives. These issues are explored in later chapters.

This chapter has shown that although there is a consensus that 'something' has happened to the global economy in recent decades, there is a great deal less agreement about what this has entailed, the extent to which it has happened and whether contemporary trends constitute a 'qualitative shift' from previous periods. The portrayal of economic globalization as a recent occurrence and the world economy as fully globalized and integrated is highly problematic. A particular problem with the first globalization analyses, to recap on the discussion in the opening chapter, was that they were undertaken with a broad brush, generally in red or blue. Capital tended to be presented as a 'new', unified, monolithic force, which is seen to display certain characteristics and aims. However, production, trade, capital flows and the composition and reach of TNCs are much less 'new' in their nature and global in their reach than is often proclaimed. Although capital is indeed spreading around the globe, its embrace is much less inclusive, far more uneven, territorialized and *contingent* than is advertised, while the forces of global economic integration – summarized as the intensification of transnational links between economies, sectors, firms, cultures and peoples – must be seen alongside the forces of global economic fragmentation and polarization.

First, at both national and world levels, the concentration of wealth has been accompanied by impoverishment, and 'a large proportion of the world's population remains more or less untouched by the forces of globalization said to characterize our time' (Wyatt-Walter, 1995: 76). Second, because of the unequal incorporation of countries, regions, industries, sectors and workforces into this global 'mosaic' (Mittelman, 1994, 1995), globalizations will be experienced differently according to their position, or rank, within this global hierarchy. While the motivating forces behind migration/unemployment/poverty may be linked to global forces, these forces are expressed nationally. Thus, while the effects of 'local' market disturbances are felt globally, individual countries, classes, genders and ethnic groups will experience these quite differently. For example, workers in the advanced industrialized countries will feel the effects of the corporate restructuring of production differently to workers in developing countries. Third, it is more appropriate to talk of global econom*ies* rather than of a global economy. These global economies reflect divisions between different fractions of capital (productive vs financial capital, investment vs speculative capital, and domestic vs international capital), national and world-regional forms of capitalism, and legal and illegal global economies – divisions which give rise to a diverse range, rather than a singular set, of interests.

3 Globalization and the State: From Defeat to Political Struggle

Although globalization has been predominantly interpreted as an economic phenomenon, there is a growing body of literature which stresses its political dimension. 'Political globalization' provides an important corrective to the claims of 'strong' globalization that the global economy is ungovernable inasmuch as it draws attention to the continuing importance of institutional and political structures of regulation and control which mediate economic flow and circulation. The present chapter, together with Chapters 4 and 5, examine the centrality of political agency to globalization. This chapter concentrates on the state, Chapter 4 examines IGOs and Chapter 5 focuses on NGOs and social movements.

Specifically, this chapter examines how far states are pushed by economic forces to act in certain ways and how far states have rescinded control of economic actors and economic activity. It argues that while states may have lessened some regulation of capital, they have not abandoned control – indeed, the normal operations of capital and the market still require the existence of strong states – and, accordingly, the continuing range of state regulation of both TNCs and markets is demonstrated. This chapter also examines state strategies as a response to globalization, illustrated through the growth of regional blocs and it argues that, for some states at least (primarily the East Asian NICs), integration into the global economy through industrialization has been decidedly a state strategy. Here, the importance of social policy as part of states' globalizing strategies is emphasized. This emphasis on state activism in regulating globalization demonstrates the dialectical nature of this relationship: just as external factors bear on the state, so the state also acts outwardly through its own strategies to the extent that outcomes are neither certain nor uniform.

Capital vs states?

Claims that the state has been marginalized and emasculated tend to follow globalist orthodoxy and take the defeat of the state and the victory of capital as a given:

> The sovereignty of nations is in peril not on account of the international economy but because of the power of corporations to invest with less restriction, to reshape public policy support of private wealth generation and, most of all, to appropriate the political culture of nations for corporate ends. The message is clear as it is simple: national 'place' has to give way to corporate 'space'. (Drache, 1996: 53–4)

However, this formulation runs up against the following objections: it posits the state as acting in opposition to globalization, and it over-estimates the power of TNCs and underestimates that of the state. Indeed, the description of TNCs as unfixed, supra-national agents locked in conflict with states, ignores the dependency of TNCs and international markets on the state to facilitate their operations.

State regulation of TNCs

A central claim of 'strong' globalization theory is that TNCs are 'free-floating' agents, somehow 'separate' from their domestic bases (Chapter 1). Much of this discussion has focused on TNCs' location policies to the neglect of wider factors and has emphasized labour costs as being a determining factor in location decisions. Chapter 2 argued that TNCs are still largely national in their composition and structure, that relocation has been more limited than claimed, and that labour costs are only one factor in a much more complex equation. Indeed, the focus of attention in the globalization literature has been almost totally on the location decisions by TNCs and the arranging of tax and other facilities to attract TNCs, to the neglect of how TNCs interact with the state in many other areas such as consumer protection, market control, environmental regulation, occupational health and safety, and competition. The development and control of new technology by TNCs, notably in the pharmaceuticals and biotechnology industries, has been decidely dependent on state sponsorship and state regulation. In biotechnology, products by TNCs such as Monsanto have been a co-production of capital and the state, and the biotechnology industry has accepted state regulation as a way of assuring the public of the safety of its products. New methods of regulating corporations have emerged on the grounds of competition, public health, occupational health and safety and environmental impact. Furthermore, states can and do impose sanctions, including criminal ones, on corporations. Corporate executives in the US can face jail sentences for cartel activity or for toxic dumping, or for homicide charges in occupational accidents. More usually, sanctions can involve substantial monetary fines for corporate misdeeds.

A further problem with these 'stateless' TNCs which are assumed to be in conflict with states is that no one seems to have told the home governments about it. States continue to press each other for the advantage of their own manufacturers and service providers, engage in negotiations and disputes about trade and barriers to trade and take protective action in cases of alleged dumping. It can be assumed that when Washington pushes for open capital markets worldwide, it is worried about the interests of its friends on Wall Street, not those in Tokyo, Frankfurt and London. In short, states and capital are as often allied as in conflict (Gordon, 1987), with capital relying on its home state to advance its interests. This alliance is most easily visible in the peripheral countries, particularly the NICs, where capital has been often directed by the state, in a quasi-military operation under martial law following the decimation of working class organizations (Steven, 1990), where the unionization of workers represented a 'threat' to the national interests that the military and secret services were interested in suppressing. In countries such as Indonesia and Burma, the introduction of multinational capital was allied with nationalist state-building; in Indonesia it was particularly associated with the colonization of West Papua and East Timor. This state activity in support of its business interests is not confined to East Asian states: the US, for example, is notorious for the lengths to which it will go to protect the interests of its businesses.

This lacuna in 'strong' globalization theory can also be seen more generally in its ascription of a unity of purpose and aim to TNCs, as it does to capital in general. However, capital is as fragmented and fractured as the forces it faces globally. For example, FDI in a productive plant, in a peripheral country, has very different interests to speculative capital that flows into real estate and currency speculation. Just as the interests of financial capital may differ from those of manufacturing capital, so Chase Manhattan's interests may differ from those of Nike, and they certainly differ from those of Toray and Asahi. Similarly, it is not possible to ascribe a unity of purpose and interest to domestic and foreign capital, or to small and medium-size enterprises (SMEs) and TNCs. Domestic capital has often been at the forefront of arguments for greater, not less, protectionism. Indeed, among the most vehement opponents of deregulation has been domestic capital, because deregulation destabilizes production and trading conditions and increases competition from foreign firms seeking entry into national markets. Accepting business power has grown does not necessarily lead to the conclusion that it is an unstoppable monolith; indeed, the extent to which businesses are able to realize their preferences will 'vary from issue to issue depending on its internal cohesion, the strength of its opponents, and the institutional arena in which policy is made' (Pierson and Leibfried, 1995: 452).

The description of TNCs trampling over nation states therefore underplays the significance of extensive state regulation of capital and market sectors. The underestimation of the pivotal role of the state in capitalist global economic development can be summed up in one word: Japan. Japan is the only non-Western country to enter the core. Japanese capitalism, like Japanese imperialism, is decidely a joint creation of Japanese capital and the Japanese state. The Japanese state has actively limited direct investment by transnational capital, and, in the early 1970s, trade and investment restrictions were in fact even more stringent than those adopted in developing countries (Evans, 1985). The export of the Japanese model of state-led industrial and economic development to East-Asia and South-East Asia led to the 'Asian miracle' – ironically the glittering jewel of globalization.

There are numerous instances of the global strategies of some of the mightiest TNCs on earth coming up against hurdles erected by bureau-crats in regulatory and competition authorities. The homeland of free enterprise, the US, provides one useful recent example. Of a proposed £4.26 billion takeover of PacifiCorp by Scottish Power, a spokesperson for the latter told the *Guardian* that the merger 'would not be a com-plicated question for regulators'. But the *Guardian*'s own enquiries implied a larger number of regulatory hurdles remained to be jumped: 'The merger could take a year to clear ten federal departments, five state regulators, governors and legislatures, maybe twenty environmentalist groups, up to a dozen tribes and even the governments of New South Wales and Victoria in Australia' (*The Guardian*, 12/12/98: 26). While many of these groups do not have the power to block the takeover, some very definitely do, or at least possess the power to inconvenience it to the extent that the economics of the takeover change. Although monopoly and competition regulators may appear to operate primarily as legitim-izing mechanisms for corporate mergers, on occasions they have strongly intervened.

Corporations face a range of restrictions on size, monopoly or oligo-poly operations, various non-tariff barriers, and tax and fraud investi-gations. Dicken (1992) identifies the two most important types of state regulation for TNCs as the granting of market access and the deter-mination of the rules of operation once access has been gained. On access barriers, he notes that non-tariff barriers now apply to about a quarter of all imports to industrialized countries. The regulation of FDI deals with both access and rules of operation:

> In controlling access, that is regulating the entry of foreign firms, governments may operate screening mechanisms to filter out those investments which do not meet national objectives, whether economic, social or political. Foreign firms may in fact be excluded entirely from particularly sensitive sectors of the economy or the degree of foreign involvement may be restricted. The operations of these firms which have been allowed a physical presence may be regulated in a whole variety of ways, including in particular, the operation of local content requirements, export levels and methods of taxing locally-derived profits. (Dicken, 1992: 305)

Even in this one area, the range of regulation is wide. Just as state strategies towards regulation differ, so do those of corporations. It is unlikely that there will be a uniform response by corporations to regulatory differences between states, as 'for the most part, responses to regulatory differences are contingent upon specific circumstances in which particular TNC strategies are especially significant' (Dicken, 1992: 309). Chapter 2 showed that corporate internationalization strategies take various forms – FDI, mergers, acquisitions, strategic alliances, international subcontracting and various forms of networking – all of which are a response to regulatory differences. Strategic alliances with domestic firms, for example, are often a means for firms to enter domestic markets. Dicken concludes that the influence of national regulatory policies on spatial strategies of TNCs is a two-way process:

> On the one hand, TNCs respond to differentials in the regulatory surface: on the other hand, the changing nature of the regulatory surface itself is, at least partly, a state response to the strategies of TNCs. (1992: 314)

Overall, despite inflated claims that TNCs have evaded the control of states, states play an important role, whether as guardians or gatekeepers, in controlling TNCs' access to their domestic markets or to other resources that TNCs would like to exploit.

State regulation of financial markets

Although most attention has been paid to the regulation of TNCs (productive capital), they are paragons of stability compared with financial capital, which represents the most globalized fraction of capital (Chapter 2). Yet, here again we find that financial globalization does not necessarily involve the reduction of state power or regulation, and as Weiss (1999) argues, 'global finance is able to impact on states only inasmuch as, states – as a result of their basic orientations and institutional capacities – enable or invite such impacts'.

In an illuminating discussion of the German stock exchange, Lütz (1998) demonstrates that globalization leads to increased state regulation, as the state undertakes new regulatory functions. She shows both that the globalization of the securities market was accompanied by the 'emergence of an increasingly dense network of regulatory interstate collaboration' (1998: 158), and that the result was a regulatory 'race to the top' rather than the feared 'race to the bottom'. This race can mainly be traced to one of the two principal initiators of international cooperation in securities regulation – the US Securities and Exchange Commission (SEC). The other major impetus for cooordination came from the EU, whose Single Market programme included the integration of EU capital markets. State regulation of these markets was encouraged by EU directives on insider trading (1989) and investment services (1993) which required EU countries to nominate a regulatory body for international cooperation.

The SEC's interest in exporting the US regulatory model came from a desire to prevent capital flight from US financial markets:

> The power of the SEC rests not only on the fact that it is the oldest regulatory agency in the securities sector, but also on the fact that the agency upholds a regulatory model seen as the most investor oriented in the world. Given the fact that this model imposes the highest costs in terms of disclosure rules and transparency standards on its domestic producers, the SEC has a strong interest in exporting it. Under conditions of increasingly globalized markets, high regulatory standards could have turned into competitive disadvantages for US investment companies. (Lütz, 1998: 159)

This fear led the SEC to increase collaboration with other financial regulatory authorities through the signing of Bilateral Memoranda of Understanding (MOU) which codified information exchange and mutual assistance procedures. The SEC's first MOU was signed with Switzerland in 1982, continuing with Britain and Japan in 1986. By 1994 the SEC had signed 20 MOU globally. Lütz notes that 'in almost all these countries, MOUs [sic] with the SEC either preceded the establishment of new public regulatory agencies or followed shortly afterwards' (1998: 159). This new surge in regulation was in effect market-driven – on the US side by the SEC's desire to protect US markets, on the other countries' side by the desire to lure to their markets the most attractive customers in the world, US investors, by providing them with essentially the same protection as was available in their home market. For these reasons the regulatory field was levelled up instead of down.

In the German case, existing regulation of the stock exchange involved 'a well established mode of self regulation with the state playing a minor role' (Lütz, 1998: 154). This self-regulation was accompanied by cartel relationships between the major actors in the stock market, the German banks (both commercial and investment banks), and between the regional exchanges, which benefited from protection from their regional governments (*Länder*), which shared co-decision rights with the federal Ministry of Finance on stock exchange matters. With an underdeveloped capital market and without a strong lobby of institutional investors, the costs of this inefficient system were passed by the banks to the investors. This cosy arrangement necessarily came under strain with the liberalization of financial markets. With a weak market at home, the German banks attempted to attract foreign investors. The lack of success in this was attributed to investor doubts about the German market: insider trading, for example, was not criminalized, nor was there a commitment to transparency, while transaction costs were high. Attempts to increase market share by selling German investment products on the US market were scuttled by the SEC, which argued that the German system was inferior in protection levels to the US. In response, the major banks began to reorganize the German securities market, pushing towards centralization and introducing new financial products and new technology. They also began pushing for a new centralized regulatory agency; a move supported by EU requirements and by the Hessen *Land* whose interests lay with the development of the dominant Frankfurt stock exchange. After much political jousting, a new regulatory agency began work in January 1995 under the auspices of the federal Ministry of Finance, though the *Länder* retained some regulatory responsibility. Shortly after this new agency came into operation, access to the US market was granted to German financial products and cooperation agreements were signed with the SEC and the Commodities Futures Trading Commission of the US (Lütz, 1998).

Although these new regulatory arrangements were brought into being by the globalization of financial markets, these arrangements show the continuation of national diversity under globalized conditions. The new arrangements included the level of investor protection, transparency and criminalization of insider trading required by international (i.e. US) standards, but the form taken was distinctly German: 'a complex regulatory structure evolved which reflects the kind of "interlocking politics" characteristic of the German model of federalism' (Lütz, 1998: 164).

State regulation of welfare markets

A recurrent theme in 'strong' globalization is the extent to which global economic integration has undermined states' capacity (and inclination) to regulate markets in the interests of social protection. Again, what we find is that just as the coherence and power of capital are overestimated, so the enduring strength of the state in mitigating social risks and regulating welfare markets is also underestimated. Nor has globalization led the state to lose any of its powers of control or regulation over the supply and consumption of welfare services. Notwithstanding the international market in certain welfare services in the sense that specialized services can be accessed internationally, the provision of health, education and welfare services 'is subject to a significant degree of regulatory intervention' (WTO, 1998a: 10).

The presence of natural persons, or the mobility of service providers such as education, health and social work professionals, is regulated by national measures relating to educational, training, accreditation and licensing systems governing professional practice, by immigration requirements and nationality conditions (e.g. length of stay, payments of taxes, needs tests), as well as by regulatory controls governing terms and conditions of employment (Harris and Lavan, 1992; Moran and Wood, 1996; WTO, 1998a). There are also a range of restrictions on consumption of services abroad. Students are directly restricted by immigration requirements, labour policies, foreign currency controls, and indirectly by the lack of portability of national degrees and diplomas (WTO, 1998a). Patients' access to international health care services is highly restricted because, first, consumption abroad is restricted by rules and practices relating to reimbursement under mandatory – public or private – insurance schemes (WTO, 1998b), and second, health and medical services tend to be provided by organizations (often multi-nationals) which charge the full market rate. Thus, it tends to be only the wealthy who consume health services abroad, and for the vast majority of people access to health care is determined by national citizenship and by any bilateral or reciprocal, or, in the case of the EU, multilateral, arrangements entered into by their government. Thus, with the partial exception of the EU, rights to health care are not portable between countries, while patients are most likely to choose services which are closest to home anyway. Thus Jordan (1998) argues that, accompanying the development of international trade in services has been the emergence of consumer classes: the rich, with international lifestyles, who rely on packages of goods and services (health farms, private clinics, private schools) provided by commercial companies; business and professional groups who are members of international networks, firms and organizations and who rely on a mixture of commercial and public services; and ordinary workers who rely on state-controlled public health services.

A wide range of 'barriers', or regulations directed at institutional suppliers of services restrict the commercial presence abroad of organizations and companies. In the field of higher education, the WTO (1998a) notes the following restrictions: the authorization of national licenses, affecting whether or not educational institutions are recognized as degree- or certificate-awarding institutions (determining students' entitlement to financial assistance, and thus the economics of studying abroad); limits to direct investment by foreign education providers, such as equity ceilings; real estate acquisition; nationality requirements; needs tests, restrictions on recruiting foreign teachers; student population to be targeted (e.g. whether foreign institutions are allowed only to enrol foreign students); the existence of government monopolies and high subsidization of local institutions. Limitations on the cross-border supply of services include restrictions on the granting of financial assistance abroad, restricting the supply of the service to foreign students in the country and nationality requirements.

In the health and medical sectors, there are a range of regulatory measures that restrict commercial presence and cross-border supply of goods and services. Thus, even countries which allow for full participation of (foreign) commercial companies and organizations in their hospital or nursing care sector at freely negotiated prices still retain extensive regulatory control over the quality of services provided, including the qualifications of employees (WTO, 1998b). Moreover, despite the advanced state of global production, marketing and sales of products such as medical equipment, pharmaceutical drugs and private health insurance, access to and operation in the health product market is primarily regulated at national level by individual governments. The pharmaceutical industry, for example, is one of the more globalized industries whose products are 'global' in both their composition and use, but 'markets are highly segmented because of national health and price regulations and the incidence of particular diseases and traditions of medical practice which leads to decentralized final production, certification and marketing functions' (Casadio Tarabusi and Vickery, 1996). The state, in conjunction with professional groups, retains a significant degree of control over what is produced, who produces it, how it is marketed and the level of sales (particularly with regard to prescription drugs, for example). Indeed, state regulation of prescription drug use – notably states' attempts to reduce costs in their public health services – is one of the causes of the recent 'crisis' in the international pharmaceutical industry which led to the recent wave of mergers in the industry.

Even from a position of strong support for the consolidation of international welfare markets, the WTO recognizes that trade agreements are not without their problems. Notably, governments tend to seek exemptions to protect their rights negotiated bilaterally giving preferential treatment with regard, for example, the movement of natural persons supplying services (professionals), the promotion and protection of investment, and the right of establishment of juridical persons (WTO, 1998a: 12). The WTO also notes the problems in subsequently implementing free trade agreements. One of the key factors here is the diversity of existing institutional arrangements onto which international trade agreements impact unevenly between sectors and countries and which affect the economics of international mobility of consumers, and individual and institutional suppliers of services. Even in the EU with its Single Market the WTO notes that

> the Union experience has not been unequivocally encouraging to date. Cross-border investment is hampered by diverging institutional structures, limiting the scope for private market participation, while labour mobility may suffer from cultural and language barriers. (1998b: 14)

It also notes the ability of national insurance regulators to segment demand for health care services.

In the case of health and medical services, the WTO is optimistic that substantial regulatory restrictions on international trade in these services can be overcome, stating that 'the picture seems to be gradually brightening over time' due to, first, changes in regulatory regimes in some countries towards stronger market orientation, thereby opening up opportunities for greater private sector involvement, and, second, to technical changes which are enabling some services to be transmitted electronically between countries and continents (WTO, 1998b: 1). It invites the WTO members to use the Millennium Round of trade negotiations to 'reconsider the breadth and depth of their commitments on health and social services, which are currently trailing behind other large sectors' (ibid.). As regards the potential for further growth in higher education, the WTO is more realistic, and notes that although 'higher education institutions are being forced to look for alternative sources of funds' and 'investors are being encouraged to enter a new industry', any attempt to further liberalize tertiary education would be likely to encounter significant political opposition:

> This situation has been perceived as involving the risk that in the rush to become market-oriented, universities might be distracted from their educational missions. On the other hand, it is questioned whether higher education can be profitable for private investors without public subsidies. In addition, while access to international education may enhance domestic institutional and human capacities and promote development, flows of people and exposure to new ideas can arguably have a challenging impact on the structure of relatively fragile societies and touch on cultural sensitivities. (WTO, 1998a: 9)

Events in Seattle showed that the WTO's caution about the difficulties of extending trade law in higher education was the more realistic political assessment of the 'cultural sensitivities' that it would encounter. Indeed, France objected to what it perceived to be a plan by US universities to infiltrate national systems of higher education (see Chapter 5).

The necessity of state regulation: from deterritorialization to reterritorialization

The discussion has so far established the importance of the state in setting the ground rules of capital accumulation as well as regulating the arena in which accumulation takes place. These very basic needs capital has for the state are too often ignored in the globalization literature, partly due to the presentation of transnational capital and state as necessarily in opposition to each other, and of globalization and national autonomy as mutually exclusive. Indeed, globalization is too often presented as capital and state in collision with each other, when they are often in collusion together. As Gordon argues, 'it is not at all clear that [TNCs] have already achieved new global structures of coordination and control which will *necessarily* enhance their power' (1987: 25, emphasis in original), because the relationship between multinationals and governments is 'both cooperative and competing, both supportive and conflictual. They operate in a fully dialectical relationship . . . locked into unified but contradictory positions, neither the one nor the other partner is clearly or completely able to dominate' (1987: 61). Thus, just as states require capital investment for economic growth, so capital is dependent

on states and political associates to perform a range of functions –
enforce property rights, provide basic infrastructure and an educated,
trained labour force, and maintain social stability – in order to facilitate
its operations (Evans, 1997; Petrella, 1996; Pitelis, 1991; Pooley, 1991). On
this last issue, we should recall that capital is selective as to where it is
prepared to locate its operations: stability, above all, is to be prized, and
this stability is normally provided by the state's monopoly over coercive
violence. It is, after all, hard to make profits in a country in which a civil
war or widespread civil unrest is going on, as Shell, for example, found
to its cost in the Nigerian delta. If the state is too fragile to guarantee
social peace, then the basic law and order required for the operation of
markets is missing. Here, the importance of the state as the organizer
and guarantor of markets must be recognized, as Lütz noted in the case
of securities markets:

> Property rights have to be guaranteed and rules have to be set up and
> monitored – tasks which obviously cannot be fulfilled by the market par-
> ticipants themselves. It is apparent that the widening of market boundaries
> requires a set of agreed or imposed rules of the game; there is no spontaneous
> implementation of market mechanisms. (1998: 165)

Indeed, despite neo-liberal fantasies, markets do not spontaneously arise
fully grown from nowhere by some form of economic immaculate
conception:

> markets are conscious constructs – in the same vein that command economies
> are deliberate arrangements – in that they are based, by design or default, on
> political principles (who gets what, why and how) and on choices of how
> individual resources, rights, aspirations, and possibilities are reconciled with
> collective ones. The assumption that markets are 'neutral' and 'natural'
> obscures the political choices that are imbedded in the institutions that govern
> the market. (Chaudhry, 1993: 247)

It follows from this that intensive institution-building is needed to construct market economies:

> At a practical level, creating and regulating markets requires myriad financial,
> legal, and civil institutions, with stable and firm long-term commitments to
> regulate the actions of producers, importers, and labour, enforce contracts,
> and ensure the free exchange of information among economic groups. Market
> relations based on competition for profits and prices are inherently conflictual,
> involving shifting interests among producers, importers, labour, consumers,
> and the government. To create and regulate markets, the government must, at
> a minimum, provide the legal context within which disputes between
> competing actors are resolved. (Chaudhry, 1993: 251–2)

As this is the minimum required for effective market operation, we may conclude that free markets and free market economies cannot exist 'without effective legal, regulatory and extractive national institutions that have jurisdiction over a given territory' (ibid.: 265). These institutions sound suspiciously like nation states.

The failure to recognize the importance of state functioning for continuing capital accumulation is an example of globalization theory's attempt to detach economic relations and activities from the social and political context in which they are embedded and from all constraints, including those of geographical location. Much of the literature on globalization has focused on unifying economic and technological processes as evidence of greater global interdependence and integration. Globalization theory places an emphasis on *flows* (particularly transnational ones) and on the erosion of impediments to these. In so doing, it has neglected to attend to how globalization 'also entails constant efforts towards closure and fixing at all levels' (Geschiere and Meyer, 1998). A salutary corrective to the emphasis on flows, circulation and deterritorialization is provided by analyses of globalization from the disciplines of geography, planning and urban studies. It is no coincidence that the interest of these disciplines is the analysis of 'space', one of the more abstract concerns of globalization. When empirical hackles rise at such phrases as 'compression of time/space', spatial analysis literally brings these theories down to earth. While theoreticians have spoken of transnational space, the useful reminder from these disciplines is that the transnational/global must touch down somewhere. Geographers balance the over-emphasis given to deterritorialization and circulation by emphasizing the infrastructure needed for all this circulation.

By way of example, in an excellent critique Brenner (1999) makes two criticisms of analyses that focus on flows, circulation and deterritorialization. First, he argues, 'they tend to neglect the forms of relatively fixed and immobile territorial organization – in particular, urban-regional agglomerations and state regulatory institutions – that enable such accelerated movement'. Second, 'they neglect the ways in which the current round of neo-liberal globalization has been intrinsically dependent upon, intertwined with and expressed through major transformations of territorial organization on multiple geographical scales' (Brenner, 1999: 432). Thus, what is involved, is not the abolition of geographical scale and deterritorialization, the 'end of geography', but a reterritorialization, or change, in geographical scale and organization: 'Cities and states are being re-configured, reterritorialized and re-scaled in conjunction with the most recent round of capitalist globalization, but both remain essential forms of territorial organization upon which the world-scale circulation of capital is premised' (Brenner, 1999: 433).

Accepting that the state retains significant control over capital and markets and that it retains its capacities to shape national and global economic development leads us to examine how states have attempted to steer globalization. In the same way as capital has adopted a variety of internationalization strategies, so too have states and governments. To put it another way, just as states are under pressure from external forces, organizations or institutions, so they attempt to influence this 'external' environment. For nations to assert themselves as 'sovereign powers', they must engage in collective action with other states through the medium of transnational cooperative frameworks. The next stage in this chapter considers how states have attempted to steer economic globalization through regional alliances and formations.

Regionalism

Regionalism is a 'state-led or states-led project designed to reorganize a particular regional space along defined economic and political lines' (Payne and Gamble, 1996: 2). It is a project distinct from regionalization which is a 'market-induced' process, the *outcome* of state strategies to 'lock in' regional divisions of labour, trade and production and develop intra-regional trade (Hout, 1996). No new claim can be made for regionalism, which has existed, for example, since the nineteenth century in the 'Far East', long pre-dating contemporary globalization, but states' contemporary strategies to regulate globalization have been distinctively regionalist in their character and a wide variety of regional formations have grown over the last three decades (Table 3.1) (Dunkley, 2000; Fawcett and Hurrell, 1995; Robson, 1993). Many of these formations have emerged during the 1990s and more are likely to emerge in the future. Among regionalist strategies are also included cooperation between sub-regional areas, such as the growth triangle of North-East and South-East Asia (Ohmae, 1995a), and the Arab Maghreb Union, a grouping of five Arab states of North Africa (Tripp, 1995); Bowles and MacLean (1996) consider the possibility of an East Asian bloc, while Whalley (1992) peruses the prospects for a WHFTA: (Western Hemisphere Free Trade Association) associating North and Latin America.

The proliferation of regional blocs is sometimes portrayed as evidence of bloc-dominated global *dis*order – essentially an anomaly in the move to an otherwise globalized, unified multilateral trading order (Bowles and MacLean, 1996). However, as we have already seen, globalization is a highly truncated, regionalized and selective process, and economic integration has been at its most intense among, and between, the three most developed regions of the world, the 'Triad'. Thus, globalization and regionalization are not mutually exclusive processes but 'complementary phenomena' (Hout, 1996: 164) – regionalization simply adds another level at which the economy operates. Indeed, regionalization is driven by the same economic logic as globalization. Market trends only loosely determine bloc formation, and political strategy is required to

Table 3.1   *Regional trade agreements (RTAs)*

Name or countries	Date of commencement or proposal	Details
European Union (EU)	1957 and extended thereafter; monetary and political union agreed to in 1992 Maastricht Treaty	Economic union and proposed political federation – Austria, Belgium, Denmark, Finland, France, Germany, Greece, Ireland, Italy, Luxembourg, Netherlands, Portugal, Spain, Sweden, UK.
Central European Free Trade Agreement (CEFTA)	1993	Free trade area: Hungary, Poland, Czech Republic and Slovakia
North American Free Trade Agreement (NAFTA)	1992	Free trade area: US, Canada, Mexico, to be extended to Chile
ASEAN Free Trade Agreement (AFTA)	Association of South-East Asian Nations (ASEAN), 1967, AFTA, 1992	Cooperation from 1967; preferential trading arrangement from 1977; proposed free trade area over 15 years from 1993, excluding agriculture and services: Brunei, Indonesia, Malaysia, The Philippines, Singapore, Thailand, Vietnam
Asia-Pacific Economic Cooperation Forum (APEC)	proposed 1989, Secretariat, 1992, Detailed goals 1994; scheduled completion 2020	Proposed free trade area for goods and investment – AFTA, Australia, Canada, Chile, China, Hong Kong, Japan, Korea, Mexico, New Zealand, Papua New Guinea, Taiwan, US
Australia and New Zealand Closer Economic Relations Trade Agreement (ANZCERTA)	1983, with subsequent addenda	Common market – Australia and New Zealand
Southern Core Common Market (MERCOSUR)	1991, operational from 1995	Customs union – Argentina, Brazil, Paraguay and Uruguay
Caribbean Community and Common Market (CARICOM)	1973, replacing 1966 predecessor	Common market – covering most Caribbean states
Common Market for Eastern and Southern Africa (COMESA)	1996, supersedes earlier RTAs, to be implemented over 10 years	Customs union and partial common market; free movement of persons and businesses: Angola, Burundi, Comoros, Eritrea, Ethiopia, Kenya, Lesotho, Malawi, Mauritius, Rwanda, Sudan, Swaziland, Tanzania, Uganda, Zaire, Zambia, Zimbabwe.
South Asian Association for Regional Cooperation-Preferential Trade Arrangement (SAPTA)	1993	Preferential trade arrangement – Bhutan, India, Maldives, Nepal, Pakistan, Sri Lanka

Source: Dunkley, 2000

institutionalize and foster certain trading patterns (Bowles and MacLean, 1996). The expansion of CUSFTA to NAFTA through the incorporation of Mexico was largely post-hoc political ratification of changes that had already taken place (Hout, 1996). While trade pacts may ratify existing capital movements, they also consolidate and shape them. The Single Market project, for example, was to facilitate European corporations that could compete globally by providing them with economies of scale and a *grand marché* over which to spread long-term risks; the result has been an increase in the share of trade and investment between member states as a proportion of total EU trade and investment (OECD, 1996a). Regional bloc formation has also forced capital to globalize or internationalize: 'companies competing in global markets were increasingly likely to establish a local presence in the three main markets of the "triad" during the 1980s' (Wyatt-Walter, 1995: 108), although 'Japan as a destination for FDI remains, even more than its trade, the big anomaly' (1995: 108).

In the same way that regionalization and globalization are complementary processes, the growth of regionalism, as expressed in the growing number and membership of regional groupings, is not antipathetic to globalism. What regional processes imply is that world capitalism can now operate at global, regional, sub-regional and national levels at the same time. Indeed, states work with a range of multi-level and multi-range institutions (Hout, 1996; Bowles and MacLean, 1996); they strategize both at international and regional levels and see no inherent contradiction between a multilateral trade order and regional trade blocs. The US, for example, has taken a leading role in international integration through GATT, and has looked also to regional integration through CUSFTA and NAFTA. During the post-War period the countries of Western Europe looked as much to regional integration as to international integration. The European Coal and Steel Community (ECSC), the precursor to the EU, was evidently a regionalist strategy, but it emerged within a broader context of the consolidation of economic and political internationalism generally, and the pursuit of a geomilitary and geo-economic strategy on the part of the US specifically. In this sense, while European integration was *conditioned and prompted* by processes of globalization, it was a state response which was more directly related to regional problems (G. Ross, 1998).

A further point of note is that globalist and regionalist strategies are also compatible with economic nationalism. Both political interests and national economic interests were of concern to the founding states. Despite the creation of an internal market in the coal and steel industries and the extensive internationalization of member states' economies (exports of goods and services as a proportion of GNP were as high as 43 per cent in the Netherlands, and between 11 and 16 per cent in France, Germany and Italy in 1950 (Milward, 1994)), the state's extensive role in economic management was seen as the best means of securing the long-term interests of manufacturing and therefore of realizing economic (and social) reconstruction. Thus, during the 1950s, France embarked on an extensive programme of nationalization, while Germany, Italy and the Netherlands kept certain industries (e.g. the car industry) under public ownership to which they granted commercial trading advantages as a means of protecting domestic markets against foreign competition (Milward, 1994). In short, national economic recovery was predicated upon a blend of nationalism, regionalism and internationalism, with a central steering role assigned to the state.

The growth in regional formations indicates a growing propensity by states to engage in collaborative, collective action not least to protect themselves against the divisive effects of transnational capital (European monetary union was in part a response to anticipated speculative attacks on EU currencies). However, the history of regionalism is also one of struggle – of both alliance and resistance – for geo-strategic economic, political and military hegemony over areas of the world. The example of Western Europe is again instructive here. Renewed European integra-tion in the 1980s 'was a complex construction which flowed from multiple motives in response to a variety of pressing problems' (G. Ross, 1998: 177), but had much to do with the strategic choices by political élites to accelerate transnational policy coordination and trade within a circumscribed economic area rather than continue exclusively with separate national strategies (1998: 179). Even so, there were clear differ-ences between governments as to the nature and extent of policy coordination – the British government in the 1980s and 1990s argued that 'regional integration should be no more than a contribution to ensuring the conditions for global expansion of capitalism' (George, 1996: 50), while France and Germany have preferred 'strategic trade' and deeper political integration between member states.

Regarding the proposed completion of the Internal Market which intended to remove the remaining barriers to the free movement of goods, services, people and capital by 1992, one of the major motivating forces was 'the declining competitiveness of European industry relative to American and Japanese rivals, especially in technology-intensive sectors, with associated structural problems of high structural unemploy-ment' (Wyatt-Walter, 1995: 89). The economics of scale involved in dominating a regional, rather than a national, market are those deemed necessary for competition on a global scale. The EU has been quite clear that the political construction of the internal market would enable European corporations to compete globally with the US and Japanese giants. This was done – crucially – in the high-tech industries which require massive capital spending on R&D to stay ahead of the game. The EU has also strongly supported specific research projects which have involved transnational cooperation between European companies in high-tech areas, as well as cooperation between the private sector, universities, and other institutions in research:

Europe (exceptionally) has increasingly engaged not only in regional trade protection but also 'regional technonationalism'. That is, the increasing perception in Europe of a need for a common response to the challenge presented by US and Japanese firms in high-technology sectors has led to the adoption of publicly subsidized, collaborative R&D programmes aimed at enhancing the competitiveness of European firms. (Wyatt-Walter, 1995: 113)

Regionalism is related to geo-political and -military dominance as much as trade or economic dominance (Sum, 1996). Thus, ASEAN was primarily political in inspiration, a result of the Cold War. In the early twentieth century Japan attempted to remap the area currently known as East Asia to persuade, or force, the countries in this region to accept a subordinate position in the Japanese empire. After World War II, the US attempted to reconfigure the region under its own hegemony. Currently, the US, Japan and China are competing for geo-political and geo-economic advantages in the region (Sum, 1996). Through these strategies, the identities and interests of the countries of East Asia are rearticulated and repositioned. In relation to future regional groupings, Bowles and MacLean argue that the most likely motive for Japan and the NICs in joining an East Asian bloc would be 'to group together as allies to counter ever more aggressive US demands for market-opening measures' (1996: 167). Revealingly, no regional formation has appeared in East Asia, though it is here that a most obvious regional political economy is apparent. The reason is political: Japan's imperialist aggression is too recent in history to allow it to lead an East Asian formation. Similar nationalistic fears are evoked by the spectre of mainland China.

Regional formations take different institutional forms. While some have been almost stateless in their existence as pure economic or trade agreements, others have developed social and political projects as well. The EU may be regarded as the most advanced example of the latter: it is the only regional bloc to have macro-economic (monetary, trade and finance) policy competences, a common currency, redistributive powers and an institutionalized 'social dimension' entailing common minimum standards and social provision. A far more limited model of political integration characterizes the regional grouping in North America – NAFTA (1994). Described as 'the most comprehensive investment treaty ever agreed to between developed states' (Appleton 1999: 90), NAFTA expanded the territorial reach of CUSFTA into Mexico and the scope of what was essentially a trade agreement to include investment, services and intellectual property. However, although it has attempted to set minimum environmental and labour standards and introduce mechanisms for their enforcement, it has not pooled macro-economic policy, established a common currency, or made social provision. There are signs that other regional formations are also beginning to develop a social dimension, although the extent of institutionalized cooperation in the social sphere is limited. Mercosur has gone furthest in developing consultative arrangements on labour and social issues, while the ASEAN, SADC and APEC fora are talking about it. The emergence of social issues onto regionalist political agendas shows that labour, like capital and governments, operates at a number of levels and in a range of fora. For Wilkinson and Hughes (2000) this socialization of regional trading arrangements attests to the influence of the labour movement's strategy to institutionally link trade and labour regulation in regional fora, and they argue that labour's regionalist strategies are a significant development in global social politics given the resistance to the involvement of global trade institutions in the administration and enforcement of international labour standards (see Chapter 4).

In the remainder of this chapter I examine how states mediate the process and effects of globalization through, first, their national economic and industrial development policies, and second, their social policies. The following treatment shall concentrate on East Asia, not only due to its status as the most successful region in the period in which globalization is said to have occurred but also due to its place in neoclassical economic mythology.

State-led economic and industrial development

A recurrent theme throughout globalization studies is the growth both of international cooperation and competition; nation states seek both to cooperate with one another but also pursue policies that maximize their national competitive advantage (Rhodes, 1991). Beyond this, though, it is clear that individual states already interacted with the structures of the global political economy in quite different ways. As Palan et al. (1996) argue, if the state is undergoing transition then it is to alternative types of state which develop different strategies for pro-actively interacting with the global system. The particular strategy that states adopt reflects their particular histories, 'factor endowments' and capacities. States will remain differentiated by their rank in the global political economy, their geo-political and geo-economic group, by the type of state, as well as by the strategies of 'niche states' which promote themselves as tax and regulation havens.

On this issue of varieties of state regulation, Chalmers Johnson has isolated a useful dichotomy of state attitudes to regulation:

> A regulatory, or market-rational, state concerns itself with the forms and procedures – the rules, if you will – of economic competition, but it does not concern itself with substantive matters. For example, the US government has many regulations concerning the anti-trust implications of the size of firms, but it does not concern itself with what industries ought to exist and what industries are no longer needed. The developmental, or plan-rational, state by contrast has as its dominant features precisely the setting of such substantive social and economic goals. (Chalmers Johnson in Dicken, 1992: 306)

Dicken argues that 'it is . . . not unreasonable to interpret many of the current politico-economic tensions in the global economy as being at least partly a reflection of a clash between these two different models of state behaviour' (1992: 306). 'Market-rational' states, such as the US and the UK, tend to be more regulatory than developmental, while 'plan-rational' states tend to be developmental, disciplining both capital and labour, and often involving strong elements of nationalism and nation state building. These states tend to be late industrializers and are exemplified by the East and South-East Asian developmental states, including Japan. Amsden (1995) has also suggested these states exemplify a successful late-industrialization paradigm of strong state intervention, industrialization by learning and diversified private firms:

> successful South-East Asian cases are part of a general 'late'-industrializing paradigm that encompasses not only fast-growing East Asia (including China) but also a culturally, geographically and historically varied set of countries encompassing Argentina, Brazil, Chile, India, Mexico and Turkey. (Amsden, 1995: 791)

Indeed, the major examples of economic growth over the last three decades, the decades of globalization, have all been state-controlled processes in which TNC involvement was heavily controlled and limited by a strong state.

If the globalization thesis were correct, it should be able to provide an explanation for what has been described as the most important change in global production and economic patterns over the last 30 years – the rise of the Asia Pacific economies. Until the recent currency crisis that undermined it, the Asia Pacific was seen as the glittering pearl of globalization, with the potential, according to the former US Trade Representative Carla Hills in 1993, to 'trigger an economic renaissance worldwide' (*Financial Times*, 13/8/93). Yet the Asian experience contradicts some of the basic tenets of 'strong' globalization:

> The process of accelerated economic growth in the NICs appears to be everywhere associated with the expansion of the public sector and the role of the state. It has not been 'free enterprise' nor multinational capital which has led the process, but the deliberate and persistent efforts of governments. Foreign companies appear as formally invited – and often barely tolerated – guests at a feast organized, supplied and supervised by Ministers; not infrequently the guests have been expropriated in the midst of the festivities. (Harris, 1986: 148)

The lack of transnational guidance in this development is confirmed by a survey by UNESCAP of the empirical evidence of the role that TNCs played in the Asian economies. It noted that, the absolute number of TNCs in most Asian and Pacific countries is relatively small, and TNCs are not the dominant source of investment in even the most internationalized and open economies of the region . . . on average, TNCs provide through their direct investment only around 3% of total investment financing in the developing Asian and Pacific countries and even this is heavily concentrated in a relatively small number of countries. (1988: 3)

Even in those East Asian countries where TNCs have been basic to state development strategies the guiding hand of the state is evident. As Henderson summarizes,

the rapid economic growth and development of Japan and the newly industrialized countries would have been inconceivable had they emerged as *market rational* political economies, as neoclassical accounts in effect would have us believe. Rather they have been heavily state-influenced or directed *plan rational* political economies. (1993: 203)

Central to these state plans was manufacturing industry and the heroes of this industrialization were industrial engineers rather than general managers. State policy designated certain industrial sectors as central to economic development:

In Taiwan and South Korea, as in Japan before them, the state has deliberately induced selected industries if these were considered essential to national economic development. Thus from the 1950s to the 1980s either by encouraging (with, for example, cheap credit) or directing private firms, using transnationals (often in joint-venture arrangements), or using state-owned enterprises, the Taiwanese state has created and continues to oversee such industries as synthetic fibres, plastics, petrochemicals, automobiles, televisions, steel, shipbuilding, electrical machinery, semiconductors, precision tools and computers. In sectors such as these the state has acted in anticipation of changes in comparative advantage; it has led the market, not followed it. (Henderson, 1993: 205–6)

The centrality of state planning can also be seen in the global growth of the petrochemicals industry, which resulted from state economic planning rather than from the globalization strategies of the TNCs which dominated the industry. The growth of productive capacity, for example, in the petrochemicals industry in peripheral countries over the last 20 years has happened 'almost entirely through NFI (new forms of investment), notably joint ventures, much licensing and some turn-key contracts' (Oman, 1989: 75). This growth and the concomitant shift in global production patterns has not been driven by transnational, 'private' capital, but by

the governments and the large state-owned or state-supported firms of the host countries and it is they who undertake the search for appropriate foreign partners. Foreign investors have never been beating at the door to take part in these new forms of investment, let alone take the initiative of proposing them. (Oman, 1989: 76)

Thus, while not discounting TNCs as significant agents of change, local capital – in particular state capital – has 'played the major role in promoting the apparent geographical spread of the industry since the 1960s' (Chapman, 1992: 19). In all these cases the initiative can be traced back to state economic planners which prioritized the development of a national petrochemical industry as necessary to provide inputs for downstream manufacturing industries.

State industrial planning used a variety of methods to direct industry, but central to these has been state control over access to capital. This control stemmed in Taiwan, for example, from an almost entirely nationalized banking system and heavy restrictions on speculative investment, while in Korea 'the banks were (re)nationalized in 1961, the development of capital markets restricted and access to foreign sources of credit rigidly controlled by the state' (Henderson, 1993: 209). If an explanation for the success of late-industrialization policies compared with their failure in Latin America is to be sought, it is surely to be found here:

> Unlike many countries which have subsidized particular industries, the Koreans and Taiwanese like the Japanese before them, have subjected com-panies in receipt of subsidies to rigorous performance standards. These have often included requirements on product quality and export contribution and have been backed up by the threat to curtail cheap credit, presaging financial ruin. (Henderson, 1993: 209)

This discipline placed on capital, with its constraints on rent-seeking and speculative investment, has also prevented the appearance of the extreme levels of income inequality that have appeared in other late-industrializing nations. Like control over labour, it has been justified by a project of economic nationalism where the interests of both capital and labour have been subsumed into the creation of a successful national economy under state guidance and direction. It may thus be concluded, with Evans, that,

> East Asian successes force us to re-examine the idea that effective participa-tion in a globalized economy is best achieved by restricting state involvement in economic affairs. They suggest that successful participation in global markets may be best achieved through more intense state involvement. (1997: 69–70)

Even the World Bank (1997a) has been forced to finally admit the importance of the state in engineering the East Asian 'dragons'. How-ever, it limits itself to an 'economic' conception of the state, and regards the state as important only insofar as it is central to achieving economic 'transition' and eventual integration into the global economy. Here, the World Bank regards the most important state roles to be: establishing a stable investment environment through a foundation of law and property rights; ensuring macro-economic stability; avoiding price distortions; 'liberalizing' trade and investment; fostering greater reliance on private markets for welfare provision and delivery, and maintaining public programmes targeted at the most vulnerable or poorest. Thus it continues its traditional practice of ignoring empirical evidence of the central importance of state industrial and social policy in the globalization process.

Before the discussion examines more fully the importance of social policy in helping the engineering of globalization, it is worth noting that many claimed the Asian financial crisis (1997) would sound the death-knell of state-led economic development. However, the success of the Asian states and local capital in creating the 'Asian miracle' is only further emphasized by the arrival of a financial and currency crisis that can be traced to state deregulation of capital controls. This deregulation, in response to demands from the OECD, World Bank and IMF, that governments strictly adhere to market principles, led to a flood of foreign investment into the area. However, much of these funds went into speculative real estate and stock market investment rather than into enhancing productive capacity and industrial upgrading. According to Bello it was only a matter of time before this 'giant speculative bubble over the real economy . . . would explode in a highly destabilizing fashion' (1998: 14). Explode it did, and led to a massive reversal of foreign capital flows, originating initially in Thailand and then spreading throughout the region and globally.

The crisis also made its effects felt in the real economy rather rapidly, in fall in output; bankruptcies; massive job losses and a rise in unemployment, under-employment and temporary work; a severe drop in wages and incomes, a sharp rise in the numbers of people in poverty, and the mass repatriation of foreign workers to their countries of origin (Bullard, 1998; Lee, 1998). In Indonesia alone, the crisis increased the number of people living in poverty by 20 million, using the World Bank's definition of US$1 per day. The crisis was felt worldwide with the collapse of commodity prices and the fall, or competitive devaluation of, currencies, while national banking sectors with loan exposure to the region, indigenous firms exporting to the region and local branches of Asian multinationals based pretty much anywhere were also affected. The crisis wiped £33 billion off leading shares in the UK alone, the drop in the FTSE-100 was the third largest fall ever (*The Observer*, 23/9/98), and the ILO estimated that the crisis cost more than 10 million jobs worldwide (*Irish Times*, 24/9/98).

The IMF's standard prescription for bailing out the financial business classes, otherwise known as stabilization and recovery programmes, in the countries with which it has concluded agreements to the tune of

US$100 billion (Thailand, Indonesia and South Korea) was based on an interpretation of the crisis as attributable to domestic factors, notably the 'crony capitalism' engendered by interventionist, even corrupt, state practices (Lee, 1998). The IMF accordingly gave primacy to restoring international confidence in the currencies affected by exchange rate devaluation, tightening domestic monetary and fiscal policy, including credit control, and increasing interest rates. This stabilization package was accompanied by a programme of structural reform involving privatization of public companies, the lifting of restrictions on foreign ownership of corporations and increasing foreign access to domestic assets (Chandrasekhar and Ghosh, 1998).

Social policy also played an important part in the overall public policy response to the crisis, albeit one principally of mitigating the impact on living standards and promoting social and political stability in the region. However, the IMF-imposed fiscal austerity measures reduced the scope for increased social expenditure at a time when need was soaring. In order to mitigate the social impact of the crisis and to 'stabilize' domestic reactions, fiscal targets were subsequently revised to allow for more social expenditure. Social expenditure increased by 1.5 per cent of GDP in Thailand and 2.5 per cent of GDP in South Korea directly as a result of the crisis. Part of this increase reflects additional foreign aid earmarked for social expenditure, while the World Bank and Asian Development Bank granted social loans to Thailand and Indonesia (Lee, 1998: 54). These increases in social expenditure were not just an outcome of greater need, but also of the expansion of state welfare during this period, at least some of which could be attributed to the crisis. Social security and health care coverage were widened, and training, education and employment measures involving substantial state expenditure on grants and loans, were extended (Lee, 1998: 56). For example, unemployment became recognized as a publicly-insurable risk in Korea, severence pay guarantees were introduced in Thailand, and national pension programmes were introduced in Taiwan (Hort and Kuhnle, 2000). Also worth noting is the variation in national social policy responses to the crisis:

> a common crisis has engendered very different outcomes, with Korea moving swiftly to a developed welfare state, Thailand and Indonesia developing a 'third way' based on community and local innovations, and Malaysia and the Philippines exhibiting less policy innovation. (Gough, 2000b: 19)

The supposed obituaries of the command Asian economies seem premature, given that the economies least affected by the crisis – China, Taiwan and India – are still highly protected economies, with strong controls over foreign investments and ownership of local companies, and insulated by the limited convertibility of their national currencies. Finally, it should be noted that Malaysia survived the crisis by its 'heretical' introduction of capital controls along the Chinese model, contrary to the advice of the IMF. Attributing the causes of the crisis to international financial markets, Malaysia gave priority to halting the economic recession and allowing the financial and corporate sectors to restructure, reintroducing capital controls, moving to fixed exchange rates, lowering interest rates and easing monetary policy (Lee, 1998: 28). The IMF was forced to reverse its earlier predictions that capital controls would have catastrophic effects on the Malaysian economy, and together with the World Bank, has pronounced them more or less a success. Indeed, the crisis considerably sharpened the debate about the role of national and international public policy in preventing a recurrence of a similar crisis in the future, and it is no longer blasphemous to entertain the idea that national regulatory authorities can exert some control over financial flows (Akyüz, 1998; Lee, 1998; Weiss, 1999).

Social policy and state industrial strategy

East Asia provides an excellent example not only of the steering role of the state in globalization, but also of the centrality of social policy to states' globalizing strategies. Although East Asian countries share a common development strategy based on export-oriented industrialization, it should be noted that their welfare regimes vary considerably (see Deyo, 1992; Goodman et al., 1998; Gough, 2000b; Hort and Kuhnle, 2000). The major focus of interest in East Asian welfare states has been the mutually supportive relationship between economic development and 'proactive' or 'positive' social policy (Deyo, 1992: 305; Castells, 1998; Chau and Yu, 1999; Goodman et al., 1998). Gough characterizes East Asian welfare regimes as examples of 'productivist welfare capitalism'. The main feature of this type of welfare capitalism is, he argues, the subordination of social policy to economic policy and the imperative of economic growth (2000b: 16):

> Social expenditures were small but relatively well targeted on basic education and health as part of a strategy of nation-building, legitimation and productive investment. The growth in welfare over the last three decades has relied on the expansion of formal employment within the orbit of strong families, plus growing payment for services. (Gough, 2000b: 16)

Although state-provided welfare is restricted, welfare outcomes are relatively good. Indeed, this 'productivist' orientation of East Asian social policies has proved relatively successful in tempering social inequalities compared with other late-industrializing countries, notably in Latin America. Comparing the two regions Deyo argues that 'East Asian industrialization . . . has been relatively more compatible with positive social policy, especially during economic restructuring and in the areas of social wage and incomes policy' (1992: 296–7). The effects of East Asian state activism in social policy can be discerned when comparing countries which embraced economic 'liberalization' and experienced 'miracle' growth (Brazil, the Philippines, Sri Lanka) with those where the state has been central to the management of the economy (notably Japan, but also South Korea and Taiwan). Whereas the former experienced increased income inequality and poverty, the latter combined growth rates with improved social and physical standards (ibid.).

East Asian social policies, especially in education and training, housing and incomes, were central to export-oriented industrialization strategies. In earlier periods, competitive advantage had been achieved through low labour costs, but this advantage was reduced by other countries also seeking to compete on these terms. East Asian governments sought to regain or maintain their competitive advantage by pursuing a strategy of high value-added production, labour force stability and productivity through upgrading the skills and education of the local workforce and improving workplace social and employment benefits (Deyo, 1992; Esping-Andersen, 1996). Education in particular was central to providing capital with skilled, educated and adaptable workforces to compete on a global scale, supporting Green's argument about the importance of education to globalization:

> as capital, goods and ideas become increasingly global, and as people and skills remain one of the few national resources which remain relatively rooted, governments may come to regard education as one of the most effective remaining instruments of national policy. It becomes increasingly essential for national economic competitiveness in a global market. (1997: 4)

Education has been the focus of most attention, but housing has also been central to the creation of globally competitive workforces. The experience of Hong Kong as a city-state is instructive in this respect. The Hong Kong welfare state is often classified as a 'residual' welfare state, in which the state has reiterated the need for private not public solutions to social problems, and only intervenes when family and market are unable to provide (McLaughlin, 1993). However, this is not British- or American-style residualism as the state substantively intervenes in key areas – particularly through its public housing programme of which Hong Kong is renowned for having one of the world's largest. Hong Kong social policy has been regarded as a significant contributory factor in the economic development of the city-state as a major centre in the global economy (Castells, 1998; Deyo, 1992). Thus, although Hong Kong maintained low corporate and personal taxation and low foreign indebtedness (Henderson, 1993), 'the fundamental contribution of Hong Kong's government to the flexibility and competitiveness of small businesses was its widespread intervention in the realm of collective consumption' (Castells, 1998: 261). The public housing programme has been significant for its main structural effect – 'to influence the reproduction and cost of labour power' (Henderson, 1993).

Housing was in fact the first social sphere in which the state became substantively involved. In the 1950s the scale of squatting rose as a result of the influx of half a million refugees from China into the city-state and of the inability of the private sector to provide sufficient housing. The public sector housing programme could not be considered primarily a 'welfare' operation, a response to housing need, as it was motivated by 'threats' to public order that squatter areas were deemed to represent and particularly by the release of valuable land for industrial and commercial development (McLaughlin, 1993: 112). The next impetus to the growth of the state's role in housing came in the early 1970s. In 1966 and 1967, civil unrest broke out, initially as a response to social conditions and increases in public transport fares, but was later directed against colonial rule. The government's concern to rebuild or reconstruct state–civil society relations after the riots involved greater community consultation and state intervention, not only in housing, but also in education, health care and social services. In 1973, a housing authority was set up to plan, deliver and manage a public housing programme, aimed at providing quality housing for 1.8 million people – 45 per cent of its population and 85 per cent of the working class – eradicating substandard housing and clearing all squatter areas. During the 1980s and 1990s, the state attempted to restructure its role in housing provision, having recourse to privatization by selling leases on land, but it still retains a substantial role in housing provision (Chan, 1996; McLaughlin, 1993).

Public housing not only led to improved living standards, through improved quality of housing, but it also helped maintain the competitiveness of goods sold internationally. Low-rent public housing enabled families to survive on low wages, holding down wage demands on businesses, and small businesses in particular. Food subsidies also kept down prices. In the absence of a social security system, public housing provided an alternative safety net of substantial indirect wage subsidies. Yu and Lai estimated that the amount of subsidy from state to public housing tenants was equivalent to about 70 per cent of household income, up from 50 per cent in the early 1970s (Yu and Lai in McLaughlin, 1993; Castells, 1998). In addition to constituting a central element of the social wage and contributing to relative industrial harmony, public housing also secured the conditions for entrepreneurialism: 'most businesses were started by workers who betted their small savings, and relied on family support, and on the safety net of public housing and subsidized public amenities to take their chance' (Castells, 1998: 263). It was these small and medium-sized entrepreneurs who proved to be 'the driving force of Hong Kong's development' (1998: 263).

Another example of the importance of state social policies is provided by Singapore which has a highly internationalized economy but which is also both 'exceptionally dependent for its local economic dynamism on foreign direct investment by transnational corporations' and 'renowned for the capacity and power of its state bureaucracy' (Evans, 1997: 69–70). Singapore's export-led growth strategy has been engineered by the state, which is also a major provider of infrastructure; it controls trade unions, regulates labour supply and wage-setting, and is a major provider of welfare services (housing, health, education and pensions). In fact, the Singapore state is 'virtually a monopoly provider for the nation and a universal welfare system' (Tremewan, 1998: 89).

Tremewan describes this large-scale provision of state welfare as 'a fundamental factor in [Singapore's] sustained economic growth' (1998: 78). Central here is the Central Provident Fund (CPF), established in 1955. The CPF is a mandatory state saving scheme for retirement. A proportion of an employee's wages is paid into the fund, with an equivalent amount contributed by employers; this proportion has increased from 5 per cent (1955) to 20 per cent (1994) of an employee's wages. However, there is no guaranteed right to a minimum pension: individuals receive back only what they paid into their 'account', plus interest paid at a nominal rate. The CPF enjoys a near monopoly over national savings as there is no alternative institutional means of saving for retirement and welfare payments are highly restricted. Although the CPF was designed primarily as a means of saving for retirement, it also serves a number of other functions such as the financing of third-level tuition fees, home ownership and health care, and provision for dependents in case of injury or death of the breadwinner.

Despite being mandatory the CPF controls the major savings and assets of only 65 per cent of Singaporeans. Nevertheless it is clearly an important instrument of domestic economic and political management. In 1990, gross national savings comprised 45 per cent of GDP; 30 per cent of these savings were made through the CPF (Asher in Tremewan, 1998: 85). This 'state system of forced saving' (Tremewan, 1998: 86) gave the government access to massive amounts of cheap capital that could be used for developing infrastructure and investing in government-owned or -approved companies and schemes. Through the CPF, the government manages both domestic consumption and production costs by varying the total wage (immediate and deferred) reducing or raising employer and employee contributions as necessary (1998: 82). This state bureaucracy successfully guided the local economy from its origins in low-skill assembly work to its current high-tech, high-skill state by actively guiding TNC restructuring:

By investing heavily in education and delivering Asia's most advanced welfare state, government planners consciously developed the preconditions for such restructuring. The *coup de grâce*, however, was delivered during the

1980s when the state doubled labour costs by forcing up employer contributions to the Central Provident Fund. The anticipated goal of shedding unskilled assembly workers and the transformation of Singapore into a high-tech 'post-industrial' society seems to have transpired. (Henderson, 1993: 212)

The CPF has been important in financing the city-state's public housing programme. The Home Ownership Scheme (1964) aimed to encourage long-term leasing of public sector dwellings, and tenants who were CPF members were permitted to use their CPF payments for the deposit required. The mass housing construction programme was economically cheap for the government, which pays little or nothing for the land (of which it owns 75 per cent). It was also politically rewarding, as it permitted the ruling party to consolidate its political base through the financing of the local construction industry. Despite having a near monopoly on housing, in the 1980s the state created an internal market by introducing an upgrading programme which permitted leased flats to be sold on (Tremewan, 1998: 96).

Through its control of wages and welfare the government has sought to stabilize working-class subsistence and exert control over workers to minimize political dissent:

> The relatively high cost of housing and its link to the forced saving regime of the CPF have compelled a high level of social discipline in that people have had to remain in formal employment in order to meet increasing costs and to provide for their future subsistence. (Tremewan, 1998: 90)

In effect, extensive state welfare is entirely compatible with economic globalization and high levels of internationalization. The state has been assigned a considerable role both in attracting foreign capital and in ensuring continued profitability on its behalf. As Tremewan points out, Singapore's attractiveness to foreign capital has been premised on

> a continuing supply of relatively cheap, disciplined workers with appropriate skills, as well as a relatively developed infrastructure being rapidly improved, a state policy constantly to upgrade the technical level of production, a strategic geographical location and a reliable government administration. (1998: 81)

Conclusions

Perhaps the most glaring defect of globalization theory is its presentation of globalization as a reality which cannot be resisted and which must be accommodated. Globalization discourse 'naturalizes the market and the economy, to such an extent that it presents the latter as [an] autonomous force to which we must bow' (De Angelis, 1997: 43). A similar analysis of the paralysing and fatalistic nature of this discourse is given by Gibson-Graham who compares the 'globalization script' to the 'rape script':

> The globalization script normalizes an act of non-reciprocal penetration. Capitalist social and economic relations are scripted as penetrating 'other' social and economic relations, but not vice versa . . . Now that socialism is no longer perceived as a threat . . . globalization is the prerogative of capitalism alone. After the experience of penetration – by commodification, market, incorporation, proletarianization, MNC invasion – something is lost, never to be regained. All forms of noncapitalism become damaged, violated, fallen, subordinated to capitalism. (1996: 125)

This defeatism is not only politically dangerous, but it does not accord with the empirical evidence which suggests the resilience and continued relevance of the state, rather than its terminal demise. The presentation of the state–capital relationship as one in which capital is essentially in conflict with the state, or hegemonic after defeating the state, is inaccurate. It posits capital always in opposition to the state, whereas it is more useful to see capital and state often allied together, as well as often in conflict (Hall in Gordon, 1987: 61). The presentation of capital as acting without regulation is also inaccurate: it is bound in various webs of regulations and governance, which it accepts grudgingly, attempts to circumvent and which it very occasionally invites. Indeed, transnational capital wishes to secure the support of the state, not to replace the state. It has an interest in strong public bureaucracies and in avoiding the real institutional marginalization of the state. As Yaghmaian (1998) points out, it has a very basic need for the state to provide the law, under which contract and other disputes between individual capitals can be resolved and sanctions enacted, and to maintain civil order. It needs the state to facilitate its operations because the state remains the dominant institution which upholds the social relations on which economic globalization is dependent:

> despite the internationalization of wage relations, class relations are largely reproduced in geographically separated fragments in specific national sites. Nation states and national state policies remain crucial for the legitimation of capitalist relations of production on national sites. (Yaghmaian, 1998: 255)

Therefore, although globalizing tendencies are occurring these are neither inevitable nor do they constitute a bulldozer with the power of history behind it, levelling all in its path. The state remains a powerful agent, in no way dominated by transnational forces. Indeed, far from being victims of the forces unleashed by a social movement for global capitalism, states have supported, driven, steered and stabilized capitalist accumulation on a global scale. The example of East Asia showed the continued possibility (indeed, the necessity) of state activism in national economic and social development, while the proliferation of regional formations indicates states' willingness to partake in collective action, pooling resources and power to control a greater area than would be the case were they to act independently.

'Strong' globalization theory is therefore incorrect in positing globalization and national autonomy as mutually exclusive (Garrett, 1998). It is precisely because the totalizing elements in 'strong' globalization theory allow for no resistance, and because the matter is not foreclosed, that there is a need for a more nuanced theory of globalization which sees globalization not as a foregone conclusion, but as a political strategy – open to contestation or even failure. Central to this is a re-evaluation of the relative strength of the state vis-à-vis transnational capital, and the recognition of TNC/state interactions as sites of struggle, with victory often as likely for the state as for capital.

4 International Governmental Organizations and Social Policy

A major theme within political globalization is the intensification of transnational policy coordination and the regulation of global resource (re)distribution by supra-national institutions. Like regional formations (see Chapter 3), international formations proliferated during the twentieth century. As Kaul et al. note, 'more treaties were signed during the four decades after the second world war than in the previous four centuries' (1999: 499), and the number of international organizations grew from around 70 in 1940 to over 1,000 by 1992 (ibid.). The contemporary global political economy is governed by a complex legal and political framework of international agreements, treaties, regulations and accords agreed through a range of transnational organizations, agencies and alliances (Table 4.1). The most prominent areas of transnational cooperation are trade, investment, finance and macro-economic policy, as well as environmental policies and social policies in employment, migration, social security, education, health and social services, population control and humanitarian aid.

The intensification of transnational policy cooperation is said to have altered the way that territories and populations are governed, a tendency most clearly seen in regional formations (EU and NAFTA) and in relations between developed and developing countries (Pérez Baltodano, 1999). However, while the influence of international institutions over national social development has been the honourable subject of extensive research in development studies, this cannot be said of academic social policy which has tended to confine IGOs to the background (Deacon et al., 1997; Townsend, 1993). However, as Townsend argues, IGOs 'do more than provide a context in which this development takes place. They initiate, guide, influence and determine as well' (1993: 102), by underwriting the conditions and patterns of international economic investment, production and exchange and setting the parameters of national macro-economic policy. Indeed, he contends that insofar as these institutions play a key role in determining how resources are accumulated and distributed globally, they form an important part of any explanation of inequality and poverty globally. The policies of the World Bank, IMF and WTO are held to be particularly significant in this respect because of their role in the transnational diffusion of neo-liberalism, as

Table 4.1   *International governmental institutions and fora*

Name	Year	Functions
Institutions		
International Monetary Fund	1944	Promotes international monetary cooperation and stability. Supervises monetary and exchange rate policies, issues policy recommendations; grants credit to countries with balance of payments difficulties
International Bank for Reconstruction and Development (World Bank)	1944	Promotes economic and social development in developing countries. Finances projects or programmes which directly contribute to economic productivity but for which no private finance can be found
United Nations UN agencies: ILO, UNICEF, UNHCR, FAO, WHO, UNESCO, UNDP, UNCTAD.	1945	Promotes peaceful relations between countries and economic and social development
GATT	1947	Promotes and maintains multilateral trade systems by laying down rules on world trade and settling disputes between members
International Finance Corporation (Sister institution of WB)	1956	Promotes private enterprise in developing countries. Grants loans, with acquisition of a direct stake in companies
International Development Association (Sister institution of WB)	1960	Promotes economic and social development. Provides very long-term loans to developing countries
Policy fora		
Paris Club	1956	Debt restructuring
OECD 29 richest countries	1960	Economic policy cooperation
G3, 5, 7, 8, 10 World's richest countries	1962+	Strengthens the coordination of international economic and monetary policy
G 24, 77 Developing countries	1972+	Discusses monetary and financial interests of member countries

Source: Bakker, 1996

most clearly seen in their mantra of international competitiveness, 'free markets' and 'free trade' (the 'Washington consensus').

   This chapter examines the international political-institutional arena as a site of political conflict over the regulation of global capitalism.

It explores the nature, scope and content of transnational policy coordination of capital (monetary policy, trade, and public and private investment) and labour and human rights by the GATT/WTO, IMF, World Bank and UN acting in conjunction with other public and private transnational and bilateral agencies. It only invokes the one international institution that has been central to analyses of transnational social policy – the EU – as an illustration or point of comparison (see, for example, Cram, 1996; Geyer, 2000; Hantrais, 1995; Leibfried and Pierson, 1995; Majone, 1993; Rhodes, 1991; Sykes and Alcock, 1998). A central theme in the literature is how far IGOs are able to steer the course of economic and social development nationally, and the discussion accordingly focuses on the financial, legal and other instruments, such as technical assistance and political agreements which IGOs use to try to set the parameters for national social development and intervene in the domestic social policy process. Like the previous chapter, this one also tempers the picture of the state as helpless in the face of rampaging international forces and the victory of neo-liberal ideology: it argues that the state lies at the heart of global governance and invokes domestic politics to explain the content of national social, political and economic reforms.

International monetary and exchange rate regimes

International monetary and exchange rate regimes have provided the context for international trade and finance and national economic development for well over a century. Under the International Gold Standard (1870) national currencies were pegged to an official gold price and 'represented the quintessential integrated economy', under which national autonomy was minimal (Hirst and Thompson, 1996: 44). Governments were required to subordinate their domestic monetary policies to international rules and conventions and to pursue policies which 'adjusted' domestic economic activity to a level that maintained the value of their currency relative to gold. By raising or lowering its discount rate, the Bank of England effectively controlled world monetary policy and economic activity more broadly. The Bretton Woods system set up after World War II was designed to stabilize the international economy and permit a greater degree of national autonomy. Exchange rates were semi-fixed against an anchor currency until 1976 when they were replaced by floating exchange rates (i.e. national currencies were 'floated' rather than fixed against a common price anchor). Formally, this flexibility permitted a greater degree of national autonomy as, unconstrained by the rigidities of a common price anchor, governments could in theory pursue monetary policies to adjust changes in the strength of their exchange rates against the dollar, pursue international trade objectives and adopt expansionary social and employment policies (Hirst and Thompson, 1996). Monetary and exchange regimes were thus a cornerstone of the 'compromise of embedded liberalism' (Ruggie, 1983) on which the post-war Western welfare states were founded.

National autonomy, be it under the semi-fixed or floating exchange rate regimes, was in practice conditioned by the domestic and foreign economic policies of other countries, notably the US, whose fiscal and monetary policies were an important determinant of interest rates and international capital flows which affect exchange rate and currency values. The effects of US domestic policies rippled across the world economies, causing fluctuations in world interest rates, worldwide recession and debt (Gilpin, 1987: 145). Furthermore, Bretton Woods institutions are controlled by the advanced industrialized countries as voting rights depend largely on financial contribution to them. Thus, the G7 countries hold more than half of the votes on the IMF's Executive Committee, and the US alone controls 18 per cent of votes on the IMF's Executive Committee, with the right of veto over any decision (Bakker, 1996). Finally, government policy *de facto* operated within the parameters set by international financial institutions and markets.

One of the problems of the flexible exchange rates regime is that governments engage in competitive currency devaluation to make their exports cheaper and foreign imports more expensive. These strategies can have a considerable global impact. In addition, national currencies have proved vulnerable to the volatile, speculative tendencies of the global financial markets, as EU, Latin American, East Asian and Russian governments have all found to their cost. In response to these problems a range of cooperative policy fora, or political clubs of countries, have emerged to establish an agreed set of rules and goals between member countries regarding monetary policy. At the regional level, the EU has gone furthest by re-establishing fixed exchange rates, introducing a common currency and centralizing macro-economic policy, although a common currency area has also been considered in East Asia. At the international level, transnational cooperation in macro-economic policy has also occurred, particularly between the advanced industrialized countries. The replacement of the G5 by the G7, for example, heralded a period of closer cooperation with more frequent meetings between finance ministers and central bank governors and a greater degree of macro-economic policy coordination (Bakker, 1996). This development has coincided with the emergence of monetarist policies prioritizing low inflation, the control of public expenditure and the reduction of debt and budget deficits, and of the 'free trade' paradigm. This globalization of economic management has been accompanied by the globalization of social and environmental management. The focus of G7 summits, for example, has widened from international monetary and budgetary policy to include international debt, structural adjustment, social development and environmental problems.

Multilateral trade regimes

During the nineteenth and early twentieth centuries cross-national trade and investment were regulated mainly through bilateral agreements, but after World War II there was a distinct move to establish regional and multilateral rules to eliminate 'discriminatory' practices against foreign trade and investment. In 1947, the GATT was set up to oversee the removal of international trade barriers and supervise the expansion of international trade. It was based on the premise that 'free trade' stimulates the expansion of international trade and economic growth faster than can even the most internationalist of national trade policies (S. Amin, 1997; Hirst and Thompson, 1996). To the extent that 'free' trade would encourage greater international economic interdependence it was deemed one of the best guarantors of both political stability and economic growth; as Kapstein puts it, 'free trade was optimal from the cosmopolitan perspective' (1999: 93). Similar motives and premises lay behind the creation of the Common Market, the precursor of the EU, in Western Europe during the same period.

The GATT is committed to market access, transparency, economic safeguards, progressive liberalization and the integration of developing countries. The central rules of the GATT are the Most Favoured Nation principle (concessions within a trade agreement must be granted equally to all nations) and the National Treatment principle (states must treat domestic and foreign firms offering like services equally) (Dunkley, 2000). The application of these principles over successive Rounds since 1947 has removed or reduced a range of tariff and non-tariff 'barriers' to international trade, such as quotas and trading practices favouring national producers that are obscured by health or administrative regulations (S. Amin, 1997; Dunkley, 2000; Hirst and Thompson, 1996; Hoekman and Kostecki, 1995).

The establishment of multilateral trade rules is associated with the growth of international trade during the post-war period. While trade regulated by the GATT covered just 7 per cent of world trade by the mid 1980s (S. Amin, 1997), the GATT's coverage of trade sectors widened, as did membership of the institution – from 32 states in 1947 to 116 states by 1994, representing two-thirds of the countries of the world. The expanding membership of GATT reflects the global expansion of capitalism which, combined with the failure of economic development in the so-called socialist countries, is now drawing into the international economic system, not only the formerly communist countries of Central and Eastern Europe and the former Soviet Union, but also countries such as China and India which have abandoned long traditions of self-sufficient development for enthusiastic integration into the global economy. This support by the 'comprador bourgeoisie of the periphery' (S. Amin, 1997: 27) for the GATT reflects their support for the principle of free trade and improved access to Northern markets.

The Uruguay Round deserves particular mention. It was the manifestation of what Dunkley (2000) calls the 'Geneva consensus' – the view that a renewed commitment to internationally-oriented economic development strategies, 'free' trade and deregulation was needed. The protracted negotiations, which spanned seven years (1986–1993), resulted in legal and institutional reforms to the international trade regime, which have profound implications for the workings of the economic and political structures of member states (Chossudovsky, 1997; Nader and Wallach, 1996).

First, existing GATT agreements, treaties, articles, codes, and clauses were brought together and bound into a single package under the control of a new institution, the WTO (1995), which was granted executive and legal powers recognized in international law. Dunkley (2000) likens this new system to a 'three-legged stool', with the WTO as the seat and the GATT, GATS (see below) and TRIPs as legs. Under the dispute-settlement procedure, governments and corporations may refer a claim to the WTO executive if they believe that other states' policies contravene international trade and investment law. The WTO is able to impose legal obligations on states to comply with international trade and investment law, and can apply trade sanctions if a government fails to make its laws or practices conform with international law. In this respect, the establishment of the WTO and its constitutionally-enshrined commitment to deregulation has been described (from a position of opposition) as a 'landmark' in the 'formalization, strengthening and politicization' of the GATT's ad hoc system (Nader and Wallach, 1996: 94).

Second, the coverage of international trade law was extended to more sectors (textiles, clothing and agriculture) and areas (investment, commercial services and public procurement). International rules and procedures were introduced or tightened, aiming to reduce or eliminate non-tariff barriers, such as: investment incentives (e.g. subsidies, grants, tax concessions); performance requirements (e.g. export and local content agreements, domestic sales requirements, technology transfer requirements, foreign exchange restrictions); and technical measures (e.g. specifications, standards, labelling). TRIMs cover measures relating to corporate activity in general which restrict foreign investors (competition policy, pricing restrictions, collusive tendering), while TRIPs establish global rules protecting intellectual property (e.g. genetic engineering, patent protection, trade marks, copyright and industrial designs). Commercial services are regulated by the General Agreement on Trade in Services (GATS). This mainly covers business services but also includes certain health and welfare services and professionals, and curtails governments' right to limit foreign investment. The Agreement on Government Procurement (GPA) enhances the rights of foreign tenderers in government purchasing policies, including those relating to public services, and covers more sectors and public entities than before (Dunkley, 2000: 49–52).

One of the key anticipated effects of international trade law is the lowering of social, health and environmental standards and their arrested development more generally. Thus, national or other international social, health and environmental regulations which conflict with international trade and investment law are prohibited. This applies both to existing and future laws. A range of regulations in the scheduled areas are to be made less trade restrictive generally (Dunkley, 2000; Hirst and Thompson, 1996; Nader and Wallach, 1996). The WTO's track record of adjudicating on environmentally-linked trade disputes offers a taste of what may be to come in social- and health-related trade disputes. Reviewing WTO panel decisions relating to TREMs (domestic environmental policies with trade implications), Dunkley finds that TREMs were judged acceptable if: they do not discriminate against exports; they are applied only within the country imposing them; they are implemented in the least trade-restricting manner possible; they are used in relation to products but not processes of production; they are proportionate to their objects, and less trade-interventionist measures have previously been sought (Dunkley, 2000: 198). In an analysis of the implications of the Uruguay Round for public health measures, Koivusalo (1999) argues that tobacco advertising bans (whether direct or indirect, such as the use of trademarks in other products) introduced on public health grounds may be deemed to violate tobacco corporations' commercial rights, and thus be subject to WTO disputes mechanisms (1999: 23). She also notes the potential for 'similar problems [to] arise if countries restricted access, imposed higher taxation or set higher prices for products with negative health impact', such as alcohol or baby milk products (ibid.). She highlights a move to make greater use of voluntary initiatives, such as the labelling of products harmful to health, rather than fiscal instruments or other pricing mechanisms, or the regulation (or banning) of advertising of certain products. These legal issues are of great political import, and international trade law will force governments to continue to make political choices rather than release them from having to do so. For example, the WTO's ruling that the US could not ban petrol imports from Brazil and Venezuela on the grounds that they did not meet US environmental (clean air) standards left the US government with the choice of amending its legislation to lower its standards or facing trade sanctions (Labonte, 1998: 7). In this context, national politics matter, and will continue to matter, immensely.

An area potentially of great significance for social policy is the extension of the National Treatment principle to a wider range of areas in public procurement. This was justified on the grounds that government purchasing policies may constitute a form of protectionism to the extent that they allow governments to establish extensive domestic preferences and discriminate against foreign providers. The *Agreement on Government Procurement* (GPA) was a voluntary agreement, but binding on governments once they signed it (most governments have done so). The GPA aims to open up public procurement of services to greater competition from providers, both domestic and foreign, and incorporates a range of government sectors, including services and construction, as well as sub-national (local) government and public utilities. Signatory governments committed themselves to non-discrimination among each other where a purchase exceeds a threshold value. The GPA restricts government subsidies for regions, local industries and firms, as well as the use of performance requirements, or any other requirements which might be construed as discriminatory against foreign providers, as a condition of receipt of public money or of selling a service (Dunkley, 2000). States are required to protect the investment rights of companies which are entitled to compensation if these rights are found to have been infringed. This provision is a significant deterrent for any government considering embarking on a programme of economic nationalism or of nationalization, whether full or partial, of an entity or service in the interests of the social rights of citizens, since both may be construed as depriving a private contractor of certain expected commercial benefits (see also Appleton, 1999 on the effects of NAFTA trade and investment law on health service provision).

Indeed, health and social services, including professional services, and state subsidies for profit and non-profit services are all potentially open to challenge under the GATS and GPA provisions. The WTO notes that the provision of these services is influenced by 'non-trade' factors such as licensing and qualification requirements; restrictions on the range of goods and services that professionals and hospitals are allowed to provide; controls or incentives intended to ensure the adequate provision of services in all regions and for all population groups; and the direct provision of minimum services to economically disadvantaged groups (WTO, 1998b: 18). Clearly, if the WTO had its way, then equity concerns would be displaced by commercial considerations, and the state would have to allow a greater role for the private (commercial) sector in health services and treat domestic and foreign health providers equally. States would have to prepare the ground for the privatization of health and social care services (Koivusalo, 1999) and thus for a two-tier service, since public provision for all (where it exists) would become public provision for the poor, high risk (i.e. less profitable) groups that the private sector is not prepared to cover.

Fortunately in this case, it is governments, not the WTO, which decide how far they wish to see 'free' trade principles extended to public services. Here, the picture is somewhat encouraging as they have tended to baulk at full liberalization. Moreover the provisions of the GPA need to be set against the special agreements and substantial restrictions negotiated for finance, transport, agricultural services, health and social services, education and recreation to which GATS and GPA principles and provisions either do not apply or only partially apply (Dunkley, 2000). Thus, the GPA only covers the procurement of entities and categories of goods and services that are included in Member-specific Annexes; the US, whose health sector is predominantly private anyway, was the only country to include health and medical services in its Annex. Similar restrictions on the application of trade law to health and welfare services can be found in regional agreements. Thus, the reservation on health and social services in NAFTA (1992) permitted governments to maintain existing measures that conflict with specific NAFTA provisions, such as national treatment or local presence rules (Sanger, 1998). The MAI and the WTO's current Millennium Round of trade negotiations – both of which aim to extend international trade in services – have also suffered serious setbacks. There is little reason to believe that popular and governmental opposition to extending the scope of international trade agreements will diminish.

However far-reaching the WTO provisions may appear, the actual impact of the law ultimately depends on when and how it is invoked, interpreted, implemented and enforced. The interpretation of the law is likely to prove particularly significant in determining the eventual scope of the provisions. In the case of NAFTA, Appleton (1999) argues that notwithstanding the reservation on health and social services, these services may yet be subject to NAFTA law after all, as the reservation is interpreted under international, not domestic, law and there is no international definition of these services. Even the WTO acknowledges that the impact of the law is likely to be uneven, and that national institutional arrangements will determine whether or not particular services' trade falls within the remit of GATS provisions (1998a: 12–13). It also acknowledges that there are a range of methods not covered by GATS that states will continue to use to regulate access to and operation within 'their' markets. Moreover, even in scheduled areas where the full range of restrictions apply, countries may find it difficult to supply proof that other countries have infringed the non-discrimination rule, other than in cases of direct discrimination (WTO, 1998a). The GPA's impact may also be diminished by its implementation which is not on the usual most favoured nation basis, but on the more restrictive reciprocal basis obliging governments to grant market access concessions *only* to governments that do likewise.

There are signs that the political limits of the trade in services issues – as well as the application of free trade principles more generally – have just about been reached. The difficulty is that governments may agree to deregulation in principle (for others) but are less inclined to support it in practice (for themselves). Thus, in principle, international trade law requires countries to make local markets accessible to foreign investors on equal terms as domestic ones, but in practice, demands by the South that the profitable Northern markets be opened up to them was met by the exclusion by the North of certain industries from trade negotiations (as a concession, developing countries are permitted to reciprocally grant each other trading preferences). To the extent that trade agreements institutionalize the exclusion of the South from Northern markets they are directly implicated in sustaining geo-economic inequalities. As Mike Moore (Director-General of the WTO) recognized: 'the world was once polarized by a cold war; it is now becoming polarized between wealth and lack of opportunity' (*The Guardian*, 3/9/99: 22).

The WTO's panacea to geo-economic inequalities is to extend free trade principles to a wider range of sectors and improve the South's access to Northern markets. The WTO has ambitiously pressed ahead with this agenda in the Millennium Round by placing agriculture and trade in services, including education and health and social services, on the negotiating agenda (WTO, 1998a, 1998b). Despite the collapse of these negotiations in Seattle in 1999 (see Chapter 5), it seems that these trade in services issues 'will remain at the forefront of trade concerns' (Deacon, 2000a: 25; see also UNRISD, 2000). However, it is not certain that these ambitions to extend the scope of international trade law will be realized, given the mounting political opposition against it and the institutions that support it (see Chapter 5).

Development assistance regimes

International financial and development institutions play a central role in facilitating developing countries' access to financial resources for public purposes. This section focuses on the provision of financial assistance in the form of loans and aid by the IMF, World Bank and UN. These institutions, in conjunction with transnational development banks and institutes and bilateral aid agencies, have sustained the major economic and social inequalities that characterize contemporary globalization; they have overseen the accumulation of unprecedented levels of wealth in the advanced industrialized countries and mass impoverishment in, and indebtedness of, developing countries. The discussion below focuses in particular on economic and social conditionalities attached to loans and aid and their social consequences.

Loans

The IMF is a key international creditor as well as a monetary institution and it provides loans to countries to resolve balance of payments difficulties. The most contentious IMF credit facility is the extended financing facility (EFF) (1974) which was designed for countries experiencing severe, structural 'imbalances' in trade and production. Receipt of EFF funds requires the recipient government to repay the loan at the market rate of interest. When it became clear that the poorest countries could not manage repayment of debt within the IMF's existing credit facilities, the Structural Adjustment Facility (SAF) was established to provide loans for economic reform programmes at a low rate of interest and long-term repayment agreements. In 1987, the Extended Structural Adjustment Facility (ESAF) was introduced and was funded by 'soft loans' and donations from around 40 of the richest countries (Bakker, 1996).

The World Bank is usually classified as a development institution because of its mission to promote economic and social development in developing countries, but it also plays an important role as a financial institution. Along with its 'sister' institutions, the International Finance Corporation (1956) and the International Development Association (1960), it provides credit and loans (structural adjustment loans (SALs) and sectoral adjustment loans (SECALs)) to finance projects and programmes which promise to increase economic productivity and inward private investment but for which no private finance can be found. The World Bank institutions work essentially as an investment bank in the sense that they depend on their standing in the credit markets and have an interest in ensuring debt is serviced (Bakker, 1996).

Governments have always faced conditionality rules when dealing with private creditors, and although WB and IMF terms of credit (e.g. interest rates) are more lenient than those offered by commercial banks, these loans come with a stringent set of economic and social conditionalities. Conditionalities are contentious because the IMF and WB are tied to the interests of advanced industrial countries and banks and because of the policy objectives and measures that these institutions favour (Kahler, 1992). Loan conditionalities include recipient governments agreeing to pursue economic and social reform programmes to remove 'structural rigidities', enhance their foreign investment climate and ensure a stable macro-economic environment conducive to loan repayment (Bakker, 1996; Kahler, 1992). Programmes of reform typically involve: currency devaluation; reduction or elimination of foreign exchange controls; deregulation and privatization of industry and services; removal of wage and price controls and subsidies on agriculture, food, energy and transport; cuts in public expenditure and social services, including transfer payments and public employment; cuts in progressive taxation and a depreciation in organizations representing workers (Lopes, 1999; Owoh, 1996; Townsend and Donkor, 1996).

SAPs have been applied throughout the developing world as a general prescription for a range of economic problems (Lopes, 1999). By the mid-1990s over 70 debtor countries, around 30 of which are in Africa, had implemented SAPs (Owoh, 1996). The livelihood of more than 4 billion people, or 80 per cent of the world's population, is directly affected by SAPs (Chossudovsky, 1997). As instruments for aiding economic recovery, their track record is disastrous. They have been severely criticized for their inefficacy in achieving positive socio-economic outcomes as well as for their overtly negative socio-economic effects (Kahler, 1992); donors have criticized the World Bank for its failure to take account of local conditions and the social effects of SAPs reforms (Lopes, 1999).

In Africa, where SAPs were first applied, structural adjustment has come to be widely regarded as the root cause of economic stagnation and falling living standards (Lopes, 1999). In 1983, 25 heavily indebted African countries accepted a 'stabilization' programme with the IMF and a SAP drawn up by the World Bank, the common aims of which were to stabilize balance of payments, extinguish debt and reduce inflation. Priority given to these objectives relegated the creation and protection of jobs, guarantees for a minimum family income and the provision of basic public services to secondary importance (UNICEF in Michel, 1993). Owoh summarizes the devastating social effects of SAPs in Africa:

> After more than ten years of structural adjustment programming . . . living standards in Sub-Saharan Africa have fallen 2 per cent annually in the last ten years and are now lower than in 1970; unemployment has quadrupled to more than 100 million, and Africa's potential productive capacity now averages only about 30 per cent across the continent. Real wages have fallen by a third and investment is now less in real terms than during the so-called lost decade of the 1980s. Indeed, economic growth in many countries has ceased and debt has emerged as the single most important cause of Africa's present inability to develop. (Owoh, 1996: 213)

Latin America and Central and Eastern Europe have also suffered the destabilizing economic and social effects of debt, loans and SAPs. In the case of Latin America, Bretton Woods policies in the 1980s induced or reinforced a severe contraction of economic activity and employment in the formal sector, particularly in the public sector, a decline in incomes and cuts in public expenditure on food, transport and public services, notably schools and hospitals. Declining real wages, unemployment and inflation pushed more people into poverty. The poverty rate in the Latin American region increased from 26 per cent in 1980 to 31 per cent in 1989 (Morely in Barrientos, 1998: 23). A similar pattern of impoverishment occurred in Central and Eastern Europe during the 1990s. Until then, Eastern Europe and the Soviet Union were regarded as part of the 'developed' North, with citizens enjoying levels of consumption, education and health broadly comparable with countries in the OECD. Following IMF reforms, levels of unemployment, poverty and mortality rates have increased and many of the countries are now categorized by the World Bank and OECD as developing countries (Chossudovsky, 1997; Townsend and Donkor, 1996). In Central and Eastern Europe wage levels have fallen by between 20 and 24 per cent and poverty rates have increased by between 1 and 6 per cent (Deacon et al., 1997). The former Soviet republics have suffered the most: in Georgia 'the average standard of living is only about a quarter of what it was' (Townsend and Donkor, 1996: 30–1); in Azerbaijan the poverty rate increased by over 50 per cent

Table 4.2 *Poverty trends: people living on less than $1 (PPP) per day (millions)*

	1987	1993	1998
East Asia and the Pacific	415.1	431.9	278.3
(*excluding China*)	*109.2*	*66.0*	*55.6*
Eastern Europe and Central Asia	1.1	18.3	24.0
Latin America and the Caribbean	63.7	70.8	78.2
Middle East and North Africa	25.0	21.5	20.9
South Asia	474.4	505.1	522.0
Sub-Saharan Africa	217.2	273.3	290.9
Total	1,196.5	1,320.9	1,214.3
(*excluding China*)	*890.6*	*955*	*991.5*

Source: World Bank in UNRISD, 2000: 11

in the space of six years (1989–1995) and wage levels fell by nearly 90 per cent (Deacon et al., 1997: Table 2.8; see also Standing, 1996).

Indeed, SAPs have been associated with, if not contributed directly to, widening inequalities, both nationally and internationally. Between 1970 and 1989, countries with the richest 20 per cent of the world population increased their share of global GNP from 73.9 to 82.7 per cent, while countries with the poorest 20 per cent of world population saw their share of global GNP fall from 2.3 to 1.4 per cent. The world's 358 billionaires possess as much wealth as the poorest 45 per cent of the world's population (UNDP, 1996). In 1998, 1.2 billion people lived in absolute poverty, defined as less than US$1 per day (Table 4.2), and this was expected to have increased to 1.5 billion in 2000 (Bradshaw and Wallace, 1999).

Given the impoverishing effects of loans and SAPs, government compliance with financing conditions is, not surprisingly, less than complete. A World Bank study into the implementation of SALs and SECALs in 15 countries showed that the full compliance rate was just 60 per cent, or 80 per cent as measured by 'substantial' compliance, and the degree of policy reform varied widely between countries and between policy areas (Kahler, 1992: 97). In fact, implementation is a weak point for any international institution because it does not have a local presence and because SAPs have to be implemented by sovereign governments often constrained by the balance of political power nationally. Thus, in Latin America, Chile and Argentina enthusiastically embraced neo-liberal policies and implemented them unrestrained by the usual domestic constraints since political opposition was banned, while democratic governments, such as in Brazil, either resisted these impositions or else faced significant internal opposition when trying to implement the measures (Huber, 1996; Stallings, 1992).

The less than spectacular record of success of IFI funding conditionalities, as measured by compliance rates, has focused attention on the role of domestic politics in impeding the implementation of SAPs. The World Bank (1997a) has bemoaned states' lack of institutional capability and outright corruption, while Kahler attributed poor implementation to 'the existence of powerful sources of conflict between the policy strictures of the external actors and the political interests of many developing country governments' (1992: 100). In fact, there may be substantial disincentives for governments to persist with SAPs and make repayments as they encounter opposition against reforms by those set to lose from their implementation, while any gains are siphoned off to service debt repayments in any case. Attempts by IFIs to directly intervene in the national politics of structural adjustment, by policing implementation or threatening sanctions, may only exacerbate domestic political conflict and further undermine the chances of full implementation. IFI policy leverage tends to be maximized when governments have committed themselves to reform in *advance* of receiving international finance, but even here there is no guarantee that programmes will be implemented as governments may encounter various 'roadblocks' during the implementation phase from a range of groups, such as the legislature, politicians, domestic capital, the military, trade unions or farmers, which may oppose the content of programmes or specific aspects of them (Killick et al. in Kahler, 1992: 96) (see 'Social Policy Dialogues' p. 116 in this chapter and Chapter 5).

Aid

Official development assistance (ODA) is a key, and sometimes the only, source of development finance for many countries otherwise excluded from global finance. In three-quarters of African countries aid is the only means of maintaining investment at a level to ensure even nil growth and essential imports to prevent starvation and severe political disruption (Amin, 1990). Out of the 49 countries that the World Bank classifies as low income, in 19 of these aid comprises one fifth or more of their GNP. In some cases humanitarian aid, along with public donations, may be the only form of inward capital; in Mozambique aid represents more than 100 per cent of its GNP (World Bank, 1997a).

Development aid is mainly financed from national budgets and is allocated to a wide range of functions – both cash and in-kind – such as: budgetary and balance of payments support; technical assistance support for infrastructure (e.g. civil engineering feasibility studies); institution-building (e.g. development of management skills) and institutional reform (e.g. advice on restructuring social protection, education and health); 'human resources' projects (e.g. developing, or facilitating the restructuring of, education and health provision), and emergency relief and food aid (Amin, 1990; Bakker, 1996). Two thirds of ODA is channelled through bilateral foreign aid programmes, while the remaining third is channelled through multilateral development and aid agencies (the UN and WB) and NGOs (Kahler, 1992; Kaul et al., 1999). As Bakker notes, 'the Bank has always been acceptable to the rich countries as one of the channels for providing direct development aid, since they can exert influence over its decisions in accordance with their economic power' (1996: 45). Recipient countries are required to match funds – they may, for example, pay for domestic labour and suppliers' costs.

Development aid is a key area affecting the global distribution and redistribution of resources. By providing a financial guarantee from donor governments and multilateral aid agencies, aid attracts foreign private capital to invest in countries which it would otherwise not consider (UNRISD, 2000: 26–7). The participation of private capital in public development projects has now been accepted by the UN, which has recently argued that private investment has been important in assisting economic recovery in certain countries and that public–private partnerships can mobilize resources for addressing a wide range of issues relating to social development (Mkandawire and Rodríguez, 2000). The WHO has also indicated that trade can be made to work for health (Koivusalo, 1999).

Aid constitutes a transfer of public resources from rich to poor countries. In 1998, OECD development aid amounted to US$52 billion. The EU's PHARE and TACIS development aid programmes to assist restructuring in Poland, Hungary and the countries of the former Soviet Union were described as 'the biggest source of direct transfer of funds from West to East' (Deacon et al., 1997: 97). The potential of aid as a mechanism for the global redistribution of resources or for the enhancement of indigenous development processes of recipient countries must, however, be put in perspective. First, official development finance from developed to developing countries declined from US$56.9 billion in 1990 to US$47.9 billion in 1998; over the same period grants fell from US$29.2 billion to US$23 billion, loans from US$15.6 billion to US$9.7 billion and bilateral aid from US$2.9 billion to US$0.8 billion (Mkandawire and Rodríguez, 2000). OECD countries' ODA declined by 4.6 per cent between 1991 and 1997, and in 1998 ODA as a percentage of members' GNP was about one third of the agreed target of 0.7 per cent of GNP (commitment 9, 1995 Copenhagen Social Summit). The world's richest countries' (G7) ODA levels have declined by 12 per cent (US$5.2 billion) since the Social Summit, and ODA represents just 0.19 per cent of their combined GDP (1997). Non-G7 countries were more generous – their ODA averaged 0.46 per cent of their combined GDP (1997) (Mkandawire and Rodríguez, 2000). These declining levels of ODA have been spread more thinly while the proportion of aid allocated to humanitarian relief, as distinct from development, grew from 1.5 to 8.4 per cent between 1991 and 1994 (UNRISD, 2000: 28).

Second, ODA is dwarfed in comparison with other areas of spending by the developed countries. OECD military spending amounted to more than ten times that allocated to ODA. In addition, ODA represents a tiny fraction of the amount owed by developing countries to developed ones: in 1995, the debt of developing countries and the former Soviet Union amounted to US$2.2 *trillion* (UNRISD, 2000). Third, a proportion of aid flows directly back to the donor countries. In the mid 1990s, one quarter of bilateral aid was used to repay multilateral lenders. Two out of every three dollars offered by the World Bank as IDA loans and grants were reclaimed as debt repayments, while the IMF reclaimed part of the remaining dollar. In some cases, governments were spending more on debt repayments than on social provision (UNRISD, 2000: 20–7).

Development aid has been widely criticized as a multi-billion pound global industry guided by the commercial interests of Northern donors – hastening capitalist development in recipient countries and promoting the development of foreign markets for donor countries – and the interests of the global middle class of aid professionals involved in delivering it (Jayaraman and Kanbur, 1999; Smillie, 1995; Stubbs, 1998). Conditionalities attached to bilateral aid programmes stipulate that recipient countries purchase technical assistance – technology and services – from donor countries, thereby ensuring that a portion of donors' funds returns home to benefit their own economies. Technical assistance integrates countries ideologically as well as economically. It provides market opportunities for foundations, research institutions and scientists in industrialized countries to provide the 'scientific' basis for the adoption of 'modernization' policies in developing countries. These policies create the conditions conducive to dependency on TNCs for technology and on imported professional expertise (Bandarage, 1997; UNDP, 1992). Technical assistance also includes advice on social policy reform. Many have been critical of the 'social policy vision' underlying this advice which reflects the particular Western liberal welfare predilections of the funding agencies and the private consultancy agencies to which they subcontract. The economic assessments provided by the WB consultants tend to 'prove' that only substantial social expenditure cuts are sustainable, while the ILO supplies them with the range of social conventions to be upheld despite the cuts (Deacon, 1998; Deacon et al., 1997).

Development aid funds, like loans, have been criticized for being less than effective at reaching target groups. One explanation of the inefficacy of development aid, supported by the World Bank, focuses on the implementation phase and the political interests of actors delivering aid: funds tend to flow from government to government, swelling inefficient public sectors; they are misappropriated by corrupt élites (public and private) and/or appropriated by recipient country governments to serve their domestic political interests. Accordingly, there is a growing preference by donors to channel aid less through governments and more through NGOs, as these are perceived to be closer to hard-to-reach populations, more innovative and more efficient (see Chapter 5 for a consideration of issues arising from this).

The problem of ensuring that aid reaches designated target groups or services must, however, be seen in the context of policy design, and it is here that a competing explanation of the inefficacy of development aid – one which focuses on policy error – is relevant. Critics point out that a growing proportion of aid has been used to support policy reforms promoting market-oriented development, which either does not benefit the poorest, or worsens their situation (Jayaraman and Kanbur, 1999; UNRISD, 2000). Moreover, donors support a range of development assistance programmes and policies which may conflict, with one another. However, even a coordinated response is insufficient to bridge the implementation gap. The example of the 20:20 initiative agreed at the Copenhagen Social Summit (1995) is instructive in this respect. This initiative entailed a mutual commitment between developed and developing countries to allocate an average of 20 per cent of ODA and 20 per cent of the national budget to 'basic social programmes'. It was supported by the main multilateral development agencies (World Bank and UN agencies) as well as by certain NGOs in developed and developing countries.

The implementation of the initiative has proved problematic, both for donor and recipient governments. On the donors' side, one problem is agreeing a definition of 'basic' social services, while donors' interpretation of their commitments has been inconsistent. While some governments took 20 per cent as an overall target for their development programmes, others stipulated that 20 per cent should be achieved in each recipient country. In addition, while some donors regard the initiative as a broad policy commitment and long-term goal, others argue that recipient governments should be sanctioned if they fail to achieve their target. On the recipients' side, the allocated funds may not actually reach target groups for a number of reasons. First, governments may simply shift funds earmarked for social and health services elsewhere (in ways reminiscent of practices of certain member states regarding the use of EU structural funds). Second, they may give priority to certain services (such as primary education which is favoured by donors) at the expense of other social services, or they may embark on infrastructure-building (e.g. schools) without having allocated adequate resources for teaching staff. Third, governments face political difficulties in delivering aid. The priority given to basic services for the poorest groups may be at the expense of maintaining existing services for a cross-section of the population and alienate working and middle classes as they are expected to pay again for private provision (UNRISD, 2000: 29–31).

International labour and human rights regimes

Labour standards are 'norms and rules that govern working conditions and industrial relations' (OECD, 1996b: 25), and they cover most aspects of labour markets – collective bargaining, wages, working time, health and safety, labour inspection, non-discrimination, child labour – and related institutions such as social security systems. Labour standards have developed within an international context of attempts by the labour movement to establish a body of international law on workers' and human rights in anticipation of the impact of global capitalism on working conditions (Evans, 1998; Herod, 1997). They can be traced to the 'free trade' vs 'fair trade' debate, which dates back to the nineteenth-century concerns about unfair terms of trade competition arising from socially unacceptable practices. In the contemporary context, they are advocated to prevent countries from basing their comparative advantage on low labour standards (OECD, 1996b). Labour standards are a core site of global social politics and, although labour standards are enshrined in international agreements and global policy discussions, they have 'remained a battleground of controversial viewpoints and diverging interests' (Sengenberger and Wilkinson, 1995: 116). Currently, the main global institutions regulating labour standards are the UN, ILO and OECD. This section focuses on the role and remit of each institution and recent policy debates regarding this area of global social policy. It concentrates on issues arising from the implementation of international labour standards and reviews recent attempts to insert a social (labour) clause into international trade agreements.

The UN has approached workers' rights as fundamental human rights. The UN Charter of 1945 set out a number of general provisions regarding human rights. Article 55 stipulated that countries should aim to strive for improved living standards, full employment, respect for human rights and basic liberties for all without distinction of race, gender, language or religion. The UN Declaration of Human Rights (1948) subsequently specified that these human rights include civil, political, social, cultural and economic rights. These were further specified in two Covenants (1966). The Covenant on Civil and Political Rights specified the right to life, liberty, freedom from torture, freedom of opinion and expression, freedom from slavery and servitude and the right to peaceful assembly and association. The Covenant on Economic, Social and Cultural Rights covered the right to: form and join trade unions; work; equal pay for equal work; education; social protection and a decent standard of living. More recently, the Covenant on the Rights of the Child (1989) contains provisions on the rights of children to special protection, healthy development and free primary education.

ILO Conventions are the most comprehensive set of international labour standards. There are over 170 Conventions and more than 180 recommendations, some of which refer to general aims, others which refer to the treatment of specific groups. First-level Conventions relate to workers' 'core' rights: freedom of association and collective bargaining; abolition of forced labour and exploitative child labour; non-discrimination in pay and working conditions. These rights are deemed 'core' because they have the characteristics of fundamental human rights: they involve the liberty, dignity and respect of the individual and they provide framework conditions (i.e. the ability to determine or influence standards freely) for other labour standards. Second-level Conventions refer to broad objectives in relation to social standards and they commit signatories to maximize levels of employment, improve living standards and establish minimum levels of living and working conditions (e.g. employment security, health and safety). ICO conventions also pertain to the institutions governing social and labour standards, such as labour administration systems (e.g. tripartite consultation and labour inspection) and social security systems (e.g. guaranteed minimum standards for social security benefits and equal treatment of women and men). Finally, Conventions may pertain to designated social groups, such as: women (maternity protection, prohibition of night work and underground work); children and young people (regulation of working hours and conditions, night work); older workers; migrant workers and tribal populations; as well as to certain occupational groups, such as shipping and fishery workers (OECD, 1996b).

The OECD is a third, albeit minor, source of international labour standards. Its Guidelines for Multinational Enterprises (1994) are recommendations addressed by governments to multinational enterprises (MNEs) providing them with a set of labour standards consistent with applicable laws (preface, OECD Guidelines). MNEs' labour practices should not be less favourable than those observed by comparable employers in the host country (OECD, 1996b: 71–2). Among the workers' rights to be observed are: freedom of association; collective bargaining; information on the company's performance; training; non-discriminatory recruitment and redundancy practices; wages; promotion and training. Currently, the Guidelines' (2000) principles of good practice as they pertain to corporate social policy include: contributing to economic, social and environmental progress and sustainable development; respecting the human rights of those affected by their activities in a manner consistent with the host government's obligations and commitments; encouraging local capacity-building through close cooperation with the local community; encouraging human capital formation; refraining from seeking or accepting exemptions related to environmental, health, safety, labour, taxation and financial issues; and developing and applying effective self-regulatory practices that foster mutual trust between enterprises and their host societies. The functioning of the Guidelines is overseen by the OECD's Committee on International Investment and Multinational Enterprises (CIME). Observance of the Guidelines by enterprises is strictly voluntary and not legally binding.

These human rights and labour codes represent the institutional expression of universal norms and values and have been a central and enduring strand in the development of global social policy. Thus, at the 1995 World Social Summit in Copenhagen, governments (re)affirmed the universality of basic workers' rights in the context of their commitments to eradicate poverty, achieve full employment and promote social development. However, while most governments accept workers' rights in principle (i.e. for other countries), they are more reluctant to implement them in their own territories. Indeed, Conventions or Covenants are not legally binding on governments until they are ratified, and ratification has been slow and far from complete. Thus, the OECD (1996b) noted that only 62 countries, including just 15 OECD countries, have ratified all ILO Conventions relating to core labour standards, while only 123 countries had ratified UN human rights Covenants relating to workers' rights. Five countries, including China, Korea and South Africa, had not ratified any ILO Conventions relating to core workers' rights, while the US had only ratified one of them (abolition of forced labour). Governments have not ratified Conventions on the grounds that they would be ineffective – a number of countries opposed the ratification of the Convention on the minimum age for child labour on the grounds that it would not safeguard against child labour exploitation. Governments may reject them in principle, as India has done, arguing that they are influenced by Western concepts inappropriate to their national contexts (OECD, 1996b: 35). Yet even when a country has ratified a Covenant or Convention, there is no guarantee that it will be enforced. In theory, Article 33 of the ILO empowers it to take action to secure compliance by a state with the terms of a Convention which it has ratified, although the practice of the ILO is not to impose sanctions but to rely on moral suasion to encourage greater compliance (OECD, 1996b). In fact, there are very basic difficulties even in *knowing* when labour standards, even core labour standards, are being enforced because 'information on this issue is sparse and incomplete'. As the OECD notes, the 'lack of reliable indicators on enforcement is especially acute regarding child labour, forced labour and non-discrimination in employment' (OECD: 1996b: 48).

One response to the institutional separation of labour and trade regulation and the patchy enforcement of labour standards is the insertion of a social (labour) clause into multilateral trade agreements. In theory this would make trade and market access conditional upon governments agreeing to meet the following 'core' labour standards which already find expression in ILO conventions: freedom of association; collective bargaining; restrictions on the use of child labour; prohibition of forced labour; and non-discrimination in employment. Social clauses would be legally binding and enforceable by institutions that regulate world trade, namely the WTO. Countries, and the industries and firms operating in them, found to breach of these standards could have the social clauses of trade agreements invoked against them and their exports restricted (Sengenberger and Wilkinson, 1995; Shaw, 1996). An environmental clause has also been proposed along these lines.

The idea of establishing institutional links between trade and labour regulation can be traced back to the proposal for an International Trade

Organization (ITO) to regulate world trade, whose cooperation with the ILO would be intrinsic to the post-war institutional framework. This proposal floundered in the face of national opposition, and trade regulation fell to GATT, while labour regulation fell to the ILO (Evans, 1998; Wilkinson and Hughes, 2000). As then, so now, responses to a social clause, or an institutional link between trade and labour, have ranged from qualified acceptance to outright opposition. It has caused division within and between the trade union movement, NGOs and governments, and none of the international institutions have been prepared to include a social clause in trade treaties and make the WTO share in the administration and enforcement of labour standards, even though OECD and World Bank regard the economic effects of core labour standards as at least neutral, and at best positive (Evans, 1998). The WTO has insisted that there is no need for a social clause because free trade will 'naturally' improve labour standards. Although it supported a global commitment to core labour standards and pledged to continue collaboration with the ILO on the issue, it reaffirmed that the WTO should be concerned only with trade and that the ILO should concentrate on labour and with mitigating the social effects of WTO legislation. The ILO, which has argued for greater consideration to be given to the effects of economic globalization on workers, has also expressed grave reservations at a sanctions-based social clause which it regards as incompatible with its traditional emphasis on moral suasion and assistance in establishing and maintaining workers' rights. It has also been concerned about a perceived encroachment on its principles and procedures by another organization (Wilkinson and Hughes, 2000).

Opponents of a social clause have objected to it on the following grounds. First, it would enforce Western cultural values on non-Western societies. Here, as in the sphere of human rights, it is alleged that Northern governments are using the ethical claims of international society as a vehicle to assert a new global hegemony (Deacon, 1999a; Wilkinson and Hughes, 2000). Second, a social clause would erode the comparative wage advantage enjoyed by developing countries when engaged in competition with industrialized countries. Third, a social clause would introduce a new form of protectionism by industrialized countries against developing countries. As Shiva argues, social (and environmental) clauses are a form of 'unilateral internationalism' which would 'function primarily as conditionalities imposed by Northern governments on Southern governments' (1995: 5). Shiva also objects to a social clause on the grounds that it would not challenge the *cause* of social and environmental degradation – free trade policies – and that it does not assert substantial social or economic rights, notably the right to work and the right to livelihood (1995: 5). Finally, a social clause would do little to help many women, since much of their work falls outside the scope of international labour regulations anyway, while the enforcement of labour standards may further negatively impact on their employment.

Thus, women workers would be pushed out of the formal sector, where they are more likely to be protected, into the informal sector, where they are not, as a consequence of companies making greater use of sub-contracted production to female homeworkers in the informal sector (Henson, 1996; Shaw, 1996).

In the face of such opposition, the debate about linking trade and labour regulation has shifted away from a punitive social clause and towards the need for a more general acceptance of, and commitment to, core labour standards and enabling workers to claim an equitable share in the benefits of free trade (Wilkinson and Hughes, 2000). Although the focus on core labour standards indicates their universal acceptance, irrespective of cultural specificities and level of economic development, it is a far cry from any legal obligation to respect core labour standards and does not address the problem of their (non)enforcement. In short, states have proved eminently capable of resisting encroachment on their autonomy on this issue. However, Wilkinson and Hughes (2000: 271–2) predict the return of the labour standards issue to the WTO via pressure from regional bodies which are playing an increasingly important role in the WTO and which trade unions are directing their efforts towards in order to develop more effective mechanisms to regulate and enforce labour standards. Many of these regional groupings have developed, or are developing, some kind of social dimension (e.g. NAFTA, the EU, APEC, SADC and Mercosur) so might be expected to press the WTO on workers' rights globally (ibid.: 272).

Given the difficulties besetting global policy-making and implementation, it is likely that the preference will, for the foreseeable future, continue to be for 'soft law', such as Charters, Declarations, codes of conduct, and political agreements, as a way of overcoming some of the political and socio-cultural obstacles to transnational social policy. Indeed, this is the experience of the EU which has the most developed system of supra-national social law and enforcement mechanisms. 'Soft' law is more acceptable to governments; it does not legally bind them to a set of norms or fixed rules and allows more flexibility in persuading or negotiating with actors to adhere to universal norms (Pape, 1999). The problem here, of course, is that social progress through 'soft' law is subject to the pitfalls of voluntaristic compliance (see Chapter 5).

Social policy dialogues

From the perspective of IGOs and donor countries, neither the control of resources dispensed to states for specified purposes nor international legal instruments are necessarily effective means of influencing national policy and provision to the extent or in the ways that they may desire. IGOs cannot impose their preferences on sovereign states and know they must negotiate with them if they want to recover their money or exert any influence over them. 'Policy dialogues' therefore constitute an important means by which international agencies attempt to foster a political climate conducive to their own interests and intervene more directly in the domestic policy process (Burden, 1998). *Social* policy dialogues in this context refer to the political visions and policy prescriptions articulated by IGOs and other agencies with regard to, for example, employment, social protection, health, reproduction, social services and education. They also include advice on policy or systems reform to recipient governments – often provided as part of technical assistance – and other interventions in political debates nationally, such as: sponsoring research, reports and conferences; providing information; auditing compliance with international standards; and adding authority to critics when domestic policies are judged to fall short of international standards (Burden, 1998).

By attempting to set the parameters of reform through the articulation of a vision of the role and structure of national social protection – visions which may be tangibly supported by the provision of technical assistance and finance – policy dialogue can be regarded as a political-technocratic strategy on the part of IGOs to intervene more directly in the domestic social policy process. Policy dialogues help international institutions to identify and foster direct, 'insider' contact with technocratic and other élites, individuals and groups who share similar cultural, political and ideological interests and orientations (Burden, 1998). They help forge 'epistemic communities' and political alliances between a cadre of national technocrats, business and political élites and IGOs and so build a 'winning coalition of support' (Kahler, 1992: 127).

IGOs attempt to construct a policy consensus, preferably in advance of structural adjustment programmes, to persuade recipient governments to engage in joint problem-solving with them and, ultimately, for governments to align their policies with those favoured by creditors (Kahler, 1992). These dialogues may have a clear institutional basis and may be established in advance of, as well as operating in tandem with, SAPs, to reinforce their objectives. The IMF, for example, set up the systemic transformation facility (STF) in 1993, for the former Eastern bloc countries 'as a paving mechanism in establishing a working relationship with the Fund and building a policy dialogue' (Bakker, 1996: 25).

Policy dialogue is also a means of drawing attention to the consequences of reforms enacted by governments, especially their impact on the poorest groups for whom the World Bank and IMF are committed to ensuring safety-net provision (Bakker, 1996). The Social Dimensions of Adjustment Unit of the World Bank was established in 1987 in response to growing criticism of SAPs as programmes for mass impoverishment, a criticism which was hindering their implementation. Its purpose was to monitor the social impact of structural adjustment and to suggest ways that states could mitigate extreme hardship, albeit without adversely affecting economic restructuring programmes. Its political support for residual, means-tested social provision has resulted in measures typically targeted at retrenched workers (e.g. civil servants and workers in state-owned enterprises), low income urban households hit by the removal of food subsidies and price increases, and the rural poor hit by the removal of agricultural subsidies and poor access to resources such as land, employment and basic services (Brydon and Legge, 1996).

The discussion now turns to two areas of social policy dialogue in which international organizations have been actively involved: fertility and population control, and pensions policies. The emergence, content and diffusion of these global social policies will be examined, as well as the various actors involved and the interests that are being served in the governance of these issues and the instruments used to advance reforms.

Fertility and population control policy

Concern with population control can be traced back to the often eugenically inclined intellectual debates and social movements in Europe and the US in the late nineteenth and early twentieth centuries. Fertility and maternity policies in Western Europe were prompted by concerns about the *quantity* and the *quality* of the population. Pro-natalist policies of various strengths were pursued in response to declining birth rates and population losses due to World War I. Maternity and/or child allowances were introduced in various forms in Sweden and Germany, where the eugenics movement was particularly strong, and in Britain, Norway, France and Italy. Concerns about mother and child welfare and the responsibilities of mothers in rearing fitter children prompted policies to improve the 'quality' of the national stock (Bock and Thane, 1991) and encourage 'the breeding of the fit and intelligent and discourage the reproduction of the weak of body and intellect' (Williams, 1989: 126). In Britain after World War II, universal family allowances, ostensibly introduced on pro-natalist grounds, were introduced on a flat-rate basis because it was believed that a sliding scale of rates, which targeted allowances at poorer parents or which increased payment rates for more children, would encourage the poor to reproduce disproportionately (ibid.). To these eugenic concerns can be added imperialistic ones, and in Britain 'welfare politicians had warned of a British population decline which, compared to India's population expansion, would endanger Britain's 'status in the world', 'genius for colonization' and 'love of political freedom' (Bock and Thane, 1991: 12). Population policies were therefore inextricably linked with nation-building and with states' globalizing strategies:

> Demographic anxiety . . . was in part a product of intensified international competition from the late nineteenth century; it seemed that nations needed fit work-forces, fit armies and fit mothers to rear them if they were to compete

effectively in an increasingly internationalized market, for imperial domination and in war. (Bock and Thane, 1991: 11)

In the 1950s and 1960s, population became established as a concern of international agencies. It was constructed from the outset as a problem of over-population, as a global problem requiring a global response. Population control was strongly supported by Western European countries, particularly Nordic countries such as Sweden, with its strong eugenic tradition, and by the US, which saw population control in developing countries as an issue of national security. The first major initiative came from a private US foundation, the Rockefeller Foundation, which established the Population Council in 1952. The same year saw the foundation of the International Planned Parenthood Foundation, one of the major actors in population control discourse over the following decades.

In the 1960s 'population crises' appeared in political discourse. This 'catastrophist' discourse has its roots in Malthusianism which explains poverty, death and environmental degradation as the outcome of population pressure on scarce resources (E.B. Ross, 1998: 1). On a popular level, 'catastrophist' theoreticians, such as Paul Ehrlich, attributed the hunger crisis to population growth, not to the concentration of economic, political and environmental resources, the unequal distribution of land, or the control of food production for private profit (Hartmann, 1993; E.B. Ross, 1998). Catastrophist concerns were firmly established by the time of the first consideration of population as a global public policy issue in the 1965 World Population Conference in Belgrade. Although this was a meeting of technical and scientific experts, rather than of official government representatives, it paved the way for the formation of global population policy by the UN and World Bank. When Robert McNamara announced the involvement of the World Bank in population control in 1968 he rationalized it as follows: 'The World Bank is concerned above all with economic development, and the rapid population growth is one of the greatest barriers to the economic growth and social well-being of our member states' (quoted in Koivusalo and Ollila, 1997: 187). The UN held its first Conference on Population in Bucharest in 1974, which led to the World Population Plan of Action. At this conference, while Northern countries pressed strongly for the adoption of population control policies, Southern countries argued that 'development is the best contraceptive'. By the second UN conference on population in Mexico City in 1984, developing countries' resistance to population control policies was weakened by their worsening economic situation and their dependence on Western aid, and many agreed to implement population control policies as a condition of receiving structural adjustment loans. Perhaps an honest expression of the interests behind population control can be found in the US National Security Memorandum on international population policy (1974), which, according to Koivusalo and Ollila, feared adverse socio-economic conditions generated by population factors could contribute to increasing levels of child abandonment, juvenile delinquency, unemployment, petty thievery, organized brigandry, food riots, separatist movements, communal massacres, revolutionary actions and counter-revolutionary reprisals. The Memorandum pointed out that such conditions would also detract from the environment needed to attract foreign capital. It also feared that rapid population growth could endanger the world's mineral supplies, which increasingly come from the developing countries. (1997: 191)

During the 1980s and 1990s, attention shifted from the hunger 'crisis' to the environmental 'crisis'. Population growth was held responsible for desertification, runaway urbanization, and the depletion of the earth's resources, while population control became a panacea for global economic and environmental problems (Koivusalo and Ollila, 1997: 192).

It is no accident that the major source of funding for the reduction of population growth in developing countries has been the North, particularly the US. During the 1970s, 'population programmes were allocated two-thirds of all US foreign assistance to the health sector, while about half of Britain's multilateral aid contributions were for population control programmes' (Chetley, 1990: 8). Funding for population programmes has steadily increased: US contributions increased from just under US$300 million in the early 1990s to US$500 million by 1994; World Bank funding increased from an average of just over US$200 million in 1989–1991 to US$450 million in 1995 (Koivusalo and Ollila, 1997: 188–9). The US currently provides around 40 per cent of total population aid, which is channelled through bilateral programmes and NGOs. USAID, which works closely with the UNFPA, IPPF and the World Bank, has been 'the most influential of the donor organizations on population projects in developing countries' (Barrett and Ong Tsui, 1999: 221; Koivusalo and Ollila, 1997). Reimer Ravenholt, the head of USAID Office of Population (1967–1980), expressed the militaristic view pervading global population discourse when he stated that 'ordering contraceptives is like ordering bullets for a war. You don't want to run out' (Bandarage, 1997: 65). The largest private foundations involved were the Rockefeller Foundation, the MacArthur Foundation, the Population Council, the Hewlett Foundation, the Ford Foundation and the Mellon Foundation, all based in the US (Koivusalo and Ollila, 1997). The population programmes of the UN and WB, the emerging global consensus in the field of demography, and the activism of INGOs, has led to the global diffusion of population policies: by 1993 some 123 developing countries had adopted population control policies (Barret and Ong Tsui, 1999: 215).

Population control measures have been criticized as internationally sponsored programmes of human rights abuses (Peters and Wolper, 1995). Women in developing countries are the targets of this global social policy, the objects of 'quick fix' solutions, advanced through monetary means, such as cash incentives to accept 'high-tech', dangerous contraceptives, or technical means such as forced sterilizations (Bandarage, 1997: 66). These reach their zenith at sex-selective abortions, supported by medical and intellectual élites using market metaphors to justify abortion, particularly of female foetuses. This, they argue, will benefit women by reducing their supply, increase their scarcity and therefore their social status and value.

Alongside these crude and dangerous methods, methods intended to 'empower' women to voluntarily control their own fertility have emerged in response to growing global opposition to population control policies. Recently there have been attempts by the population control lobby to co-opt green and feminist concerns – or at least their language. In relation to the latter, Koivusalo and Ollila (1997) note that core feminist demands, such as women's empowerment or control of their reproductive capacities, were accepted by fundamentalists of all religions, right-to-life organizations and population control agencies at the most recent UN population conference, the International Conference on Population and Development in Cairo (1994). While some have claimed this represents a major step forward, critics – doubting the commitment of international institutions to these principles as anything but a tactical appropriation of a new vocabulary – 'have claimed that gender equality has become the social tool by which the UN seeks to ensure that its goal of population control is achieved' (Koivusalo and Ollila, 1997: 198).

Population control policy is one of the earliest examples of global social policy. The major push for this policy has been at the international level; the major international development institutions (governmental and non-governmental) have developed population policies, while that international institution with a vengeance – the Catholic church – as well as other, often fundamentalist, international religions and their institutions have also been involved. The delivery of this global social policy has involved the public, commercial and voluntary and community sectors at the international, national, and local levels. Bandarage (1997) has depicted the global governance of population control as a triangular hierarchy. Donor countries of the North sit at the apex, disbursing financial and technological aid, and women of the South sit at its base, receiving the aid. Between these are an intermediate layer consisting of a global network of international agencies – NGOs, UN agencies, development banks and private foundations – below which lie the states of the South. On the national level, where the policy is implemented, are the government, the private sector and national NGOs; at sub-national level are the hospitals and clinics, including those provided by local NGOs. The interaction of these institutions, with the women whose fertility is being controlled, involves the use of family planning providers and motivators, including local community leaders and the use of mass media for 'social marketing'.

Pensions

The major actors in this field are the ILO, World Bank (and associated development banks) and IMF. For much of the twentieth century, the dominant actor in this area has been the ILO, which has emphasized that the primary goal of social security should be to ensure access to a minimum standard of living and raise living standards overall. The ILO has recommended a tripartite PAYG model. The first pillar consists of a compulsory basic, universal flat-rate pension provided by a public scheme. The second pillar consists of a public, compulsory, defined-benefit (earnings related) scheme financed on a PAYG basis from payroll contributions. The third pillar is a voluntary, fully funded, defined-contribution scheme for people who wish to supplement the two schemes (Amparo Cruz-Saco Oyague, 1998; Otting, 1994). A sub-stantial role is envisaged for the first pillar, and a smaller role for the second and third pillars. This model, along with ILO legislation and recommendations, gained international acceptance and was influential on the legislation used by developed and developing countries alike (Osui cited in Kay, 2000). The ILO has insisted that pension reforms should improve upon existing provision by ensuring adequate coverage, unified and standardized entitlements, and rates of payment linked to earnings.

The arrival of the World Bank and IMF into pensions policy reform debates displaced the ILO as the dominant IGO in social security policy. Both the World Bank and IMF have been at the forefront of attempts to foster a political climate conducive to the residualization of state welfare and the promotion of private and voluntary initiatives (Deacon et al., 1997). This has meant recommending cutting state pensions to ensure minimal provision for the poorest and enhancing private pension provision for the rest of the population. The IMF has warned that failure of governments in developed countries to undertake such pension reform would have global consequences:

> the aging of the population has started to contribute to serious fiscal stresses in most of the major industrial countries . . . the industrial countries face daunting deficits and the prospect of heavy debt accumulations that in the absence of policy adjustment could adversely impact on global financial flows and interest rates. (IMF, 1996: 32)

The IMF's reminder to developed countries of their global responsibility to privatize pensions must be seen alongside the World Bank's similar insistence that comprehensive, publicly-funded and -provided pension systems are neither desirable nor viable and that the private sector offers the best solution to the pensions 'crisis'. Indeed, the World Bank's endorsement of privatization and its application to pensions in the mid-1990s 'symbolized pension privatization's transformation from a radical idea to a mainstream, global policy prescription' (Kay, 2000: 192). The Bank favours a subsidiary role for the state and a substantial role for the private sector in the management and provision of pensions and has recommended that 'industrial countries need to create an institutional framework that minimizes the threat of inadequate savings by ensuring that social security schemes are fully funded and by discouraging early retirement' (World Bank, 2000: 35). It regards the legitimate role of the state as limited to regulation of the pensions industry and to the provision of a minimum state pension for the poorest of the population. It advocates a three-pillar model. The first pillar consists of a low-level, means-tested state pension, publicly-managed and tax-financed. The second pillar consists of mandatory personal pensions, privately managed, based on individual funding and defined contributions. The third pillar consists of voluntary supplementary schemes, based on defined contributions and individually funded, to top up income in old age. The World Bank envisages a greater role for the second and third pillars in pension provision, and a smaller, residual, role for the first tier. This type of advice has been offered to advanced industrialized and developing countries alike, but it holds particular sway for countries which are dependent on IGOs and the North for development finance. Indeed the World Bank has not only offered such advice but has devoted substantial institutional and financial resources to realizing pension privatization in Central and Eastern Europe (Deacon et al., 1997; Deacon, 2000b), Latin America (Amparo Cruz-Saco Oyague, 1998) and China (World Bank, 1997b).

In Latin America, the 1980s debt crisis gave creditors (governments, private banks and IFIs), which had not previously insisted on conditionalities, an enormous amount of leverage over national governments. Further lending to debtor governments was restricted; creditors demanded that debt be serviced and that balance of payments deficits be stabilized, and imposed SAPs on governments as part of debt servicing arrangements. These programmes included the deregulation of trade, the privatization of state enterprises, the reorientatation of production towards exports and the reduction of external and internal budget deficits, including cuts in social security, pensions and food subsidies (Huber, 1996). Bretton Woods institutions assumed the role of coordinators debt service policies (IMF) and creditors of further structural adjustment loans (WB) to repay these debts. In effect they became authorities for the provision of technical advice in the countries of the region (Amparo Cruz-Saco Oyague, 1998; Huber, 1996; Stallings, 1992).

In tandem with the Inter-American Development Bank (IDB), the World Bank supported national pro-privatization campaigns by supplying governments with the expertise and financing for transition to a privatized system. The World Bank and IDB provided policy expertise, technical advice and funding in Argentina and Uruguay. IFI resources were used to fund and staff programmes of research which were critical to developing reform proposals, drawing on local consultants outside of the civil service who had no personal incentive to defend the existing PAYG system. The IDB made loans to the government in Uruguay for facilitating the transition costs to a private pension system, establishing a regulatory framework, improving administrative efficiency and assisting the development of capital markets. Such financing would not have been available for PAYG-only reform. This international support for privatization proved crucial in securing government control of the policy agenda as the national forces of opposition to the privatization of pensions lacked similar funds to support their campaigns. The dominance of the Washington consensus was unchallenged by an alternative model of pension reform as the ILO did not play a significant role in national policy debates at this time (Kay, 2000: 192–3, 195).

Although policy dialogues are used as a means of persuading governments to adopt and implement policy reforms they cannot bridge the 'implementation gap' because technocratic policy alignment, like structural adjustment, may not be sustained during implementation. The focus on policy-makers as the principal agents of reform neglects those subsequently charged with implementing the policy, such as civil and public servants and NGOs, who may hold significant bureaucratic and political power, but also different ideological beliefs from those charged with making policy. Moreover, popular opposition plays a key role in determining how far reforms are implemented. Thus, policy dialogues may provide legitimacy and support for new 'policy templates' (Kahler, 1992), but much still depends on the national political context as to how far, and in what form, these are actually implemented. The factors determining the implementation of global social policy are examined in Chapter 5.

Conclusions

This chapter has emphasized, in common with much of the globalization literature, the ways in which international agreements and policies impinge on state autonomy and impose severe costs on them and their populations. In this reading, IGOs are held responsible for 'free trade' and the liberalization of investment, while states are responsible for policing and enforcing international agreements and managing the domestic social and political consequences of these. Yet this interpretation is only part of the story. The missing dimension is why do states take part in these agreements at all? One reading of this area would see the relationship between IGOs and states in terms of the variety of state strategies to regulate the global economy. While states increasingly cooperate in certain areas through collective means, 'national interest' remains as strong as ever. Indeed, global political and legal agreements accommodate, if not protect, national interests as much as they override them. Governments pursue policies that maximize their national competitive or comparative advantage, negotiate derogations or reservations from international treaties whenever they can, and generally try to limit the 'encroachment' of international institutions on their public policy powers. Those who claim that states have minimal space for action contradict themselves when these states decry global agreements and fora as advancing the interests of Northern over Southern countries. The guiding role of the US in this regard is consistently remarked upon critically.

Those who argue that globalization erodes the state also fail to appreciate that the world political system is still inter-governmental and is premised on constitutionally-sovereign states. Despite the proliferation of supra-national and international institutions and agreements, there is no centralized international mechanism to enforce treaty obligations worldwide. International institutions are, at the end of the day, inter-governmental. The IMF perhaps comes closest to a nascent international state insofar as it carries out a number of state functions, such as the allocation of funds and the regulation of some aspects of international finance. However, while the IMF may have the technical capacity of a state, it lacks the political resources and coercive capacity of states (Pooley, 1991). Thus, claims that international institutions are 'reducing to zero the space in which states and particularly Third World states can exercise management' (S. Amin, 1997: 30) and that 'we have entered a new era characterized by a separation between the globalized space of capitalism's economic management and the national spaces of its political and social management' (1997: 32) are a gross exaggeration.

Regarding claims that economic and political interdependence lead to a substantial restriction of state autonomy and capacity, international cooperation is premised now, as it has always been, on interdependency. Indeed, international cooperation is, at the end of the day, the cooperation of sovereign states. As Drache argues, 'cooperative activity . . . does not necessarily imply that the cooperating actors somehow fade into the background' (1996: 53), while James states 'the extent to which [international cooperation] finds expression in agreed programmes of action, that action has to be coordinated or conducted by states' (1999: 469). The power of the state to enforce international law remains unrivalled, and this division of labour between states and international institutions means that the latter cannot – and do not seek to – replace the 'internal' functions of the state, including social policy functions.

Therefore, when both critics and supporters of international agreements claim that these agreements interfere with state autonomy – as even the IMF and World Bank admit that they do to some degree (Kapstein, 1999) – they are to a certain extent correct, insofar as government policies and practices are required to be consistent with international trade and investment law. But they are not specific enough. First, not all countries are equally vulnerable to policy leverage and these agreements interfere with the autonomy of some states far more than others. It is, in the main, Southern countries which receive financial aid and which are forced to accept SAPs. The successful implementation of multilateral agreements, policies and programmes nationally depends on the issue or policy area involved and country characteristics such as government ideology, political and social institutional regimes, interest group organization and mobilization, state capacity and strategic location (Stallings, 1992). When developments in economic, demographic and social structures are also taken into account, even broadly similar pressures facing governments will provoke quite different national responses.

Second, the idea that non-state actors may have some impact on states' actions does not constitute evidence that state autonomy has been substantially eroded or that the state no longer has regulatory powers. While it is important to note that governments may not be able to fully rely on some 'traditional' methods of regulation, such as trade, exchange and investment controls, it is also important to note that they have been able to secure a range of important concessions, restrictions and exemptions for important sectors and industries in international treaties. Regarding the effects of the WTO, as Dunkley (2000) notes, even if OECD countries fully implement their liberalization programme, which commits them to completely liberalizing market access in one third of sectors, and partially in one half of them, they will still retain considerable control over remaining sectors. States' obligations to treat 'local' and 'foreign' capital equally certainly renders their regulatory control of privatized services in the interests of social protection more difficult, but not impossible, and they still retain a range of regulatory powers in a range of areas.

Of particular importance as regards the formation and implementation of global policy is that although domestic public policy has to take account of international trade and investment law, it also has to take account of national and international *social* laws and agreements, as well as the legislature and politicians, NGOs, electorates, military and domestic business interests which may oppose IGO-sponsored reforms or win important concessions from them. Therefore, international actors do not always determine the shape or outcomes of domestic policy reform, while states still retain a considerable degree of control over capital and markets. Indeed, any changes in the regulation of the *domestic* operations of capital and labour still needs to be explained by reference to the balance of political power nationally. This is the subject of the next chapter.

5 The Globalization of Social Conflict and Political Struggle

My argument so far has been that 'strong' globalization theory's emphasis on the overwhelming constraints of global capital on domestic politics and policy-making both assigns disproportionate weight to economic forces (Chapters 2 and 3) and underplays political factors, especially national states (Chapters 3 and 4). However, this needs to be taken further as there is no 'clear-cut sovereignty game for all states' (Sørensen, 1999: 597). The ways in which states promote, 'receive' and react to globalization differ according to their position, or rank, within the global political economy (e.g. 'core' or 'periphery', strategic economic or military location), their institutional, cultural and historical traditions and arrangements, and the national balance of power between the state, labour, capital and civil society. Thus, while globalizing forces may straddle (part of) the globe, they also have to manifest themselves at the regional, national and local levels, at all of which they may run into trouble and opposition and to the extent that outcomes are never certain in advance. Any explanation of the globalizing strategies of capital and states, and of the consequences of globalization for social policy, must therefore take account of the social, economic, cultural, political and institutional *contexts* in which these are developed. The continuing importance of 'closure', state regulation and 'territorialization' have therefore been highlighted in contrast to 'strong' globalization's fixation on circulation, flows and deterritorialization because

> The conventional notion of globalization as an advancing force bulldozing the world around it is clearly at odds with the multiplicity of forms encountered or engendered in diverse contexts. Confusion occurs when one overlooks the way that centralizing elements of globalization fuse with distinctive local and regional conditions. (Mittelman, 1996: 232)

This chapter examines the importance of social conflict and political struggle – and of politics and political agency more generally – in the regulation of globalization, and the range of levels at, and spheres in, which global politics and political action take place. It examines the importance of the 'local' context and factors such as the nature and strength of ideologies, cultural and religious values and traditions, social, religious, political and environmental movements, the strength and balance of political power between political parties, and between labour, civil associations and capital, and the political compromises between them (Esping-Andersen, 1996; Garrett, 1998; Hay, 1998; Pierson, 1998; Rhodes, 1996). It is shown that although globalization may indeed be a key influence on public and social policy, it is only one among many other influences, and its implementation is likely to be tailored to fit the national context. This emphasis on the importance of the 'local' context is not to deny the global one, nor is it to posit 'global'/'national' and the 'local' as exclusive categories (Scholte, 2000; Swyngedouw, 1997), nor is it to suggest that 'local' precludes transnational links; it merely seeks to draw attention to how victory, defeat or compromise depend on the *context* in which struggles occur.

The discussion also highlights the range of actions taken by the voting, consuming and productive populations to regulate or oppose globalizing strategies at a number of levels (local, national, regional, international) and in a number of spheres (institutional, economic). These actions, which form part of the context in which globalization is negotiated, mean that global forces do not steamroll over domestic factors and forces. Such actions can restrict the margin of operation of both the state *and* capital. Indeed, globalization has thrown up structures for contestation, resistance and opposition which mediate the process and effects of globalization and create space for an alternative politics of globalization. The political parameters are not as narrow as the catastrophist and triumphalist positions within 'strong' globalization would have us believe.

The institutionalist bias of global governance and political globalization

If 'strong' globalization theory has assumed a heavily economistic flavour, then many analyses of political globalization and global governance have assumed a strongly institutionalist flavour. Thus, global governance predominantly refers to the range of 'efforts to bring more orderly and reliable responses to social and political issues that go beyond capacities of states to address individually' (Gordenker and Weiss, 1996a: 17), and the focus of attention tends to be on IGOs, regional formations and states. Bretherton, for example, defines political globalization as 'a growing tendency for issues to be perceived as global in scope, and hence requiring global solutions; and to the development of international organizations and global institutions which attempt to address such issues' (1996: 8).

Important though IGOs are, the issues of global governance and political globalization embrace a much broader range of agencies, actors and actions. Governance has been defined as 'the sum of many ways individuals and institutions, public and private, manage their common affairs' (Commission on Global Governance, 1995: 2) and as 'the control of activity by some means such that a range of desired outcomes is attained' (Hirst and Thompson, 1996: 184). Governance need not be associated with statist institutions, nationally or internationally, at all and can be performed by a range of public and private, state and non-state, national and international institutions and practices (1996: 184). It includes 'formal institutions and regimes empowered to enforce compliance' as well as 'informal arrangements that people and institutions either have agreed to or perceive to be in their interest' (Commission on Global Governance, 1995: 2).

Indeed, in its broadest sense, global governance refers to *all* non-state sources of 'authority' which have the power to allocate values and influence the distribution of resources: business organizations and networks, both legal (TNCs) and illegal (TCOs); professional associations; transnational authorities in sports, art, music; the global mass media; transnational social, political and religious movements, NGOs and other citizens' movements (Commission on Global Governance, 1995; Strange, 1996). The particular configuration of actors involved in governance varies according to the area, market or sector in question. By way of illustration, all of the following participate in the governance of one particular commodity market, the sugar and sweeteners sector: transnational firms, national and international authorities in charge of competition policy, the International Sugar Council (a global group with specific responsibility for trade), local voluntary associations, plantation workers, beet farmers and dietitians (Commission on Global Governance, 1995: 3).

Global governance and global politics involve a multitude of actors operating at a number of levels and in a range of spheres. The realm of politics should be understood as actions which aim to influence collective economic, social and political practices and extend far beyond the practice of governments or, in the case of global politics, IGOs. Thus, social movements and NGOs certainly act in the *institutional* realm of governance, where they seek to influence and participate in policy-making and implementation, but they also act in the *economic* realm, engaging in strategies of protest and orchestrating public outcry to oppose corporate (re)location or persuade corporations to adopt socially- and environmentally-acceptable practices (Wapner, 1995: 329; Williams and Ford, 1999).

Snyder's (1999) concept of 'global legal pluralism' is consistent with this broader notion of governance as structures and processes of power and authority:

> Global legal pluralism involves a variety of institutions, norms and dispute resolution processes located, and produced, at different structured sites around the world . . . These relations of structure and process constitute the global legal playing field. (1999: 342–3)

Snyder argues that scholarship on global governance has tended to stress legal contracts between parties either in a bilateral/multilateral form, or in 'vertical', hierarchical form, in terms of multi-level governance; that consequently it has paid less attention to the ways in which transnational economic networks are governed, or regulated, as much by socio-cultural norms and 'soft law' as by contract law. Snyder's approach highlights multiple sites of global economic governance: some sites are market-based, others are polity-based, but each has distinctive institutional and normative characteristics which shape the production, implementation and sanctioning of rules (Snyder, 1999: 372). The concept of 'global legal pluralism' also brings political agency to the fore by emphasizing the norms, values and standpoints of strategic actors, such as governments, businesses, NGOs and international institutions.

This widening of global governance and global politics to include actions in the economic sphere as well as in the institutional-political sphere is a welcome and useful development. The former types of actions are not well captured by an institutionalist definition of global social policy such as that offered by Deacon et al. (1997) who focus primarily on the supra-national or international institutional sphere. Although the international sphere is where the most obvious attempts are being made to formulate global social policy, the primacy Deacon accords it is also a result of the institutionalist tendencies within academic social policy itself which privileges state institutions and the more institutionalized sectors of opposition movements. Consequently, the emphasis on the forces and initiatives to modify 'globalization from above' neglects those against 'globalization from below' (Falk, 1997). It confines our view to the social dialogue that takes place at the level of international summits and meetings and excludes other 'social dialogues' taking place at different levels and in various locations and sites outside the boardrooms and bureaux of international institutions, dialogues which also 'influence the outcomes of international relations at least by interacting in and shaping the *political processes* that generate global policy' (Smith et al., 1997: 74, original italics). In the realm of environmental politics, for example, NGOs have demanded greater participation in the WTO, while 'less institutionalized grass-roots movements . . . are taking a confrontational attitude and challenging the WTO and notions of trade liberalization *per se*' (Williams and Ford, 1999: 283). The institutionalist bias in global social policy analysis must therefore be supplemented by accounts which emphasize social conflict, struggle and protest, to account for the range of levels and spheres in which global social politics are fought out.

Social conflict and political struggle

One glaring omission from globalization theories, and one which is puzzling due to globalization's fixation upon economics, is the existence of social conflict, and specifically, class conflict. Transfixed by the mobility of capital, some have failed to notice the instrumental role of the trade union movement in facilitating globalization (Herod, 1997), or that one impetus to capital mobility was the wave of industrial and other struggles that swept the advanced industrialized countries in the late 1960s. This missing class conflict is due to the (often unarticulated) belief that, just as the nation state has been defeated, so has the working class. Globalization theory is vulnerable to claims that it has failed to account for class conflict, yet as Moran argues, 'class conflict and/or class alliances involving the state, national capital and the working class are an integral factor in explaining the timing and course of globalization' (1998: 53).

In a useful discussion of the role of the labour movement in globalization, Herod (1997) argues that US trade unions have a long history in acting globally; they played a central role in structuring geopolitical discourse and practice throughout the nineteenth and twentieth centuries, which paved the way for corporate restructuring abroad, and in generally facilitating US economic expansionism and the spread of US capital and culture in Europe (e.g. by supporting the Marshall plan), Latin America, the Caribbean, Asia and Africa. US unions took a leading role in expanding US control over regional economies and labour forces, particularly in Latin America and the Caribbean, by setting up regional organizations in opposition to anti-capitalist labour movements and supporting pro-US political forces there. They played a crucial role by funding local political campaigns, running labour education programmes, providing aid in setting up credit unions, workers' banks, producer–consumer cooperatives and building housing for members of pro-US local unions. While these activities were more to do with anti-communist political concerns than with the activities of TNCs, they were nonetheless crucial in ensuring a more receptive investment climate for US capital. In this respect, US unions were central to the genesis of globalization, but they were also partners of US government and capital in the expansion of US economic and political influence globally.

In similar vein, global economic restructuring began, at least in part, in response to the development of class conflict in the 'core' countries. The most obvious example is the car industry, which restructured from strongly unionized and combative environments in metropolitan countries, to rural and peripheral locations in these same countries as well as internationally. This restructuring did not simply involve relocation of production, but also involved smaller plants, often with two plants dedicated to making the same component so that no single strike affecting one particular operation or factory would succeed in stopping production. Thus, it may be argued that the move offshore to global factories was caused as much by the search for increased control of labour as by a search for cheaper labour (see also Chapter 2) and that,

> rather than 'cutting loose' TNCs have employed globalization as a weapon in the domestic space of class conflict; they have threatened to exit but have sought to restructure class relations in the home politico-economic space to their advantage. (Moran, 1998: 68)

This emphasis on globalization as a means of labour discipline is supported by London and Ross's (1995) work which found the control of labour, as well as the cost of labour, to be an important determinant of the location of FDI. They argue that flows of capital from core to periphery are

> motivated in part by political considerations associated with the shifting bargaining-power positions of capital and labour . . . Capital searches for propitious investment sites in the periphery not only to revitalize rates of profit but also to discipline labour at home. The most favoured sites for mobile capital possess a certain combination of economic and social characteristics: acceptable market size (especially in the case of import-substitution investment), adequate infrastructure, and a favourable balance of class forces . . . By finding that, from 1967–1978, foreign capital, net of level of development, was attracted to places with less protest and fewer strikes, and also attracted to states that were more repressive (up to a limit), we found constant support for that part of the theory that emphasizes the control of labour. (London and Ross, 1995: 212)

Globalization should also be recognized as having been built on the defeat of the organized working class. Moran notes that the deregulation of finance in Britain, a state which was regarded as central to the expansion of international finance, 'was dependent on defeating the organized union movement' and that it 'will be dependent on this in countries such as France and Germany in which this is yet to occur' (1998: 68). Noting that the Big Bang of 1986 was preceded by the defeat of the steelworkers in 1980, the rail unions in 1982, the print unions in 1983 and finally the miners in 1984–1985, he argues that

> The Big Bang of 1986 was fuelled to a great extent with the equity issues arising from the privatization of British Gas, British Telecom, electricity utilities, etc., issues which could not have been made had organized labour maintained the institutional strength of say, the union sector in Germany. (1998: 69)

Class conflict is not the only conflict that globalization engenders. Integration into the global economy is premised on the intensification of work (Howard, 1995: 301), but while this affects both men and women, its consequences are distinct for women. Chapter 3 showed that global manufacturing and service economies dominated by TNCs rely on the 'flexible', cheaper labour of women. The ways in which globalization is premised on the intensification of women's labour worldwide can also be seen in relation to SAPs. First, loan conditionalities which require the curtailment of programmes of redistribution through state services are disproportionately likely to affect women as employees of the state (nurses, teachers and administrative staff). Second, the integration of local economies into the global economy also affects women as subsistence farmers since the greater reliance on exports for income entails a structural shift in the local economy to their detriment. Economic integration incorporates subsistence and non-money economies into the market economy and changes the structure of economic production, from self-sufficient production for domestic or local consumption, to industrialized production for export to foreign markets. This process invariably entails the transfer of the ownership of capital or assets (e.g. land) from subsistence (women) farmers to (male) property owners internally within the country at the same time as developing countries' resources are distributed to the industrialized countries (Korten, 1995). Third, as primary providers of informal care and welfare, women are disproportionately affected by cuts in health, education and food subsidies leading to increased nutrition rates, higher infant and child mortality and reduced life expectancy.

The social and economic costs of 'austerity', 'stabilization', or structural adjustment programmes are largely absorbed by the unpaid labour of women, as the ILO has recognized:

> The recession reveals in all their [sic] amplitude housework's importance and strategic nature . . . Economic welfare (understood as an available volume of goods and services to satisfy needs) still depends to a considerable degree on work carried out in families on the margin of market relations. (ILO in G.F. Dalla Costa, 1993: 114–15)

Insofar as reduced financial and service support renders women's unpaid labour more important to maintaining their family's standard of living, SAPs can be said to be premised on the exploitation of women's labour (Bandarage, 1997; Dalla Costa, 1993; Mies and Shiva, 1993; Rajput and Swarup, 1994). Thus, cuts in state health spending require women to spend more time caring for sick, disabled and elderly family members. Women substitute for formal social services cut from the public budget as they accompany family members to hospitals and clinics and provide meals for those in hospitals when catering services are withdrawn. Switching to cheaper foods (pulses, unrefined cereals) takes longer in preparation and cooking time, adding to women's domestic labour and time inputs necessary to maintain the household's standard of living (Elson, 1987, 1994). Greater reliance on women's unpaid work has, in South America and Asia, as in Britain, been accompanied by a return to 'family values'. In Venezuela, for example, this has taken the form of measures aimed at controlling social reproduction, reviving notions of the family, the sexual division of labour, notions of 'bad' motherhood and generally controlling women's behaviour more tightly (Dalla Costa, 1993). Thus, as with EPZs (p. 46, Chapter 2), globalization 'piggy-backs' on local patriarchal structures.

The globalization of social conflict: protest and opposition

With these processes and effects spreading throughout the world, different groups – from farmers to feminists, from indigenous peoples to environmental activists – have organized to oppose globalization at local, national and international levels. Central to this political global-ization has been the creation of global awareness and analyses. Environ-mental activists, for example, recognized from an early stage the need to view their subjects on a global basis, due to the interconnectedness of ecological systems; as Sauvin argued, 'the scale, spread and dynamics of contemporary environmental degradation are historically unique and global in nature' (1996: 93). With the ecological system conceptualized as global and interconnected, global analyses were called for: the environ-mental crisis was quickly defined as a global one and global solutions pressed for. As early as the mid-1970s,

> awareness of national problems had grown to the point where it was now clear that there were many environmental problems that were either common to more than one country, or were transnational, regional or even global in their scope. Issues such as marine pollution, whaling, fisheries, desertification, acid rain, threats to the ozone layer and carbon dioxide build-up could not be solved by individual states acting alone. (McCormick, 1995: 225)

It is important to recognize that the political response to these problems as global, rather than national or local in origin and nature has been a selective one. Shiva's (1994) analysis of the World Bank's Global Environmental Facility shows that political calculation was behind the selection and definition of some problems as global (greenhouse gas emissions, biodiversity, pollution in international waters, and ozone layer depletion) to the exclusion of others (notably toxic waste and hazardous emissions from nuclear and chemical industries). However, this selectivity does not detract from the general point that the growth of opposition groups and of social movements against globalization has been integral to – even accelerated by – the globalization process:

> The globalization of civil society precipitates resistance from disadvantaged strata in a changing division of labour. The losers in global restructuring seek to redefine their role in the emerging order. In the face of the declining power of organized labour and revolutionary groups, the powerless must devise alter-native strategies of social struggle. They aim to augment popular participation

and assert local control over the seemingly remote forces of globalization. New social movements – women's groups, environmentalists, human rights organizations, etc. – are themselves a global phenomenon, a worldwide response to the deleterious effects of economic globalization. (Mittelman, 1996: 325)

The relationship between globalization and the increase in social conflict is supported by Rosenau (1990), who argues that not only has the world become more integrated since 1945, but that it has also become more turbulent, at least in part due to growing global interdependence. There is reasonable empirical evidence to support this position. Tarrow (1995) reports evidence of increasing magnitude, simultaneity and coordination in contentious collective action by European social movements since the early 1960s, while the 1980s – a period of economic crisis and reform – marked 'a new wave of urban political mobilization' (Walton, 1987: 468) as inhabitants of countries responded to restructuring with civil and political unrest, with the result that 'the new uprisings of the world's poor have altered the international political economy' (1987: 384). Indeed, there is evidence of increased growth in transnational social movement organizations (TSMOs) – social movements which 'involve conscious efforts to build transnational cooperation around shared goals that include social change' (Smith et al., 1997: 60). Over 60 per cent of all TSMOs active in 1993 were formed after 1970 (Smith, 1997: 46); 42 per cent of environmental TSMOs were formed after 1985 and 80 per cent were formed after 1970 (1997: 48). Keck and Sikkink also report that the number, size and professionalism of what they call 'transnational advocacy networks' have grown dramatically in the last three decades, along with the density and complexity of their international linkages with intergovernmental organizations and other NGOs (Keck and Sikkink, 1999: 92). These new social movements are increasingly cooperating and coordinating on the global level, in addition to the national level, most often in the sharing of information and debate, but also in their actions. Transnational movements are essentially oppositional in challenging corporate power and inter-governmental institutions and practices of regulation. Indeed, they provide an important countervailing force against the centralization of power, especially bureaucratic and economic power (Tarrow, 1995).

Paradoxically, one of the tools that is a medium for globalization is also a medium for counter-globalization. The importance assigned to technology in globalization has already been noted (Chapter 1), but in the present context, communications technology also plays a role in social conflict of both a criminal and political kind engendered by globalization, from drug cartels and illegal arms merchants to social movements and advocacy networks (Cleaver, 1999; Keck and Sikkink, 1999). Rosenau (1990: 360) attributes the 'marked increase in the number of spontaneous collective actions' and their rapid spread around the world as at least partly due to new, and increasingly globalized, media, while Ganley argues that 'the advent of personal electronic media has coincided and is interacting with an age of massive political upheaval' (1992: 7).

Waterman highlights 'the growing import of networking, communication and culture in the development of a new kind of global solidarity' (1998: 373); indeed, global social dialogues have been particularly facilitated by developments in communications technology, such as the internet. This technology makes global communication, information exchange and dialogue easier and cheaper for highly disparate and isolated groups, many of whom cannot afford international travel. Technology has also been central to domestic political conflict and struggle. Ganley (1992) points, for example, to the use of cassette-recorded speeches by the Ayatollah Khomeini during the Iranian revolution. Similarly, some authoritarian regimes, such as China or Singapore, have responded cautiously to the internet due to its potentially destabilizing role. New technological and media systems are rapidly adopted by activists. Those who organized the Carnivals Against Capitalism and the anti-MAI, -WTO and -IMF campaigns (see below) did so to a large extent over the internet. Indeed, 'in conflict after conflict, e-mail and web pages have been cited by protagonists on both sides as playing key roles' (Cleaver, 1999: 10), while Hoechsmann notes that 'as a communications tool for activists located in far-flung corners of the world but united in the struggle for social justice in the brave new global economy, the Internet is a powerful new technology' (1996: 34).

It should be noted that opposition forces to globalization are not necessarily always progressive, at least in the accepted Western sense. Responses to the disruptive effects of globalizations have included not only a renaissance in national and ethnic movements, in xenophobia and racism, but also a growth in religious fundamentalism. On the latter, while Islamic fundamentalism is the example which is usually cited in the West – rather than as a movement against neo-liberalism – it also includes the growth in the US of a bible-bashing militia movement, with their paranoid visions of black helicopters, ZOG (Zionist Occupation Government) and a UN-led New World Order. Faced with the loss of security associated with globalization, individuals retreat to older forms of certainties to anchor their existence. In the remainder of this chapter I examine in some detail the range and form that local struggles against globalization have taken and the political struggles and actions to construct alternative agendas and courses of action for global reform.

Struggles against globalization

'Local' counter-struggles and protest against globalization are fought by a range of groups and organizations: trade unions; women's groups;

environmental groups; tribal and indigenous groups; consumer groups; human rights groups; civil liberties groups, and anti-nuclear groups. These provide an important source of countervailing power to global-izing actors and groups (Fox Piven and Cloward, 1995: 314). Indeed, a major aspect of their work may consist of targeting market processes and influential associations affiliated with trade, culture, religion, science and production using 'the realms of transnational social, cultural and economic life' (Wapner, 1995: 313). These movements and groups 'identify and manipulate nonstate levers of power, institutions, and modes of action to alter the dynamics of domestic collective life' (1995: 315). They employ a wide range of strategies: lobbying legislators; letter-writing campaigns; exposing illegal activities; class action suits through the courts; demonstrations, strikes and riots; consumer boycotts, and physical attacks on products, centres of consumption and infrastructure. In the discussion that follows it is considered how opposition move-ments have mobilized against the globalizing strategies of capital, international institutions and governments and how these have been forced to address movement criticisms of the social, health and environ-mental consequences of their actions and movement demands placed upon them.

Capital

There has been a reported rise in labour internationalism, with issues relating to health and safety and women and child workers the subjects of international campaigns. Trade unions have 'successfully challenged *at the global scale* the actions of transnational corporations' (Herod, 1997: 192, emphasis in original) through: developing international coordina-tion in contract bargaining; arguing that workers around the world should enjoy similar health and safety conditions at work; rights to union representation and collective bargaining; encouraging mergers between unions in certain industries in order to present a more unified position against management; investing resources in developing databases on corporate operating and bargaining practices around the globe to facilitate affiliates' corporate campaigns (Herod, 1997: 182-3). A major impetus to transnational labour activism was NAFTA (Carr, 1999), while US unions have been prepared to undertake innovative actions, such as 'corporate campaigns' and participate in new alliances and coalitions with consumer and environmental groups, among others. Some (Moody, 1997; Scipes, 1992; Waterman, 1998) have reported the emergence of new labour movements in peripheral countries which they call 'social movement unionism'. Social movement unionism refers to the active lead taken by unions and their members on issues of direct concern to them, as well as on issues affecting those less able to sustain self-mobilization. Of note here are attempts by trade unions to establish international connections at the shop-floor level rather than through union secretariats. One example of this is the emergence of labour-led, grassroots anti-apartheid groups in the mid-1980s, which forged links with black trade unions in South Africa; apartheid was an issue in several strikes in the US against TNCs that operated in that country (Herod, 1997).

Many strategies to socially regulate globalization take the form of direct action using the market mechanism. Market-based strategies of resistance to global capital include international campaigns by consumer groups and NGOs to bring about improved standards for groups of workers in particular industries. For example, one successful campaign, targeting working conditions in textile factories in Guatemala subcontracting to The Gap (a North American retail chain), involved the National Labour Committee, the textile union UNITE, religious and women's groups, along with allies in Central America. These campaigns have the best chance of success against companies such as Nike that depend on consumer brand loyalty. Cavanagh and Broad (1996) see countervailing power to that of global corporations emerging in these new coalitions of movements, which are coordinating across labour, environmental, consumer and other social sectors, on one axis, and across geographical boundaries on the other axis. They cite the importance of transnational links in victorious campaigns such as the following:

> In May 1995 religious, labour, consumer and other US groups that make up the Child Labour Coalition, launched a consumer boycott of Bangladeshi clothing exports after investigations revealed widespread child labour in the industry. The threat of a boycott led the Bangladesh Garment Manufacturers and Exporters Association to sign an agreement with UNICEF and the ILO to move some 25,000 children out of the clothing industry and into schools. (Cavanagh and Broad, 1996: 22)

Market-based strategies work by persuading consumers to redirect their spending power away from the products of companies or countries perceived to be abusing the environment, workers' rights or human rights. Consumer, trade and labour boycotts, social- and eco-labelling of products, and investor initiatives have brought about corporate codes of conduct in global industries such as baby foods, drugs, textiles, garments and footwear (Shaw, 1996; Vander Stichele and Pennartz, 1996). Consumer boycotts have 'helped people to make connections between global problems and their own mundane shopping trip' (*Ethical Consumer*, 1996: 21) and generated social concern among both businesses and consumers. To the extent that they heighten awareness that 'buying is politics' (Bennholdt-Thomsen and Mies, 1999: 121) they offer a means for leveraging public effort (Diller, 1999). A review in *Ethical Consumer* (1996) listed five fully successful UK boycotts, seven partially successful UK boycotts and four successful US boycotts which were supported by

UK consumers. However, Friedman argues that 'while in theory consumer boycotts offer the ecological strategist a powerful weapon for prompting corporations to work towards the realization of a sustainable future, in practice, the boycott tactic may have limited usefulness' (Friedman, 1995: 214) He notes that often it was not the boycott itself, the economic leverage of consumers, that determined success, but media coverage of the practices of offending firms (1995: 213).

Investor initiatives are investment-related decisions that seek to encourage socially-responsible corporate behaviour (e.g. the adoption of codes and labels) while maintaining the level of economic return. They grew from 'socially-responsible investment' movements in some developed countries, and many initiatives now serve as catalysts to advance law and policy by raising the threshold for best practice (Diller, 1999: 111). Snyder suggests that codes of conduct drawn up by TNCs or sectoral trade associations, often in response to NGO pressure, 'may be much more important in practice than formal national or local legislation' (1999: 361). In his study of global commodity chains in the toy industry, Snyder argues that codes of conduct can be considered 'analogous to multilaterally negotiated treaties which are then applied as standard-form contracts laid down by the leading firms in a particular market' (1999: 363). Dominant buyers are susceptible to political pressure to adopt codes, while they are also in a powerful position to contractually impose codes of conduct on their suppliers because of their control of brands and marketing.

The limitations of these forms of action also need to be pointed out. In a review of action on child labour, McClintock concluded that:

> Corporate codes of conduct and product labelling efforts, while having the advantage of being market-based, suffer from the risk of capitalist shirking. Better governance mechanisms to eliminate child labour are likely to require not only enhanced codes of conduct but also the upgrading and more effective enforcement of national labour laws plus the use of supranational institutions to implement international labour standards tied to trade policy. (1999: 516)

These drawbacks are symptomatic of those that arise from all forms of industrial self-regulation. Voluntary introduction of codes of conduct by TNCs may be intended as PR gestures with no real content, aiming only to delay state regulation, depoliticize political issues by redefining them as technical issues, and fudge the issue to be regulated (CornerHouse, 1998; Diller, 1999; Vander Stichele and Pennartz, 1996). In addition, the content and operation of codes of conduct vary enormously. In a review of 215 codes of conduct, occupational health and safety was the most frequently addressed issue (75 per cent), while refusing to contract with companies that used forced labour (25 per cent) and freedom of association and collective bargaining (15 per cent) were the least addressed issues. A similar degree of selectivity was found in social labelling programmes, where child labour was the most frequently targeted issue (Diller, 1999: 112–13). Diller also found that national law is the most frequently cited reference source for code standards, followed by international standards (general human rights or labour-specific standards) and industry standards (1999: 115). However, she also found that there was great diversity in content and that 'most self-definitions [of standards] differ from, and even contradict, international labour principles' (1999: 116). In short, these 'private', voluntary initiatives may depart from, and may even undercut, public efforts to improve labour regulations while abrogating corporate responsibility for a substantial range of employment rights and standards and obligations. In short, they may represent the 'pursuit of a private form of social justice for private gain' (Diller, 1999: 100).

Once adopted, codes of conduct pose significant implementation, enforcement and monitoring problems. Although many corporations prefer self-policing methods for monitoring and implementation, code implementation systems tend to lack adequate human resources, participation by workers, and transparency in application (Diller, 1999). Without effective mechanisms and institutions for monitoring and verification, including real sanctions for failure, they are of little use (Vander Stichele and Pennartz, 1996: 15). However, it should be recognized that outside pressure from critics and labour rights groups can sometimes prove effective in enforcing implementation. In recognition of these limitations, a range of proposals are currently being developed by international institutions to standardize private sector initiatives and develop better coordination of public and private actions. These range from the establishment of a universal set of social principles to guide industry (OECD, World Bank, UN Commission on Sustainable Development) to more regulatory approaches (e.g. the European Parliament has proposed a legally-binding model code of conduct for European businesses operating in developing countries) (Diller, 1999: 123).

A further issue is that, given that these codes are intended to respond to different constituencies, they may come to be used as a vehicle for more powerful constituencies to gain over less powerful ones. On this issue Deacon notes that,

> Codes of conduct are supposed to address the demands of the Northern consumer, NGOs, the company shareholder and the Southern worker. Where these claims conflict, it has, in some cases been the interests of the Southern workers which have suffered. Companies respond to the consumer's demand for immediate action rather than the worker's need for gradual improvements. In order to be effective, codes have to be constructed and implemented in a way which surmounts these contradictions and addresses the needs of the least powerful. (1999b: 32)

Regulatory strategies may be reformist in the sense that they aim to gradually improve working conditions in established sites of production, but they also include outright opposition and disruptive action at the local level. Numerous examples of such action, many of which are actions against local branches of TNCs, can be cited: various tribal and indigenous groups and NGOs have taken their concerns to the AGMs of transnational companies such as RTZ (Rio Tinto Zinc), Shell, BP and Monsanto, while international institutions may be called on to back up local opposition – for instance, a US labour union (OCAW) recently lodged a complaint against a German chemical company (BASF) operating in Louisiana (US) with the Paris-based OECD. Plans for new production methods, factories and other corporate facilities are facing organized local opposition with a vengeance and may constitute an important constraint on capital's 'footloose' inclinations. Indeed, while many states increasingly offer themselves as locations for capital's projects, some have had the occasion to complain that their efforts have been hindered or betrayed by 'unrepresentative' environmental or community groups who oppose the facilities the state has worked so hard to attract. Whether the problem is conceived as one relating to the community (summarized as NIMBY, Not In My Back Yard), or one relating to the proposed activity itself (summarized as LULU, Locally Unwanted Land Use), it is a growing problem, not only in the core countries, but also in the peripheral countries. Global corporations operating locally may face strong contestation from the local population, up to and including armed opposition, as RTZ mining in Bougainville, Shell extracting oil in the Nigerian Delta and BP and other corporations operating in Colombia have discovered to their cost.

With genetic engineering, for example, which can be expected to have far-reaching social, economic and environmental effects, the introduction of new technology by capital on a global scale, often aided by permissive state regulation, has encountered a range of popular opposition strategies. In relation to genetically modified foods, the types of resistance vary geographically: in Britain, consumer boycotts and activist attacks on test crops have been the principal forms of resistance; in Asia and Europe, opposition has developed on an ideological level, often with a religious basis; in India resistance has taken the form of attacks on companies by mass farmers' organizations. Here, again, the 'global logic' of capital finds itself in conflict with local forces. While in general it may seem that capital is the victor in these struggles, it is fair to say that there have been numerous inspiring examples of victory for local forces over transnational capital.

The state

Events around the world demonstrate that strong campaigns can still be mounted against the state to defend welfare rights and entitlements. Drawing on the examples of pensions policy and taxation policy, this section shows how, for both 'developed' and 'developing' countries, the fate of globalization is often decided 'locally' rather than globally, is mediated by class struggle and is dependent on the national balance of power.

In France, although one in every 12 French workers was unemployed and one in every five French workers was in a part-time or temporary job, a major strike protest by public sector workers and popular mobilization more generally prevented proposed pension reforms from being realized (Bensaïd, 1996; Bonoli, 1998; Jefferys, 1996). The reasons for this defeat of a globalizing policy can be found in national factors, one of which was the shared view between the classes of a 'neo-Bonapartist stress on the leading role of a dynamic state embodying the common interest' (Jefferys, 1996). This ideology was central to the post-war development of France which saw the setting up of a state welfare system, minimum wage, and included 15 significant nationalizations, involving coal, electricity, gas, the four main banks, Air France and Renault. These were followed by a further wave of nationalizations in 1981 and 1982, which affected banking, steel and strategic companies in electronics, information technology, aerospace and chemicals. This newly expanded public sector employed 25 per cent of all industrial workers, yielded 30 per cent of industrial turnover and expanded the number of firms dependent on both government favours and orders (Jefferys, 1996: 10). Accompanying this state involvement in the economy was a dirigiste ideology shared by the élite managers of both state and capital:

> Building on a traditional *Jacobinism* that stressed the transforming role of the group who controlled the state, [the] Liberation Gaullists were *dirigistes*, believing the state should intervene and plan to create a renewed, greater France, while leaving the market in place. (Jeffreys, 1996: 9, emphasis in original)

In the 1995 French election, the only candidate who called for rolling back the welfare state received just 5 per cent of the vote. Chirac, having learned his lesson from his defeat in 1988, when he had campaigned on a more explicitly liberal programme, emphasized his commitment to the welfare state. After his victory, in October 1995, Chirac abandoned his election promises to prioritize the fight against unemployment. The previous month Juppé had declared he would impose a public sector wage freeze in 1996. Growing pressure from the international exchange markets for the state to comply with the 3 per cent Maastricht budgetary deficit target prompted Juppé to propose, on 15 November, cuts to social security and reform of its management, along with increases in taxation.

In response to these proposals there were three waves of mobilization involving a wave of one-day public sector strikes and demonstrations against the proposed reforms, combined with indefinite or renewed strikes against the means of circulation (transport and communication sectors were those most affected). The strike wave did not reach into the private service or manufacturing sectors where trade unionism had effectively disappeared (Jefferys, 1996: 19) but was supported by 'extraordinarily high levels of participation in street demonstrations, especially in provincial cities' (1996: 16). On 12 December, the day of greatest mobilization, 270 cities and towns in France were hosts to demonstrations involving around 2.3 million people; Grenoble, a city with a population of 250,000, saw 70,000 people demonstrate. These demonstrations were led by striking workers, supported by striking students and those on one-day strikes, as well as by large numbers of non-strikers from the private sector, and sometimes by organizations of the unemployed and the homeless. The strikes soon took on the character of a popular uprising: 'from the issue of defending social security, the mobilization grew within a month into a movement of general opposition to commercial globalization and the neo-liberal offensive, and their effects' (Bensaïd, 1996). The outcome of these demonstrations was that the proposed pension changes involving the railways, the post office, city transport, France-Telecom and EDF-GDF (electricity and gas boards) were withdrawn and talks were promised on social security reform. After nearly a month of strikes, the government shelved elements of its proposal (for example, the extension of contribution periods for public service workers) but retained other elements relating to social protection (for example, the freeze in family allowances and increases in health insurance payments for the unemployed and elderly).

Events in France show how the impact of globalization at national level is crucially dependent on the national balance of power and institutional orientations, and that reports of the death of the labour movement are greatly exaggerated. Indeed, the 'problem' for reforming governments, even those which are not dependent on coalitions with other parties to pass legislation or embedded in corporatist political systems, is that they are mostly not able to fully realize their desired reforms due to adverse political costs and institutional impediments. In Britain, despite the Conservative party's strong electoral position and large majorities during the 1980s and early 1990s, the full extent of welfare reforms and expenditure cuts was curtailed by vigorous opposition from political parties, professional and other interest groups (Pierson, 1994). Indeed, Pierson argues that the prospects for radical change in the welfare state – due to globalization or any other pressure – are ultimately weakened by domestic factors because social programmes generate their own constituencies, advocacy and interest groups whose 'presence dramatically increases the cost of pursuing retrenchment initiatives' (1994: 165). Attempts to radically overhaul the welfare state may only solidify public support for it and increase the electoral costs to the party in power that tries to enact and implement such reforms.

The fate of social security pension reforms in Latin America, a region in which IFIs have been key actors in social policy reform, provides another useful reminder of the enduring importance of domestic political factors in determining policy outcomes. Here, IFI influence over government policy was greatest in countries where there was a severe economic crisis (high debt, rapid economic decline, high inflation) and where there was an urgent need for financial assistance, but this influence was also contingent on the institutional and political context which facilitated or impeded reforms (Huber and Stephens, 2000; Kay, 2000). In countries where parliamentary scrutiny of reform proposals was exercised, domestic political forces, such as interest groups with an immediate stake in reform and political institutions, were 'instrumental in determining the final policy outcomes', so that the process of reform not only took much longer but the reforms differed quite significantly from the proposals (Barrientos, 1998: 31; Kay, 2000: 195). The interest groups involved included businesses, pensioners and labour unions. In countries where the labour movement and civil society were stronger, groups were able to force concessions from governments. Indeed, many groups gained full or partial exemption from reforms: the military and police (throughout the region); professionals, bank employees, judicial employees and notaries (Uruguay); public employees (Brazil); oil workers (Mexico and Colombia), and chauffeurs and employees of the public fishing company (Peru) (Huber and Stephens, 2000; Kay, 2000).

In addition to the capacities of domestic actors, political institutions were also determinant:

> Where political institutions afforded interest groups greater opportunities to veto policy, reforms were limited, while political institutions which prevented interest groups from acting as veto players provided governments with greater oppotunities to implement fundamental reforms. (Kay, 2000: 196)

Relevant factors here include electoral laws, the referendum, interest group influence within the social security bureaucracy and the powers of the executive relative to the legislature (Kay, 2000). The concentration of political power in the hands of the executive was a factor in the pension reforms in Chile and Peru (Huber and Stephens, 2000). In Chile, the dictatorship was able to push through its reforms in a matter of months due to the absence of political opposition, although even here the military secured exemptions for itself from the reforms. In Mexico, where political power was also concentrated, the president's party had a majority in congress and party discipline was high, ensuring that proposals were pushed through largely unopposed (Huber and Stephens, 2000). In Argentina, where Menem's party controlled the senate but not the chamber of deputies, and where lack of party discipline allowed labour representatives to gain concessions, the presidential decree was liberally used to bypass the legislature and override these concessions (Huber and Stephens, 2000; Kay, 2000: 199).

Despite the supposed dominance of the Washington consensus in international and national policy circles in Latin America, only Chile's pension system comes closest to the World Bank paradigm. Bolivia, El Salvador and Mexico fit the World Bank paradigm partially, while other countries forged their own paths – Argentina and Uruguay have mixed systems, Colombia and Peru have parallel systems – and enacted reforms closer to the ILO than to the World Bank paradigm (Amparo Cruz-Saco Oyague, 1998; Barrientos, 1998). Costa Rica has been able to construct a relatively unified system with only civil servants having a separate system, and has resisted orthodox economic prescriptions due to a combination of its strategic location within the region (which encouraged US aid and thus a degree of protection from IFI pressures for radical reform), the president's social democratic commitments and his ties to organized labour, and popular protests against some of the government's proposed reforms. Overall, such is the diversity of reforms in the region that Kay has argued that 'while there is a trend towards privatization in the region, there is no uniform Latin American route to pension reform' (2000: 200). He suggests that the reforms in this region are particularly notable for the way in which 'privileged groups have managed to use their political influence to retain their benefits' (2000: 201).

The importance of national political factors in mediating the impact of globalization on welfare states is also visible in corporate taxation, an area where the (downward) converging effects of globalization are expected to be seen. The structural dependence of states on internationally mobile capital is expected by some to force governments into tax competition with each other and force tax rates downwards (Hallerberg and Basinger, 1998; Swank, 1998). On the surface, the evidence would appear convincing:

> Beginning with the Tax Reform Act of 1986 in the US, every OECD country except Switzerland and Turkey lowered its top marginal rate on personal income tax between 1986 and 1991. Many states reduced their corporate tax rates during this time as well, and they often accompanied these moves with efforts to expand their tax bases and to end many common tax loopholes. (Hallerberg and Basinger, 1998: 321–2)

Hallerberg and Basinger note that although these changes in tax policy are generally ascribed to globalization, closer inspection reveals the continuing importance of *national* factors in determining how sweeping reforms actually have been. Of the expected convergence, none was there to be found: while the spread of corporate income taxes narrowed, a wide gap remained between the highest marginal rate (50 per cent in Germany) and the lowest marginal rate (25 per cent in Canada). These authors draw attention to the omission of political explanations from the standard globalization explanation of these changes. Political factors include the partisan orientation of the government or the internal structure of the state, but particularly the institutional and political structure of a country:

> countries that had only one veto player, or only one institution or party whose approval was necessary for a bill to become law, enacted more sweeping reform than states that had more than one veto player. These results suggest that even when international or domestic economic factors might 'dictate' a change in policy, reform will not be as sweeping in countries in which agreement among several institutions and/or parties is necessary. (Hallerberg and Basinger, 1998: 324)

Thus globalization is tempered once again by national political factors. By way of further illustration of this, in an empirical study of statutory business income taxation (social security, payroll taxes and corporate tax) in 17 advanced democratic nations over the period of 1966 to 1993, Swank notes a change in tax policy orientation from market-regulating to market-conforming policy rules. However, this emphasis on 'the creation of a level playing field where the market will allocate investment appropriately' (1998: 679) – a shift which is often read as being in favour of business interests – did not lead to a reduction in the overall business tax burden. Indeed, business tax rates have proved resilient. In the early 1990s, corporate profits taxation, as a percentage of operating income, was on average only marginally higher than in the late 1970s, although social security and payroll taxes increased from 13 per cent in the mid-1960s to 34 per cent in the early 1990s. Swank offers two explanations for this. The first is that tax policy emphasized cuts in tax rates on corporate profits, but also insisted that overall changes should be revenue-neutral to the treasury; it also included the broadening of the tax base as well as the elimination of investment reliefs, allowances, credits and exemptions for businesses. The second reason for the increase in the average business tax burden, particularly the rise in social security and payroll taxes, is attributed to the following:

> Substantial economic and demographic pressure and popular opposition to cuts in social insurance schemes, as well as the desire to move toward fiscal balance generally and in social security schemes in particular (e.g. through reforms in the direction of full-funding of pensions) proved barriers to notable reductions in social security tax burdens. (Swank, 1998: 680)

Overall, the evidence points to the continuing importance of the domestic sphere in any explanation of the relationship between globalization and welfare state change. Analyses have become more sophisticated in their recognition of this complexity. Thus, Esping-Andersen (2000) states that 'all welfare states have responded to the new economic and social challenges mainly by muddling through, by building on traditional premises rather than radically redesigning their welfare architecture' (2000: 7), while Pierson forcefully argues that the 'focus on globalization is to mistake the essential nature of the problem' (1998: 540). Even Scharpf, who otherwise appears to accept many of the basic premises of 'strong' globalization, argues that although countries may face similar pressures to restructure their welfare states,

> these pressures are affecting countries that differ greatly with regard to levels and structures of employment, levels and structures of welfare state spending, and levels and strutures of public sector revenue. As a consequence, national welfare states differ greatly in their vulnerability to international economic pressures, and in the specific problems which they need most urgently to address – and they differ also in the policy options that they could reach under the path-dependent constraints of existing policy legacies, and under the institutional constraints of existing veto positions. (Scharpf, 2000: 224)

International institutions

'Globalization' is increasingly perceived by a range of groups to present an obstacle to their movement goals – be they the preservation of eco-systems, respect for human rights or demilitarization – and has 'taken hold as a common integrating force and foe for contemporary social movements' (Lynch, 1998: 155). Those IGOs which are perceived to be actively implicated in promoting globalization, particularly the growth of corporate power, have been targeted by protest movements and a number of 'global social dialogues' have been going on between social movements in the shadow congresses that now regularly accompany meetings of the G7 and G8. For example, the International Encounter against Neoliberalism brought together social and political activists from a wide variety of countries in response to calls from Zapatistas. These social dialogues also accompany the meetings of the OECD, IMF, World Bank and WTO, which have faced opposition by a coalition of various groups aiming to block meetings and suspend negotiations. These social dialogues have involved creative and flexible forms of global organization and political action – public campaigns, street demonstrations and protests – by citizen groups. The People's Global Action Against Free Trade was launched to coordinate resistance globally, making use of the internet in between major gatherings. More generally, Ritchie notes 'the organized and increasingly massive presence of NGOs throughout all phases of world conferences' (1996: 183). An international conference, for example, one organized by the UN, spawns months of intensive lobbying by thousands of groups mobilizing to influence national and international agendas. At the 1995 UN Summit on Social Development in Copenhagen, Owoh notes that nearly one thousand NGOs and people's movements organized around a broad range of issues, calling for fairer distribution of resources and restructuring of the world order so that the poor and disadvantaged might have stronger say in decisions that determine their well-being. (1996: 217)

These campaigns have also been organized against some of the most basic elements of the international economic order. One transnational campaign, Jubilee 2000, aimed at a major effect of globalization – developing countries' indebtedness – involved massive national and transnational organizing for the cancellation of the unpayable debts of the world's poorest countries. It united religious and development lobbies, trade unions, consumer and environmental activists and political and cultural celebrities. The campaign successfully placed the issue of this debt on the agenda of the 1999 Cologne G8 meeting, resulting in a further US$70 billion reduction in the debt. While realists pointed out that the full figure of Jubilee 2000's 52 countries' debts amounted to US$370 billion, and cynics pointed out that most of that debt was not being serviced anyway and so cancelling it cost nothing, the campaign did succeed in making a massive transnational issue of a basic issue in development economics which would not normally attract such interest.

One of the clearest expressions of the social movement against globalization has been the anti-MAI and anti-WTO campaigns. The anti-MAI campaigns, to begin with, set the stage for a battle that saw 'for the first time active public participation in the shaping of international relations' (Grimshaw, 1997: 38), a battle which continues to be fought at the doors of most of the IGOs. Conceived in 1995 and negotiated by the OECD, the MAI was designed to provide a single, comprehensive, multilateral framework for the regulation of international investments. Described as 'the constitution of a single global economy' by the OECD and 'a legally enshrined and enforceable bill of rights for transnationals' by Grimshaw (1997: 38), the MAI covered all areas and sectors of the economy, including investment incentives, such as public grants and subsidies, with the exception of national security and defence and monetary and exchange rate policies.

The extension of the 'free trade' and non-discrimination principles to larger areas of investment than already covered by the WTO Uruguay Round would mean that, all investors – be they small companies or TNCs – would henceforth have to be treated equally. In an area of concern to social policy, foreign-based health or social services providers operating in one of the signatory countries would be entitled to receive public grants and subsidies on the same terms as a national-based provider (Sanger, 1998: 5). As UNRISD recognized (from a position of opposition), the MAI

would have allowed foreign private providers to challenge national government prerogatives to provide free services or to subsidize national non-profit providers. The scheme would have embraced the full range of health and social services, including childcare centres, hospitals and community clinics, as well as private labs and independent physicians. (2000: 15)

The MAI would have outlawed performance requirements which entail the attachment of conditions to the receipt of public money. This would mean that governments would no longer be able to: prescribe levels of exports of goods; set levels of domestic content in production; require that foreign businesses must be joint ventures with local partners, or stipulate that a given level of R&D be achieved. All of these conditions are necessary to ensure that the local economy benefits from inter-national trade. Governments would also be prohibited from restricting investors' access to national markets on the basis of their unethical operations elsewhere in the world. The MAI would have replaced all existing agreements between signatory states and overruled all laws that came into conflict with it, such as social and environmental laws. It would have permitted potential investors the right to directly challenge domestic laws and national or local governments if they judged these to breach MAI provisions or (likely to) cause them loss or damage. Thus, governments deemed to have interfered 'unreasonably' with the use of private property of an individual or business would be required to pay compensation. Such cases could arise if, for example, commercial pro-viders of health or social services claim that their business is, or is likely to be, adversely affected by government plans to expand state services (Appleton in Sanger, 1998: 8). The MAI did not include reciprocal procedures that would have permitted legal action to be taken by governments against transnationals, although TNCs would still be subject to national laws which did not conflict with the MAI.

Not surprisingly, given the far-reaching implications of the MAI, negotiations were not concluded by the original deadline of May 1997, and the French government withdrew from negotiations in October 1998. This failure to reach an agreement was largely due to opposition to the MAI on social and environmental grounds by NGOs and an 'upsurge of activities from a broad coalition of consumer, farmer, labour, church, women's, environmental, development and other citizen groups in Europe, the United States, Canada and Australia' (Khor, 1998: 25). Khor also notes the spread of opposition against the MAI within the advanced industrialized countries – at first critics of the MAI came principally from NGOs and governments in developing countries. This worldwide coalition of NGOs and citizen groups was joined by 'out-raged parliamentarians' and some provincial governments and city authorities who declared their territories 'MAI-free' and refused to recognize the MAI if signed by their government. In addition, govern-ments themselves were reluctant to concede control over key areas of their economies – as judged by over one thousand pages of country-specific objections which were lodged. Subsequent concessions made in a revised MAI negotiating text, notably the inclusion of non-binding provisions such as an acknowledgement of the principle of core labour standards and of the role of the ILO in regulating these and a provision entitled 'Not Lowering Standards', were intended to allay criticisms of the MAI but were not enough to put the negotiations back on track (Wilkinson and Hughes, 2000).

Alongside governments' cautious responses and the organized public protests which had successfully disrupted the schedule of MAI negotiations, there was growing preference for the negotiations on the deregulation of investment to take place within the WTO on the grounds that it is a global institution (the OECD only has 29 members), that it has expertise in negotiating trade and investment agreements, and that it already engages with civic groups (Grimshaw, 1997; Khor, 1998; Wilkinson and Hughes, 2000). The global citizens' campaign that had disrupted the MAI undertook a massive mobilization against the WTO's Millennium Round of trade negotiations, on whose agenda agriculture and trade in services, including health and social services and education services, were placed. The 5,000 delegates to the WTO from 150 countries were met by a programme of seminars, rallies, walkouts and civil disobedience simultaneously in Seattle (US) and in other countries. The transnational nature of mobilization against the Millennium Round can be seen in the list of locations of action reported on the London N30 website: Brisbane, Australia; Manila, Philippines; Delhi, Bangalore and the Narmada Valley, India; Bangor and Cardiff, Wales; Limerick, Ireland; Dijon, France; Amsterdam; Milan; Berlin; Rome; Prague; Iceland; Israel; Halifax, Leeds, London, Manchester and Totnes, England; and Baltimore, Boston, Los Angeles, Nashville, Washington – not forgetting Seattle – in the US. The 'N30' events, the biggest protest against globalization yet, succeeded in disrupting the talks, and by the end of the week governments left without an agreement.

The variety of causes of the failure of the Seattle talks needs to be stressed, as must their political nature. The most obvious cause was the failure of the national delegations to agree on the need for a new Round, while the arrival of delegates in Seattle without an agreed agenda was an early indication of the likelihood of failure. To this can be added the continuing articulation of concern over TRIPs and TRIMs by many national social movements since the Uruguay Round, and disquiet over the 'cultural imperialism' and disguised protectionism some claimed to see in the demand for labour and environmental clauses (Shiva, 1997), as well as NGOs' disgust at being excluded from some of the closed-room negotiating sessions.

National governments were also relevant here. Attending peripheral nations were dissatisfied with the meagre benefits they had gained from previous trade rounds, as well as with 'the high-handed way some negotiations seemed to ignore their voice', in the case of ACP states, which were still smarting from 'the condition of good governance imposed on them by the EU in recent preferential tariff reduction talks' (Deacon, 2000a: 25). On the US side, the forthcoming US elections, along with a resurgent labour movement which Gore/Clinton needed to keep on side, determined the strong American line on labour clauses which alienated the peripheral nations even further. The regional fractions within global capitalism were also apparent, with the French Education Minister accusing the US of using the trade negotiations to brainwash the world by trying to open US universities around the globe, while the EU delegation was split over the proposed liberalization of agriculture – the UK favoured dropping all agricultural tariffs, and not just some as proposed by the EU, disadvantaging the poorest countries (Deacon, 2000a). Meanwhile, other national delegations were under strong pressure from their own social movements, trade unions, environmental groups and development lobbies (Bayne, 2000). These causes of failure, combined with the well-organized blocking of the opening day and the demonstration of mass opposition (involving an estimated 30,000 people), showed that the push to open markets is not inevitably successful. Political, not economic reasons stopped progress.

That said, the round has only been delayed. Prior to the Seattle meeting in November 1999, Mike Moore firmly rejected attempts to allow NGOs a greater say in this process: 'Non-governmental organizations have a valid role to play . . . but this is an organization of sovereign governments, run by nations' (*The Guardian*, 3/9/99: 22). Following Seattle, the free-traders have concluded that ignoring civil society was perhaps not the most sensible move on their part and there is likely to be a strong attempt made to co-opt these opposition groups and their issues in a WTO civil society forum. Co-option is unlikely to succeed given the basic nature of some of the issues involved. While some opposition groups believe the possibility of a dialogue exists, others believe it would be a dialogue of the deaf, given the free traders' position that what is needed is to use the power of argument to convince civil society of the benefits of free trade – in the words of Tony Blair, 'We cannot afford another Seattle but nor can we afford to postpone the massive gains that a successful new trade round would deliver' (*The Guardian* 29/1/00:30). This position can be expected to result in an intense propaganda and PR campaign for free trade, rather than an actual dialogue where positions might be shifted.

The establishment of institutionalized social (policy) dialogues between IGOs and the more reformist-inclined NGOs has been one of the key responses to the more populist dialogues engendered by opposition movements. From the perspective of international institutions, contestations and criticisms of the social and economic effects of globalization by trade unions, NGOs and economic nationalists provide a context in which a potential backlash against globalization and further deregulation can occur. Thus, one of the problems of a globalized, structurally interdependent economy is that local crises will impact globally, so the social and economic costs, for example, of the latest financial crisis – in Asia in 1997–1998 – were experienced both 'locally' (within the region) and 'globally' (in the West). Consequently, there is a need to manage the economic and social issues placed on the international agenda by its critics as well as the worst social excesses of globalization. IGOs fully recognize the importance of underwriting the social costs of economic restructuring to secure the necessary level of local political and popular support for their reforms. This can clearly be seen in relation to the reforms planned by the OECD and EU for Central and Eastern Europe. The OECD Centre for Cooperation with the Economies in Transition stated that 'in the absence of a quick and effective policy response to the emergence of major social and labour market problems at the beginning of the transition, there is a risk that the ongoing reform process may be impeded, delayed or some steps even reversed' (cited in Deacon et al., 1997: 93), while the EU stated that

> co-operation between the Union and the CEE countries on the social dimension of transition is essential to reduce the risk of the population rejecting democracy and the market economy because the social and human costs are too high. (1997: 93)

For citizens' groups, participating in the policy process at the international level can be a means of exerting political influence over decisions taken at this level. NGOs use international organizations to place pressure on their own or other governments to set – and adhere to – standards on humanitarian and social issues in the international arena, make up for deficiencies in national policies, as well as persuade international agencies to take more account of human rights or environmental issues in international trade. These attempts at persuasion 'often involve not just reasoning with opponents, but also bringing pressure, arm-twisting, encouraging sanctions, and shaming' (Keck and Sikkink, 1998: 16).

NGOs have been encouraged to direct their political action to the global inter-governmental realm. The EU and UN in particular invite these communities of interest to consider themselves as part of an international community of transnational politics and networks. EU funding for social development projects builds in cross-national exchanges and the transfer of good practice and so facilitates linkage between grassroots projects and movements in different countries. Both the EU and UN fund transnational networks and provide an international forum through which the profile of particular issues can be raised. The UN, for example, has sponsored international congresses on human rights (Vienna, 1993), population (Cairo, 1994), gender equality (Beijing, 1995), NGOs (Vienna, 1995), the environment (Rio de Janeiro, 1996) and poverty and social development (Copenhagen, 1995 and Geneva, 2000). These fora have drawn NGOs into the technocratic process of participating in IGOs' search for solutions to the problems caused by globalization. Although the extent of NGO participation and the nature of their relations with IGOs vary by policy area or issue, they are central to the international policy process, being involved in global agenda- and norm-setting, policy-making as well as policy implementation or execution.

Regarding policy formation, some NGOs enjoy official consultative status with international agencies which may be sympathetic to their aims, working through the UN NGO Committee and the Commissions on Human Rights and the Status of Women (Gordenker and Weiss, 1996b: 220; Willetts, 1996). One of the earliest NGOs, Save the Children Fund, was responsible for drafting the 'Declaration of Geneva' on the rights of children which was adopted by the League of Nations in 1924 and subsequently incorporated into the UN Charter (Longford, 1996). NGO influence has also been 'remarkably strong' in the drafting of Environmental Conventions (Convention on International Trade in Endangered Species; the Conventions on Desertification and on Biological Diversity) (Ritchie, 1996: 185). Gaer argues that human rights NGOs are 'the engine for virtually every advance made by the United Nations in the field of human rights since its founding' (1996: 51). Thus, it was NGOs which pushed for the initial insertion of human rights into the Charter of the UN in 1945 and subsequently for the Universal Declaration of Human Rights in 1948. The 1948 Declaration was, and arguably still remains, the most important global affirmation of civil, political, social and economic freedoms and rights, such as freedom of speech and belief, of association and religion, the right to an adequate standard of living, to education, work, social security and equal pay, which it states shall apply to all irrespective of 'race, colour, sex, language, religion, political or other opinion, national or social origin, property, birth or other status' (Article 2). NGOs have also been instrumental in the subsequent expansion of the human rights agenda to push for the Convention against Torture and other Cruel, Inhuman and Degrading Treatment and the Convention on the Rights of the Child (Ritchie, 1996). In the area of women's rights, 'the human rights agenda has expanded to include areas such as violence against women, both in the public and private sphere, and other gender-specific abuses' (Connors, 1996: 147).

NGOs have also been instrumental in pushing for the establishment of inter-governmental machinery to combat human rights abuses, and have contributed, often decisively, to the work of human rights committees. Ritchie notes that NGOs 'elicit, foster and provide substantial and substantive input at many levels of the UNESCO secretariat' (1996: 180). Furthermore, while the mandate of the Commission on Human Rights authorizes it 'to seek and receive credible and reliable information from governments, the specialized agencies, and intergovernmental and non-governmental organizations', in practice 'the mechanisms rely almost exclusively upon NGO information' (Gaer, 1996: 55). Gaer also argues that 'the impact of nongovernmental organizations is now greatest as a source of independent information that triggers special mechanisms and engenders action by UN special rapporteurs' (1996: 64).

This IGO dependency on NGOs may also be seen in humanitarian aid and relief. As Smillie points out, around the world

> Governments have . . . become increasingly dependent upon NGOs for much of their poverty programming, and in many countries for more than half of their support to refugees, food aid and emergency planning. (1993: 29)

NGOs' local presence renders them a crucial link, or channel of communication, between locally expressed populist 'social dialogues' and international institutions. International organizations 'collaborate with and often rely on NGOs to deliver services, test new ideas, and foster popular participation' (Ritchie, 1996: 181). They are useful to IGOs in the implementation stage because these institutions do not have a local presence, while NGOs do. Consequently, NGOs may be drawn with varying degrees of scepticism towards collaboration with state institutions, rather than, or as well as, in opposition to them.

These national or local groups have in a number of cases proved instrumental in persuading international institutions to reform their policies and emphasize a more socially oriented model of development. As regards the World Bank, for example, its acknowledgement of the destabilizing effects of its policies and its greater emphasis on poverty resulted from criticisms by international and national NGOs and, notably, from local food riots and the threat of social unrest and disruption. The Bank's strategic response was to engage civil society in 'dialogue' and 'partnership'. The Bank 'funded a vast organizing process of bringing hundreds of large and small NGOs together to meet and develop a critique of the WB and an alternative development plan' (Midnight Notes, 1999: 11) and it established an NGO-Bank Committee consisting of selected NGOs (Ritchie, 1996). It has strategically promoted the work of national and local NGOs and their participation in a globally sponsored social development strategy. Since 1997, 38 per cent of World Bank projects had provision for NGO collaboration, compared with 6 per cent over the period of 1973–1988, while the Bank pledged to appoint more 'NGO liaison officers' to ensure that NGO concerns are adequately reflected in Bank policy (Wilkinson and Hughes, 2000). Consultation with these organizations serves the useful purpose of testing the local social and political foundations before SAPs are implemented, while social dialogue with IGOs channels political (class) struggle into productive activity and engages NGOs directly in the capitalist development process, albeit 'with a human face' (Midnight Notes, 1999).

This growing participation of NGOs in international policy formation and implementation is often heralded as a measure of the democratization and socialization of global politics and evidence of an emergent global civil society. Liberal political theory posits civil society as providing an important counterbalance both to state and economic interests and as a key democratizing force which actively forges new relationships between states and citizens (Riker, 1995). European governments in particular view civil society as a 'counterweight to state power by opening up channels of communication and participation, providing training grounds for activists promoting pluralism' (Hulme and Edwards, 1997: 6). The emergence of a wider and more pluralistic range of institutions and structures, of which NGOs are a part, is said to facilitate trends towards liberal democracy, nationally and internationally. In East Asia and Latin America, for example, NGOs have been essential to a thriving civil society and a conduit for democratization; in the EU, NGO participation in policy formation has been a key tenet of the EU's strategy to address the 'democratic deficit'.

The emergence of NGOs as key actors in social development, particularly at the service delivery end of the policy spectrum, has also been integral to neo-liberal economic projects. Citing Keane, Api Richards argues that part of the neo-liberal attack on the state 'includes an advocacy of the democratic potential of civil society attributed with such values as self-interest, hard work, flexibility, freedom of choice, private property and distrust of state bureaucracy' (1999: 148). Thus, funding NGOs plays a crucial role in creating a civic culture of freedom of choice and association, to restrain the reach of state politics and provision, counterbalancing the power of authoritarian states and contributing to political stability (1999: 149). Indeed, international development aid from IGOs and other donor agencies is increasingly channelled through the NGO sector. This is partly a response to the poor performance of government development plans but is also a result of a belief in the democratizing forces of civil society, the potential of NGOs to forge pro-poor political coalitions and provide internal support for SAPs, and their greater efficiency and effectiveness more generally in delivering welfare services.

Owoh regards the proliferation of non-profit NGOs as being 'spawned from neoliberalism's global agenda' and as 'the handmaidens of market-driven private welfare' (1996: 217). Most social development NGOs are oriented towards local poverty relief work rather than policy advocacy work at national and transnational levels. They have been encouraged 'to fill the gaps, providing services for the poor and rural communities where the market is too risky to attract for-profit providers' (Owoh, 1996: 216), while the involvement of the NGO sector as a whole may be used to give new strength to residualist social welfare strategy dressed up in the language of social development, participation, empowerment and civil society (Deacon et al., 1997; Deacon, 2000a; Vivian, 1995). Funding NGOs to deliver social development programmes makes use of their grassroots links with 'hard to reach' populations (the poorest) and with other local movements. It also gives the NGO sector a role in social policy and delivery issues as well as an interest in limiting comprehensive state provision which could displace NGOs' 'market share' (Deacon et al., 1997). Thus, NGOs may support government policies targeted at the poor, leaving a substantial role for private health and welfare provision for the remaining population. Indeed, Deacon argues the World Bank believed that:

> an alliance could be struck between itself, the excluded poor and the International NGOs and development lobby to bypass and let wither these incipient welfare states in favour of a targeted and residualized safety net approach to social policy. (1999b: 18)

Thus, NGOs have been encouraged to challenge state-dominated development policy (Riker, 1995), voice criticisms of existing welfare arrangements and generate demands for policy and institutional reform, often in opposition to corporate, trade union and producer interests nationally. An added twist to this is that 'many northern-based NGOs support their southern "partner" NGOs on funds provided by northern governments – the very governments that endorse the [World] Bank's policies' (Owoh, 1996: 217).

A final problem with the uncritical equation of NGOs with democratization and empowerment, is that the NGO universe comprises a wide range of interests, activities and perspectives on trade and development issues. For example, the aims and interests of the International Association of Pharmaceutical Manufacturers and those of Consumers International, two NGOs working in the health field, are quite different (Koivusalo and Ollila, 1997). It is also unclear whether NGO participation in policy formation has strengthened the role of citizens to influence the actions of state and international actors (Api Richards, 1999: 161), although it is clear that the collaborative process benefits an increasingly global middle class of aid professionals as much as it does refugees, displaced persons and those living in poverty. As Stubbs argues,

> The idea that the development of an NGO sector as a major employer is, actually, a major inhibitor of civil initiatives, and, even of civil society, rather than the fulfilment of it, is an uncomfortable one. (1998: 80)

Struggles against globalization and *for* global reform

As we have seen, social and political movements have taken advantage of the political 'disjunctures' that have emerged from undemocratic forms of public power, and, in addition to contesting de-democratizing tendencies, they are formulating democratic alternatives to globalization which maximize human health and welfare globally (Goodman, 1998). Global social reformism embraces a variety of ideological and political positions, but the two positions dominating global political and intellectual agendas are guided by social liberalism ('thin' reformism) which seeks to stabilize the global economy by ameliorating the worst effects of major social harms caused by globalization, and social democracy ('thick' reformism) seeking to harness globalization to realize a progressive redistribution of global resources (Scholte, 2000). The discussion below focuses on social democratic-inspired positions and agendas since global social liberalism has already been covered earlier in this chapter as well as in Chapter 4. These social democratic positions are contrasted with the global social reform agendas of what are often considered to be 'anti-globalist' nationalist and localization movements.

The strand of global social reformism which is currently enjoying prominence within global socio-political discourse is perhaps best exemplified by the work of Deacon and his colleagues carried out under the auspices of the Globalism and Social Policy Programme (GASPP). Deacon (2000a: 30) identifies four tendencies within the global political paradigm that indicate a pressure for welfare residualism: the belief of the World Bank that governments should only provide minimal levels of social protection; the view of the OECD's Development Assistance Committee that funding should be targeted on basic education and healthcare; the self-interest of NGOs in substituting for state services; and the moves within the WTO to forge a global market in private healthcare, education and social insurance. It is worth quoting him at length on the consequences of failing to overhaul this paradigm:

> In the context of withering state provision, the middle classes of developing and transition economies will be enticed into the purchase of private social security schemes, into the purchase for their children of private secondary and tertiary education, and into the purchase even at the expense of subsequent personal impoverishment of private hospital medical care. The providers of such private services will be North American or Western European. The potential to build on cross-class social contracts from the colonial era, or to fashion new ones in countries in transition, in order to build new welfare states will be undermined by the existence of a global market in private social provision . . . The result is predictable. We know that services for the poor are poor services. We know that those developed countries without universal provision of public healthcare and education are not only more unequal but also more unsafe and crime-ridden. (Deacon, 2000a: 30)

For Deacon a central challenge in global politics is to recreate at the supra-national level the social bond between classes that 'ensured social justice within [advanced industrialized] countries during the twentieth century' (2000a: 30). A socially progressive politics of globalization from a social democratic perspective would make poverty eradication and global redistribution of resources a main priority. This necessitates reform of the major institutions of global governance to strengthen global social regulation, redistribution and empowerment. It includes a shift in development and social policy analysis from the condition of the poor to the interests and privileges of the rich. It requires major institutional reform, with the UN and its agencies to be funded out of global taxes and powered to work with the new Group of ten countries, the IMF, World Bank, WTO and regional groupings 'to *plan* in an accountable way for equitable global development' (Deacon, 2000a: 31 emphasis in original). This brand of global social reformism encompasses stronger regionalist strategies as it would necessitate 'major intra-regional and inter-regional, public and private resource transfers to finance this type of public provision at all levels', in addition to internationalist strategies aiming to strengthen global social regulation and 'ensure standards of service and accessibility to all (through government subsidy) of private health, education and social services, where they exist in lieu of public provision' (2000a: 30).

Although this more ambitious reformism has infiltrated enough governance agencies to render it 'almost mainstream' (Scholte, 2000: 290), many social movements from both developed and developing countries criticize it as being predicated on the (false) assumptions that global markets and the global economy are irreversible and that public institutions at national and international levels can be harnessed to better reconcile globalization with human welfare and security. They claim that this reform agenda, ambitious though it is, is at best misguided and at worst ill-fated, and that the cause of global social reform is not met through an accommodation with the institutions that govern economic globalization, but through resistance and opposition to them, including any expansion or strengthening of their powers, even in the sphere of social policy. Thus, while these movements call for globalization from the bottom up – notably from civil society – to push for the reconstruction of economic structures and social relations globally, their task is conceived primarily in terms of transforming globalization by opposing these institutions, rather than readjusting or expanding the powers of global institutions to better regulate globalization. This transformation may entail 'dialogue' with global institutions, but it tends to be more of the oppositional kind than the negotiation-and-persuasion kind favoured by the institutionalized reformists, while their vision of a transformed globalization differs quite markedly from that of social democrats. In the discussion below nationalism and localization movements are focused on as examples of this position.

Nationalism is one response to globalization as judged by its resurgence globally. It is important to recognize that although not all nationalisms are engendered by globalization as some are reactions against regional political dominance, such as the countries of the former USSR, or against incorporation into a national formation, such as Wales,

Scotland and Northern Ireland into the 'United Kingdom', some nationalisms most certainly are. As Holton argues, 'the nationalism of former colonial countries of Africa and Asia . . . may be read as resistance to aspects of capitalist or Western globalization' (1998: 158), as can Islamic fundamentalism, a form of religious nationalism (Moghissi, 1999). Far from national or ethnic identity and culture being flattened as 'strong' globalization theory predicts, they have flourished in reaction to the pace and nature of economic and social change. Thus, in reaction to the growth of widespread economic insecurity and poverty entailed by Central and Eastern Europe's transition to a 'post-communist' or market economy 'most countries in the region had re-elected ex-communist parties' by 1995 (Deacon et al., 1997: 92). Economic nationalism also tends to be disparaged as a reactionary position supported by domestic sectional interests fearful of international competition, but it can also be regarded as a legitimate and understandable response to chronic unemployment and under-employment, job insecurity and the effects of structural change on small-scale, domestic production, income distribution and welfare services, all of which are commonly attributed to globalization (Dunkley, 2000). Economic nationalism forms part of an established body of thought and practice that advocates localization and self-sufficiency as an alternative model of social and economic development to the prevailing globalist one. Localization focuses on 'the viability of smaller-scale, localized and diversified economies, which may be hooked into, but not dominated by outside forces' (Mander, 1996: 18), and includes New Protectionism, Self-Reliant Trade, local economic cooperation and subsistence approaches.

New Protectionism entails 'a return to the security provided by a local self-sufficiency that emphasizes local economic control and local production for local consumption' (Hines and Lang, 1996: 486). Self-Reliant Trade aims to 'put governments at local, regional, and national levels back in control of their economies and to relocalize and rediversify these economies' (Dunkley, 2000: 490). Both propose the (re)introduction of controls on capital, trade and competition. Neither of these are anti-trade but are based on the partial negation of certain forms of trade. Specifically, both reject heavy dependence on long-distance international trade for key capital, consumer, food, energy, cultural or social requirements on the grounds of security and autonomy. Since most of this trade is in luxuries, consumer and capital goods, restrictions on it would stem over-consumption in the North and encourage local production for local markets in the South. Krugman calculates that the reduction of world trade by 50 per cent would reduce world income by just 2.5 per cent since national living standards derive primarily from domestic productivity and not from trade per se (Krugman in Dunkley, 2000: 256). Since developing countries rely most on transnational trade, they would be most affected but they are also most able to withstand the impact. In time, self-reliance would reduce transport requirements and their environmental costs, lessen dependence on TNCs and lessen pressure to appease countries with poor human rights records (Dunkley, 2000).

Advocates of this position are not short of suggestions for domestic measures to localize the economy: the introduction of import and export controls at national and regional bloc level to ensure that localities and countries produce as much of their own food, goods and services as they can; the encouragement of local savings and banking systems, and local control of capital (banks, pensions, insurance and investment funds) to ensure that the majority of funds are invested within the locality where they are generated and/or needed; controls on TNCs' activities to prioritize local needs; a competition policy which ends domination by big companies and guarantees local competition; the transformation of GATT into a General Agreement for Sustainable Trade to reorient trade, aid and technological transfer towards the cultivation of sustainable local economies and maximum employment; and the introduction of resource taxes to fund economic transition (Hines and Lang, 1996: 490–1). A Citizen's Income, or Basic Income, also forms a key part of these measures (Hines, 2000). Although Basic Income has been advanced in a variety of contexts as a means principally of decoupling the relationship embodied in most social protection systems between the satisfaction of social needs and participation in production, in the context of localization it surfaces as a means of facilitating voluntary exchanges and fostering autonomous economic cooperation whilst guaranteeing economic security. A variety of schemes have been advanced, but one variant is a universal (global) basic income (Jordan, 1996). The material expression of a global charter of human rights, and a major redistributive measure, it would be funded internationally, and would correspond with the resources necessary for survival in the world's poorest country; on top of this minimum, each nation or region would have its own system of redistribution that guaranteed individuals' welfare within that particular economic system (1996: 248).

All of these alternatives aim for systems which preserve local economies, communities and livelihoods and guarantee a minimum standard of living, but some also specify changes to social relations. Bennholdt-Thomsen and Mies (1999), for example, argue that a more efficiently managed, democratic globalization is a myth and that 'to preserve the foundations of life on earth, equality, justice and solidarity, new models of society and economy are needed that can lead towards true sustainability' (1999: 62). They advocate a subsistence perspective the starting point for which is 'the view from below of the globalized, expanding, patriarchal-capitalist economy' (1999: 5). The subsistence perspective, like other localization perspectives, also aims to construct an alternative model of development which permits local control over production, but it differs from them in a number of respects. First, although localization approaches contain a subsistence orientation, they take their starting point from an urban milieu of (male) wage labour, whereas the subsistence perspective takes its starting point from land, agriculture and the centrality of female labour (re)production (Bennholdt-Thomsen and Mies: 1999: 80). Second, the guiding principles of social organization from a subsistence perspective are cooperation, not competition, and an equal respect for all creatures on earth (1999: 5). Third, the subsistence perspective requires an alternative set of social relations between: women and men; generations; urban and rural classes; social classes; different peoples, and humans and nature. Indeed, Bennholdt-Thomsen and Mies argue that 'nothing can remain as it is now' if the central concern of economic and social activity changes from 'the accumulation of dead money' to 'the creation and maintenance of life on this planet' (1999: 7).

Here again, we find that action at the local, national and international levels is inextricably linked in these reform agendas. Action at international level is deemed a necessary component of localization, entailing the reorientation of global institutions to ensure that local, state and regional governments control access to markets (Hines, 2000). Thus, for Norberg-Hodge, international institutions are key to the success of diverse, local initiatives 'that will *promote small scale on a large scale*' (1996: 394; emphasis in original). Financial incentives that currently subsidize globalization can be reoriented away from large-scale production towards localized production, from: long-distance road travel to public transport, bike and foot paths; large-scale energy installations to locally available renewable energy sources; large-scale industrial agribusinesses to small-scale diversified agriculture; corporate superstores to public markets; mass telecommunications businesses to facilities for local entertainment; investment in centralized remedial health care systems and businesses to frontline, smaller clinics and prevention. Regulation at national and international levels would be needed to eliminate discrimination against small businesses and primary producers in existing 'free' trade policies, tax regulations, lending policies of banks, land-use regulations and zoning regulations, and to encourage localization and decentralization, as well as to protect the interests of citizens.

At the local level, self-help groups, community groups and cooperative movements have mobilized to fill in the gaps left by the failure of capitalism to provide sufficient quality and quantity of employment. In developed and developing countries alike new forms of local economic organization and cooperation have emerged among the poor (Bennholdt-Thomsen and Mies, 1999; Norberg-Hodge, 1996; Rowbotham and Mitter, 1994). Norberg-Hodge (1996) cites a range of initiatives striving to organize production around local needs: community banks and funds to increase capital available to local residents; 'buy local' campaigns; self-support cooperatives; local currency schemes; local exchange trading systems (LETS); tool lending libraries; producer–consumer associations; ecovillages and training in locally adapted agriculture, architecture and artisan production. LETS and local currency schemes aim to relocalize the economy and enable people to acquire the goods, services and care they need. In Britain in 1995, some 400 LETS schemes were in operation across 200 cities and towns involving some 20,000 members engaged in exchange of services (Bennholdt-Thomsen and Mies, 1999). Although they are relatively small in coverage, LETS can be regarded as a symbolic and practical 'response to the local social and economic consequences of globalization', namely, 'the economic and political marginalization of people and places marginal or unnecessary to the capitalist development process' (Meeker-Lowry, 1996; Paccione, 1997: 1179–80).

Conclusions

'Local' forces, notably NGOs and popular social movements, are central to any account of the political economy of globalization, constituting as they do an important factor in the political process which 'marshalls social responses to global issues' (Choucri, 1993: 103). Since globalization is a strategy both of ideological and economic integration, it is premised on the political 'defeat' of those who oppose this integration. However, globalization has engendered a surge of protest and oppositional movements, only some of whose demands can be accommodated within existing or reformed institutions. NGOs' links with a wide range of constituencies, such as farmers, tribal groups, women's groups, academics, professionals, labour unions, environmentalists and human rights groups have disrupted the globalizing strategies of capital, international institutions and states through a sustained critique of these strategies and more direct forms of opposition. Political mobilization, resistance and struggle can, like actions directed against local branches of TNCs, be considered global politics or 'global social dialogue'. Attention only to the 'high politics' of the global institutional arena belies the true scale of opposition against globalization taking place at local level and over what ostensibly appear to be 'local' issues. Where parliamentary politics has been perceived as having failed to make a difference, popular and professional groups and organizations are turning to extra-parliamentary forms of social dialogue through resistance and protest and various methods of direct action, demonstrations, strikes and riots to raise the political and economic costs of restructuring borne by local élites who attempt to speed through reforms (Mohan, 1996; Walton, 1987).

The power of these social movements must be put in perspective. For some, these protest movements amount to no more than 'a rearguard action which could halt the agenda of retrenchment only temporarily' (Mishra, 1999: 71). Similarly, Markoff (1998) argues that social movements, even transnational advocacy networks, still primarily work in their own national areas targeting national governments, and while this does not mean that they are ineffective,

> what it does mean is that social movements are not acting directly on the new centres of power and there does not seem to be much in the way of signs of movement in that direction. When we consider the webs of transnational finance, the element of democratic accountability not only vanishes completely, but the points of possible leverage for democratization are far from obvious. (Markoff, 1998: 25)

Speaking in August 1998, Markoff cannot be blamed for failing to predict the N30 and subsequent actions, although his question as to whether social movements have the capacity to successfully democratize the emerging global order and constitute a powerful transnational counter-hegemonic network or coalition is an important one. While the resolution of this question awaits the judgement of history, and accepting that the opposition forces described above may not be capable of defeating globalization, they do indicate that the path forward for globalization is not as smooth, untroubled and inevitable as many of its theorists assume. 'Local' forces – the nature and strength of ideologies, social movements and traditions within countries – play a key role in determining the extent to which capital investment is welcomed or resisted, the extent to which pro-globalization policies are implemented, and in curtailing the state's 'room for manoeuvre' more generally. While the significance of social movements' actions and strategies is usually judged in relation to how far they directly effect change in government policy, this is to underestimate the political power that opposition groups are still able to wield in the market and institutional spheres in shaping the perception of problems and global and national political responses to them. 'Local' social conflict and political struggle on the part of strong civic groups in the analysis presented in this chapter constitute an important countervailing power system which places significant and very real limitations on the powers of the state, international bureaucracies and capital, all of which have been forced to negotiate with these groups and make concessions to them.

Conclusions

For the purposes of this concluding chapter, I shall not attempt to summarize the substantial evidential material that informed the discussion but shall recap on the aims of the book, the main elements of the analysis, the principal concerns and the arguments presented. The principal aim of this book, then, was to bridge the gap between globalization studies and social policy analysis: to bring globalization into the study of social policy and social policy into the study of globalization. In so doing, my approach emphasized the continued importance of political agency, social conflict and struggle in determining the pace, course, timing and impact of globalization. This approach led me to analyse the relationship between globalization and social policy in the following ways. First, the discussion explored the impact of social politics and policy on globalization in order to supplement existing accounts which mostly emphasize the impact of globalization on social policy and politics. Second, my emphasis on globalization 'from below' and on the non-institutional sphere supplemented existing accounts which mostly attend to globalization 'from above' and to the institutional realm, while it also drew attention to their interconnections. My principal concerns lay with the contemporary structures and processes of global social governance, and the discussion accordingly highlighted the various 'actors' involved, both institutional and non-institutional (state, capital, labour, international bureaucracies, NGOs, households, consumers); the interests they represent; the levels at which they are involved (sub-national, national, regional, international, transnational); the spheres in which they operate (institutional, market) and the political strategies they adopt to determine the course of globalization.

The discussion was organized around a critique of the 'strong' globalization thesis. My examination of the evidence behind this thesis cast doubt on its sweeping assertions and on the politics of defeatism which it embodies. 'Strong' globalization was criticized as being wildly overstated: it significantly overestimates the power and unity of capital, underestimates the continued strength of the national state and other oppositional forces, and overgeneralizes from short-term or local changes involved. In relation to economic activity trumpeted as proof of globalization, much of the activity asserted to be new appears, on closer examination, not to be so; the evidence points to regionalization and localization of economic activity, while large areas of the globe are untouched by global capital. Like any model, what is excluded is as interesting as what is included. In this case, geographically what is excluded from globalization is Africa and other 'non-performing' regions such as the Middle East and Central and Eastern Europe where TNCs do not generally invest. Globalization is highly selective and only incorporates capital's 'most favoured nations'; many are called but few are chosen. Mittelman's conclusion on the new international division of labour seems generalizable to most current economic activity:

> There is no single wave of globalization washing over or flattening diverse divisions of labour both in regions and industry branches. Varied regional divisions of labour are emerging, tethered in different ways to global structures, each one engaged in unequal transactions with world centres of production and finance and presented with distinctive development possibilities. Within each region, sub-global hierarchies have formed, with poles of economic growth, managerial and technical centres and security systems. (1995: 279)

This emphasis on the continuing importance of territorial factors and location does not deny increased 'supraterritoriality' (Scholte, 2000) of trade, finance and production, or of commercial, voluntary and governmental organizations for that matter. Nor does it deny the challenges that supraterritoriality poses to the (territorial) state. It only places this in context and highlights the relative nature of deterritorialization. TNCs are far more territorially rooted and less 'free-floating' than advertised. Moreover, they operate within a defined social, political and institutional context in which the state is central. In this respect, I concur with Scholte:

> to say that social geography can no longer be understood in terms of territoriality *alone* is not to say that territoriality has become irrelevant . . . supraterritorial phenomena still have to engage at some level with territorial places, territorial governments and territorial identities. (2000: 59)

I have shown that territoriality does not merely *co-exist* with supraterritoriality, but that it is a *prerequisite* for supraterritoriality. States have to provide the minimum required for effective market operation and uphold the social relations on which economic globalization is dependent: free market economies cannot exist 'without effective legal, regulatory and extractive national institutions that have jurisdiction over a given territory' (Chaudhry, 1993: 265). At the end of the day, 'supraterritorialism' is dependent on territorial politics, and is mediated by regional, national and local contexts and interests.

My criticism of the 'strong' globalization thesis particularly highlighted the continued relevance, indeed resilience, of national states in the globalization process. States may have been 'decentred' but only *relatively* so, and there is no compelling evidence that the state is in terminal decline. States have enjoyed ideological and popular revival, and, if anything, national political divisions have hardened, lending support to nationalism. State regulation of TNC activities on competition, health and safety, environmental and social grounds remains extensive, while the growth of global financial capital does not in itself deny states the power to regulate it or any other fraction of capital. Far from capitulating to globalization, states are pursuing a variety of strategies to steer globalization and advance their national interests. These strategies range from the now unfashionable dirigiste control of national economies, exemplified in the developmental states of East Asia, to active participation in the formation of regional and international blocs to establish a set of common rules governing exchange, accumulation, distribution and development.

This globalization of political action by states, as well as by TNCs, professional, labour, voluntary and trade associations, has altered how trade, territories and populations are governed. Certainly, international monetary, trade, investment, labour, aid and development regimes bear on national social policies and provision. Certainly, international and transnational actors intervene in the domestic policy process. Certainly, global institutions have succeeded in steering the political choices of *some* governments. However, the extent to, and ways in which these regimes, actors and movements impact nationally is contingent on decidely domestic factors. First, the ways in which states promote, 'receive' and react to globalization are structured by their position, or rank, within the global political economy. Second, states' room for manoeuvre in pursuing and implementing globalizing strategies is mediated by national social, demographic, cultural and economic trends, institutions and traditions. Third, states' margin of operation is determined by the balance of political power between the state, labour, capital and civil society. Put simply, there are strong differences between what different states can 'get away with'. Despite the supposed overarching power of globalization, the national balance of political power may be decisive in respect of how far national states can accommodate globalization.

With regard to the supposed hegemony of neo-liberalism globally, liberalizing forces are not the only ones at work, nor are they necessarily always the most dominant ones, nor are they able to trample over the opposition. Although neo-liberal globalization undoubtedly finds much political and institutional encouragement, it also faces significant opposition from states, international bureaucracies, fractions of capital, and groups and movements within civil society. Its impact outside the traditional homelands of free market economics is weaker than proclaimed:

> The most ardent adherents and steadfast practitioners of free-market economics find their home in London, Canberra, and Washington, not Paris, Bonn or Tokyo. Outside the English speaking world, the contours of change reflect the tenacity of pre-existing régime orientations and arrangements which have more in common with symbiotic views of the state-market relationship than with Anglo-American approaches to economic openness. (Weiss, 1999: 129)

If the 'strong' globalization thesis that national states and domestic politics no longer matter were correct, then we should have seen convergence between the welfare states of the Triad countries where globalization is at its most intense – between the EU, US, Japan, and, to a lesser extent, East Asia. We should also have seen convergence among countries of other regions, such as Latin America, where IGOs have been active. Yet this clearly has not happened, nor is it likely to happen. In Latin America, for example, I noted that social reforms have been more distinctive for the retention of benefits by privileged groups than for their strict adherence to IGOs' policy prescriptions (Kay, 2000). Indeed, there is *no need*, nor is there any likelihood, that all states will adopt the same reform strategy, starting as they do from different historical, cultural, political and economic positions. While some governments *are* adopting similar strategies such as fiscal austerity, marketization, privatization, economic openess in trade, investment and finance, by no means have all governments followed the neo-liberal route (Esping-Andersen, 1996; Weiss, 1997, 1999).

Along with direct channels of communication between various civil society groups and international bodies, the globalization of political action has spawned a political force of a wealth of single issue groups protesting against various features of globalization. Many of these groups work on more than a national scale. One of the clearest expressions of contemporary global social politics can be seen in the international mobilization that led to the Battle of Seattle, organized under the motto 'May our resistance be as transnational as capital'. Here, the same tools of international communication that facilitate globalization are used in opposition to globalization. The multitude of issues and agendas – strictly national as well as global – that came together in opposition to the WTO in Seattle, illustrate the diversity of sources of opposition to globalizing strategies of capital and states, particularly to those strategies which ignore health, social and environmental protection.

Global social politics can also be found in the opposition to globalizing strategies at national and local levels. Around the world, governments attempting to recast national economic and welfare institutions and provision have been forced to engage in 'social dialogue' with a variety of protest groups unconvinced of the merits of globalization. These dialogues have taken a variety of forms, ranging from popular social protest (urban uprisings, mass demonstrations, strikes and boycotts) to direct participation in the policy-making process. These dialogues are not only conducted with governmental institutions, but also with local branches of TNCs, and have made use of market as well as institutional mechanisms. While these may not have the capacity in every instance to act as a counterweight to capital's or governments' globalization strategies, they can succeed in blocking or impeding parts of the strategy's progress and in shaping how problems are defined and responded to. Different local and national balances of power determine which of the many possible outcomes of the encounter come to pass.

Overall, then, globalization is uneven in scope, depth, intensity and impact. This is not to suggest that there are no common responses or trends occurring, or that the balance between local, national, supra-national or global influences remains unchanged. My emphasis on the contradictions of globalization points to the complexities of what 'globalization' is and how states and other interests respond to it and shape it. This emphasis on multiplicity rather than uniformity, on divergence rather than convergence, rescues globalization from the dangers of a crude economic determinism where all Chinese walls are destroyed by the untrammelled power of global capital. Rather, we discover various stages at which a multiplicity of actors' interests inter-act in various ways, at various levels, and with various outcomes, none of which is predetermined.

This analysis of the social politics of globalization suggests that social movements *for* globalization cannot simply steamroll over states and populations, or bulldoze national institutions and remould them in their preferred fashion. Social reforms have never been inevitable or easy, and there is no reason to believe that it is any different now. Globalization has not de-politicized social reform: on the contrary, political struggle has been extended to other levels and spheres. Whatever one's position on globalization or on how to proceed with global reform it is important to recognize that politics still matter and that political struggles at different levels and in different spheres are globally interconnected, so a variety of strategies is needed.

There are good reasons to believe that the global market economy constitutes a powerful pressure to *expand* rather than reduce the state's role in the provision of welfare. Extensive health and welfare provision remains popular with electorates, and even political parties that are elected on a mandate to retrench public welfare institutions have found many of their ambitions thwarted by opposition not just from electorates, or from traditional defenders of the welfare states, but also from business interests on certain issues. Moreover, welfare spending has increased during periods of open free trade (Rieger and Leibfried, 1998), and the OECD now recognizes that 'one of the effects of global-ization could be to increase the demand for social protection . . . a more useful blueprint for reform would be to recognize that globalization reinforces the need for some protection' (OECD in Deacon, 1999a: 16). Despite the World Bank's emphasis on means-testing and private provision to protect populations against the social risks of globalization, or the UN and its agencies' apparent capitulation to this agenda (Deacon, 2000a), there is no reason to believe that the political pendulum could not in future swing in favour of forces emphasizing redistribution and comprehensive public provision.

Domestic and international political pressures to protect populations against the social effects of globalization are likely to force new forms of state intervention in the economy and new forms of collective action and provision to the top of the political agenda (Garrett in Rhodes, 1996: 319; Rieger and Leibfried, 1998). There is greater acknowledgement now that globalization creates a higher level of systemic risks, and that there is a need to re-engineer current structures of cooperation to ensure the adequate provision of global public goods, such as financial stability, peace, distributive justice, equality and health, to minimize and protect against the destabilizing social and political costs of globalization (Kaul et al., 1999). Global redistribution is also on the political agenda, including proposals for international taxation such as the Toibin Tax (a tax levied on international financial transactions), an energy tax (a worldwide tax on carbon emissions), and an eco-tax (levied by governments on imported goods made using environmentally unfriendly production processes).

However, it must be acknowledged that historical, cultural, ideological, religious and institutional differences render the pursuit of 'universal' public goods, or an agreed global cosmopolitan form of social progress, particularly difficult. As Pape (1999) shows, an attempt to establish international competition rules will have to resolve fundamental differences in conceptions of 'competition'. The differences between Western countries, such as France, the US and Germany, pale by comparison with non-Western cultures, such as those in Asia, and especially in Islamic countries, in which a competition culture (in the accepted Western sense) is anathema to traditional values. Unless these differences can be reconciled, international law will simply reflect Western values and approaches and provoke renewed religious, cultural and political opposition to globalization and to international law and norms. Global universal social standards may similarly be resisted on the grounds that they constitute a new form of social protectionism against the South by the North, or that they embody and impose Western concepts and approaches on countries of very different cultural, political, economic and social contexts (Deacon, 1999a; Mishra, 1999). Thus, current attempts to export European models of social protection to China may ultimately flounder on cultural differences because individual rights are anathema to Confucian concepts (Wong, 1998).

As Phillips and Higgott (1999) argue, it is not clear that all states will acquiesce to a consensus on global public goods in the manner to which the international community aspires. First, the globalization backlash is constituted by actors antipathetic to the agents of Western capitalism, particularly in Asia, which renders it difficult, if not unlikely, that a consensus as to what constitutes global public goods let alone how to achieve them will be arrived at. Second, the global public goods debate has been mainly conducted in international arenas from which developing countries are excluded, such as the G7, or within which their influence is limited, such as the Bretton Woods institutions. Third, state policy élites' willingness and ability to provide public goods or participate in their provision at global level is limited by the negative consequences of globalization itself. Many countries do not have the resources to forge international agreements and honour their commitments (Kaul et al., 1999).

Whatever the outcomes of these processes may be, we can be sure that any settlement will reflect the particularities of national histories, problems and circumstances, as well as the political strategies followed by various groups and the social aims that these strategies seek to advance. In the end, the major contribution that this book has sought to make has been to return political agency to the centre of debates about globalization and its implications for social policy, both in movements for and against globalization. In this task, I have added to the growing scepticism of defeatist depictions of globalization as a reified economic mechanism operating outside of any social and political context. On the continued possibilities of social politics under globalization, it seems appropriate to reiterate, with UNRISD, that:

> In the last analysis, action depends on people's interpretation of what is possible and right. Thus the longer-term nature of mobilization for sustainable development depends not only on activism, but on dominant views about where the world could – and should – be going . . . Questioning extreme individualism and the unbridled power of money – reasserting the value of equity and social solidarity, and reinstating the citizen at the centre of public life – is a major challenge of our time. The 'invisible hand' of the market has no capacity to imagine a decent society for all people, or to work in a consistent fashion to attain it. Only human beings with a strong sense of the public good can do that. (2000: xix)

References

Akyüz, Y. (1998) 'The East Asian financial crisis: back to the future', in K.S. Jomo (ed.), *Tigers in Trouble: Financial Governance, Liberalisation and Crises in East Asia*. London: Zed.

Alber, J. and Standing, G. (2000) 'Social dumping, catch-up, or convergence? Europe in a comparative global context', *Journal of European Social Policy*, 10 (2): 99–119.

Albrow, M., Eade, J., Dürrschmidt, D. and Washbourne, N. (1997) 'The impact of globalisation on sociological concepts: community, culture and milieu', in J. Eade (ed.), *Living the Global City: Globalisation as a Local Process*. London: Routledge.

Allen, J. and Thompson, G. (1997) 'Think global, then think again – economic globalization in context', *Area*, 19 (3): 213–27.

Amin, A. (1997) 'Placing Globalization', *Theory, Culture & Society*, 14 (2): 123–37.

Amin, S. (1990) *Maldevelopment: Anatomy of a Global Failure*. London: Zed.

Amin, S. (1997) *Capitalism in the Age of Globalization: The Management of Contemporary Society*. London: Zed.

Amparo Cruz-Saco Oyague, M. (1998) 'Introduction: context and typology of reform models', in M. Amparo Cruz-Saco Oyague and C. Mesa-Lago (eds), *The Reform of Pension and Health Care Systems in Latin America: Do Options Exist?* Pittsburgh: University of Pittsburgh.

Amparo Cruz-Saco Oyague, M. and Mesa-Lago, C. (eds) (1998) *The Reform of Pension and Health Care Systems in Latin America: Do Options Exist?* Pittsburgh: University of Pittsburgh.

Amsden, A.H. (1995) 'Like the rest: South-East Asia's "late" industrialisation', *Journal of International Development*, 7 (5): 791–9.

Andrews, D. (1994) 'Capital mobility and state autonomy: toward a structural theory of international monetary relations', *International Studies Quarterly*, 38: 193–218.

Api Richards, G. (1999) 'Challenging Asia–Europe relations from below? Civil society and the politics of inclusion and opposition', *Journal of the Asia Pacific Economy*, 4 (1): 146–70.

Appleton, B. (1999) 'International Agreements and National Health Plans: NAFTA', in D. Drache and T. Sullivan (eds), *Health Reform: Public Success, Private Failure*. London: Routledge.

Araghi, F.A. (1995) 'Global depeasantization, 1945–1990', *Sociological Quarterly*, 36 (2): 337–68.

Axford, B. (1995) *The Global System: Economics, Politics and Culture*. Cambridge: Polity.

Bairoch, R. (1996) 'Globalization myths and realities: one century of external trade and foreign investment', in D. Boyer and R. Drache (eds), *States Against Markets: The Limits of Globalization*. London: Routledge.

Bakker, A.F.P. (1996) *International Financial Institutions*. London: Longman.

Baldwin, P. (1997) 'State and citizenship in the age of globalisation', in P.

Koslowski and A. Follesdal (eds), *Restructuring the Welfare State: Theory and Reform of Social Policy*. Berlin: Springer.

Bandarage, A. (1997) *Women, Population and Global Crisis: A Political-Economic Analysis*. London: Zed.

Barff, R. and Austen, J. (1993) '"It's gotta be da shoes": domestic manufacturing, international subcontracting and the production of athletic footwear', *Environment and Planning*, 25: 1103–14.

Barrett, D. and Ong Tsui, A. (1999) 'Policy as Symbolic Statement: International Response to National Population Policies', *Social Forces*, 78 (1): 213–34.

Barrientos, A. (1998) *Pension Reform in Latin America*. Aldershot: Ashgate.

Barry, K. (1995) *The Prostitution of Sexuality: The Global Exploitation of Women*. New York: New York University Press.

Bayne, N. (2000) 'Why did Seattle fail? Globalization and the politics of trade', *Government and Opposition*, 35 (2): 131–51.

Beck, U. (2000) *What is Globalization?* Cambridge: Polity Press/Blackwell.

Bello, W. (1998) 'The end of a miracle: speculation, foreign capital dependence and the collapse of the South-East Asian economies', *Multinational Monitor*, 19 (1–2): 10–16.

Bennholdt-Thomsen, V. and Mies, M. (1999) *The Subsistence Perspective*. London: Zed.

Bensaïd, D. (1996) 'Neo-liberal reform and popular rebellion', *New Left Review*, 215: 109–16.

Blackburn, R. (1999) 'The new collectivism: pension reform, grey capitalism and complex socialism', *New Left Review*, 233: 3–65.

Bock, G. and Thane, P. (eds) (1991) *Maternity and Gender Policies: Women and the Rise of the European Welfare States 1880s–1950s*. London: Routledge.

Bonoli, G. (1998) 'Pension politics in France: patterns of co-operation and conflict in two recent reforms', *West European Politics*, 20 (4): 111–24.

Bonoli, G., George, V. and Taylor-Gooby, P. (2000) *European Welfare Futures: Towards a Theory of State Retrenchment*. Oxford: Polity.

Bowles, P. and MacLean, B. (1996) 'Regional blocs: can Japan be the leader?', in R. Boyer and D. Drache (eds), *States Against Markets: The Limits of Globalization*. London: Routledge.

Boyer, R. (1996) 'State and market: a new engagement for the twenty-first century?', in R. Boyer and D. Drache (eds), *States Against Markets: The Limits of Globalization*. London: Routledge.

Bradshaw, Y.W. and Wallace, M. (1999) *Global Inequalities*. Thousand Oaks, CA: Pine Forge.

Brenner, N. (1999) 'Globalisation as re-territorialisation: the re-scaling of urban governance in the EU', *Urban Studies*, 36 (3): 431–51.

Bretherton, C. (1996) 'Introduction: global politics in the 1990s', in C. Bretherton and G. Ponton (eds), *Global Politics: An Introduction*. Oxford: Blackwell.

Brydon, L. and Legge, K. (1996) *Adjusting Society: The World Bank, the IMF and Ghana*. London: Tauris Academic Studies.

Buelens, F. (ed.) (1999) *Globalisation and the Nation-State*. Cheltenham: Edward Elgar.

Bullard, N., with W. Bello and K. Malhotra (1998) *Taming the Tigers: The IMF and the Asian Crisis*. CAFOD/Focus on the South, London.

Burden, T. (1998) *Social Policy and Welfare: A Clear Guide*. London: Pluto.

Carr, B. (1999) 'Globalisation from below: labour internationalism under NAFTA', *International Journal of Social Science*, 159: 49–59.

Cary, W.L. (1974) 'Federalism and corporate law: reflections upon Delaware', *Yale Law Journal*, 83: 663–705.

Casadio Tarabusi, C. and Vickery, G. (1996) 'Globalisation in the pharmaceutical industry', in OECD, *Globalisation of Industry: Overview and Sector Reports*. Paris: OECD.

Castells, M. (1998) *End of Millennium*. Oxford: Blackwell.

Castles, S. (1998) 'New migrations in the Asia-Pacific region: a force for social and political change', *International Journal of Social Science*, 156: 215–27.

Castles, S. and Miller, M.J. (1993) *The Age of Migration: International Population Movements in the Modern World*. Basingstoke: Macmillan.

Cavanagh, J. and Broad, R. (1996) 'Global reach: workers fight the multinationals', *The Nation*, 18/3/96: 21–4.

Cerny, P. (1995) 'Globalisation and the changing logic of collective action', *International Organization*, 34 (2): 595–625.

Cerny, P. (1996) 'What next for the state?', in E. Kofman and G. Youngs (eds), *Globalization: Theory and Practice*. London: Pinter.

Cerny, P. (1997) 'Paradoxes of the competition state: the dynamics of political globalization', *Government and Opposition*, 32 (2): 251–74.

Cerny, P. (1999) 'Reconstructing the political in a globalising world: states, institutions, actors and governance', in F. Buelens (ed.), *Globalisation and the Nation-State*. Cheltenham: Edward Elgar.

Chan, R.K.H. (1996) *Welfare in Newly-Industrialised Society: The Construction of the Welfare State in Hong Kong*. Aldershot: Ashgate.

Chandrasekhar, C.P. and Ghosh, J. (1998) 'Hubris, hysteria, hope: the political economy of crisis and response in Southeast Asia', in K.S. Jomo (ed.), *Tigers in Trouble: Financial Governance, Liberalisation and Crises in East Asia*. London: Zed.

Chapman, K. (1992) 'Agents of change in the internationalisation of the petrochemical industry', *Geoforum*, 23 (1): 13–27.

Chase-Dunn, C. (1989) *Global Formation: Structures of the World-Economy*. Oxford: Blackwell.

Chau, R.C.M. and Yu, S.W.K. (1999) 'Social welfare and economic development in China and Hong Kong', *Critical Social Policy*, 19 (1): 87–108.

Chaudhry, K.A. (1993) 'The myths of the market and the common history of late developers', *Politics and Society*, 21 (3): 245–74.

Chetley, A. (1990) *A Healthy Business? World Health and the Pharmaceutical Industry*. London: Zed.

Chiesa, V. (1995) 'Globalizing R&D around centres of excellence', *Long Range Planning*, 28 (6): 19–28.

Chossudovsky, M. (1996) 'Globalisation and the criminalisation of economic activity: the business of crime and the crimes of business', *Covert Action Quarterly*, Fall: 24–30, 54.

Chossudovsky, M. (1997) *The Globalisation of Poverty: Impacts of IMF and World Bank Reforms*. London: Zed/Third World Network.

Choucri, N. (1993) 'Political economy of the global environment', *International Political Science Review*, 14 (1): 103–16.

Clarke, J. (2000) 'A world of difference? Globalization and the study of social policy', in G. Lewis, S. Gewirtz and J. Clarke (eds), *Rethinking Social Policy*. London: Sage/Open University.

Clarke, S. (1990) 'New utopias for old: Fordist dreams and post-Fordist fantasies', *Capital and Class*, 42: 131–55.

Cleaver, H. (1999) 'Computer-linked social movements and the global threat to capitalism', (www.eco.utexas.edu/Homepages/Faculty/Cleaver/polnet. html).

Cleves Mosse, J. (1993) *Half the World, Half a Chance: An Introduction to Gender and Development*. Oxford: Oxfam.

Commission on Global Governance (1995) *Our Global Neighbourhood*. Oxford: OUP.

Connors, J. (1996) 'NGOs and the human rights of women at the United Nations', in P. Willetts (ed.), *The Conscience of the World: The Influence of Non-Governmental Organisations in the U.N. System*. London: Hurst.

CornerHouse, The (1998) *Engineering of Consent: Uncovering Corporate PR*. Briefing 6, Sturminster Newton, Devon.

CornerHouse, The (1999) *Internal conflict: Adaptation and Reaction to Globalisation*. Briefing 12, Sturminster Newton, Devon.

Cox, K.R. (ed.) (1997) *Spaces of Globalization: Reasserting the Power of the Local*. London: Guilford.

Cram, L. (1996) *Policy-Making in the EU: Conceptual Lenses and the Integration Process*. London: Routledge.

Crow, G. (1997) *Comparative Sociology and Social Theory*. New York: St. Martin's Press.

Curry, J. (1993) 'The flexibility fetish', *Capital and Class*, 50: 99–126.

Dalla Costa, G.F. (1993) 'Development and economic crisis: women's labour and social policies in Venezuela in the context of international indebtedness', in M. Dalla Costa and G.F. Dalla Costa (eds), *Paying the Price: Women and the Politics of International Economic Strategy*. London: Zed.

Deacon, B. (1995) 'The globalisation of social policy and the socialisation of global politics', in J. Baldock and M. May (eds), *Social Policy Review 7*. Social Policy Association. Canterbury/Kent.

Deacon, B. (1998) 'Consultancy companies and transnational policy advice: the depoliticisation of social policy?', paper to GASPP seminar: International NGOs, Consulting Companies and Global Social Policy: Subcontracting Governance?, December, Helsinki.

Deacon, B. (1999a) *Towards a Socially Responsible Globalization: International Actors and Discourses*. GASPP occasional papers, no. 1. Helsinki, Finland: STAKES.

Deacon, B. (1999b) *Socially Responsible Globalisation: A Challenge for the European Union*. Helsinki: Ministry of Social Affairs.

Deacon, B. (2000a) *Globalisation and Social Policy: The Threat to Equitable Welfare*. Occasional paper 5, Geneva: UNRISD.

Deacon, B. (2000b) 'East European welfare states: the impact of the politics of globalisation', *Journal of European Social Policy*, 10 (2): 146–61.

Deacon, B. and Hulse, M. (1996) *The Globalisation of Social Policy*. Leeds: Leeds Metropolitan University.

Deacon, B., Hulse, M. and Stubbs, P. (1997) *Global Social Policy: International Organisations and the Future of Welfare*. London: Sage.

De Angelis, M. (1997) 'The autonomy of the economy and globalisation', *Common Sense*, 21: 41–59.

Deyo, F.C. (1992) 'The political economy of social policy formation: East Asia's newly industrialised countries', in R.P. Applebaum and J. Henderson (eds), *States and Development in the Asian Pacific Rim*. London: Sage.

Dicken, P. (1992) 'International production in a volatile regulatory environment: the influence of national regulatory policies on the spatial strategies of TNCs', *Geoforum*, 23 (3): 303–16.

Dicken, P. (1993) 'The growth economies of Pacific Asia in their changing global context', in C. Dixon and D. Drakakis-Smith (eds), *Economic and Social Development in Pacific Asia*. London: Routledge.

Diller, J. (1999) 'A social conscience in the global marketplace? Labour dimensions of codes of conduct, social labelling and investor initiatives', *International Labour Review*, 138 (2): 99–129.

Drache, D. (1996) 'From Keynes to K-Mart: competitiveness in a corporate age', in R. Boyer and D. Drache (eds), *States Against Markets: The Limits of Globalization*. London: Routledge.

Dunkley, G. (2000) *The Free Trade Adventure*. London: Zed.

Eade, J. (1997) 'Introduction', in J. Eade (ed.), *Living the Global City: Globalisation as a Local Process*. London: Routledge.

Elkins, D.J. (1999) 'Think locally, act globally: reflections on virtual neighbourhoods', *The Public Javnost*, 6 (1): 37–53.

Elson, D. (1987) *The Impact of Structural Adjustment on Women: Concepts and Issues*. London: Institute for African Alternatives.

Elson, D. (1994) 'Micro, meso, macro: gender and economic analysis in the context of policy reform', in I. Bakker (ed.), *The Strategic Silence: Gender and Economic Policy*. London: Zed.

Esping-Andersen, G. (ed.) (1996) *Welfare States in Transition: National Adaptations in Global Economies*. London: Sage.

Esping-Andersen, G. (2000) 'The sustainability of welfare states into the twenty-first century', *International Journal of Health Services*, 30 (1): 1–12.

Esty, D.C. and Geradin, D. (1998) 'Environmental protection and international competitiveness: a conceptual framework', *Journal of World Trade*, 32 (3): 5–46.

Ethical Consumer (1996) 'Making it into the mainstream', January/February: 20–22.

Evans, J. (1998) 'Economic globalisation: the need for a social dimension', in D. Foden and P. Morris (eds), *The Search for Equity: Welfare and Security in the Global Economy*. London: Lawrence and Wishart.

Evans, P.B. (1985) 'Transnational linkages and the economic role of the state: an analysis of developing and industrialised nations in the post World War II period', in P.B. Evans, D. Rueschemeyer and T. Skocpol (eds), *Bringing the State Back In*. Cambridge: CUP.

Evans, P.B. (1997) 'The eclipse of the state? Reflections on stateness in an era of globalisation', *World Politics*, 50: 62–87.

Falk, R. (1997) 'Resisting "globalisation-from-above" through "globalisation-from-below"', *New Political Economy*, 2 (1): 17–24.

Fawcett, L. and Hurrell, A. (1995) *Regionalism in World Politics: Regional Organization and International Order*. Oxford: OUP.

Folkerts-Landau, D. and Ito, T. (1995) *International Capital Markets: Developments, Prospects and Policy Issues*. Washington, DC: World Economic and Financial Surveys, IMF.

Fox Piven, F. (1997) 'Welfare and the transformation of American politics', paper to Social Policy Association, Lincoln, July.

Fox Piven, F. and Cloward, R. (1995) 'Normalizing collective protest', in A.D. Morris and C. McClurg Muller (eds), *Frontiers in Social Movement Theory*. New Haven and London: Yale University Press.

Fransman, M. (1997) 'Is national technology policy obsolete in a global world? The Japanese response', in D. Archibugi and J. Michie (eds), *Technology, Globalisation and Economic Performance*. Cambridge: CUP.

Freeman, C. (1997) 'The national system of innovation in historical perspective', in D. Archibugi and J. Michie (eds), *Technology, Globalisation and Economic Performance*. Cambridge: CUP.

Friedman, M. (1995) 'On promoting a sustainable future through consumer action', *Journal of Social Issues*, 51 (4): 197–215.

Fröbel, F., Heinrichs, J. and Kreye, O. (1980) *The New International Division of Labour*. Cambridge: CUP.

Fukuyama, F. (1992) *The End of History and the Last Man*. New York: Basic Books.

Gaer, F.D. (1996) 'Reality check: human rights NGOs confront governments at the UN', in T.G. Weiss and L. Gordenker (eds), *NGOs, the UN and Global Governance*. London: Lynne Rienner.

Ganley, G.D. (1992) *The Exploding Political Power of Personal Media*. Norwood, NJ: Ablex.

Garrett, G. (1998) *Partisan Politics in the Global Economy*. Cambridge: CUP.

George, S. (1996) 'The European Union, 1992 and the fear of "fortress Europe"', in A. Gamble and A. Payne (eds), *Regionalism and World Order*. Basingstoke: Macmillan.

George, V. (1998) 'Political ideology, globalisation and welfare futures in Europe', *Journal of Social Policy*, 27 (1): 17–36.

Gereffi, G. (1996) 'Commodity chains and regional divisions of labor in East Asia', *Journal of Asian Business*, 12 (1): 75–112.

Gereffi, G., Korzeniewicz, M., and Korzeniewicz, R.P. (1994) 'Introduction: global commodity chains', in G. Gereffi and M. Korzeniewicz (eds), *Commodity Chains and Global Capitalism*. Westport, CT: Greenwood Press.

Gereffi, G.S. and Wyman, D.L. (eds) (1990) *Manufacturing Miracles: Paths of Industrialisation in Latin America and East Asia*. Princeton, NJ: Princeton University Press.

Geschiere, P. and Meyer, B. (1998) 'Globalization and identity: dialectics of flow and closure', *Development and Change*, 29: 601–15.

Geyer, R. (1998) 'Globalisation and the (non-) defence of the welfare state', *West European Politics*, 21 (3): 77–102.

Geyer, R. (2000) *Exploring European Social Policy*. Cambridge: Polity.

Gibson-Graham, J.K. (1996) *The End of Capitalism (as we knew it): A Feminist Critique of Political Economy*. Oxford: Blackwell.

Giddens, A. (1990) *The Consequences of Modernity*. Cambridge: Polity.

Giddens, A. (1999) 'Globalisation', Reith Lectures, number 1, www.lse.ac.uk/ Giddens/lectures.htm

Gilpin, R. (1987) *The Political Economy of International Relations*. Princeton, NJ: Princeton University Press.

Golding, P. and Harris, P. (1997) *Beyond Cultural Imperialism: Globalization, Communication and the New International Order*. London: Sage.

Goodman, J. (1998) 'Transnational contestation: social movements beyond the state', paper to XIV World Congress of Sociology, Montreal.

Goodman, J. and Pauly, L. (1993) 'The obsolescence of capital controls? Economic management in an age of global markets', *World Politics*, 46 (1): 50–82.

Goodman, R. (1992) 'Japan: pupil turned teacher?', *Oxford Studies in Comparative Education*, 1: 155–73.

Goodman, R. and Peng, I. (1996) 'The East Asian welfare states: peripatetic learning, adaptive change, and nation-building', in G. Esping-Andersen (ed.), *Welfare States in Transition: National Adaptations in Global Economies*. London: Sage.

Goodman, R., White, G. and Kwon, H. (1998) *The East Asian Welfare Model: Welfare Orientalism and the State*. London: Routledge.

Gordenker, L. and Weiss, T.G. (1996a) 'Pluralizing global governance: analytical approaches and dimensions', in T.G. Weiss and L. Gordenker (eds), *NGOS, the UN, and Global Governance*. London: Lynne Rienner.

Gordenker, L. and Weiss, T.G. (1996b) 'NGO participation in the international policy process', in T.G. Weiss and L. Gordenker (eds), *NGOS, the UN, and Global Governance*. London: Lynne Rienner.

Gordon, D.M. (1987) 'The global economy: new edifice or crumbling foundations', *New Left Review*, 168: 24–64.

Gough, I. (2000a) 'Welfare regimes: on adapting the framework to developing countries', Global Social Policy Programme, Institute for International Policy Analysis, University of Bath.

Gough, I. (2000b) 'Globalisation and regional welfare regimes: the East Asian Case', Global Social Policy Programme, Institute for International Policy Analysis, University of Bath.

Gough, I. (2000c) *Global Capital, Human Needs and Social Policies: Selected Essays 1994–99*. London: Macmillan.

Green, A. (1997) *Education, Globalization and the Nation State*. Basingstoke: Macmillan.

Grimshaw, C. (1997) 'The emperor's new clothes. The multilateral agreement on investment', *Corporate Watch*, 5/6: 36–8.

Hallerberg, M. and Basinger, S. (1998) 'Internationalization and changes in taxation policy in OECD countries: the importance of domestic veto players', *Comparative Political Studies*, 31 (3): 321–52.

Halliday, F. (1991) 'Hidden from international relations: women and the international arena', in R. Grant and K. Newland (eds), *Gender and International Relations*. Milton Keynes: Open University Press.

Hallwood, C.P. and MacDonald, R. (1994) *International Money and Finance*. Oxford: Blackwell.

Hantrais, L. (1995) *Social Policy in the European Union*. London: Macmillan.

Harris, N. (1986) *The End of the Third World: Newly Industrialising Countries and the Decline of an Ideology*. Harmondsworth: Penguin.

Harris, R. and Lavan, A. (1992) 'Professional mobility in the New Europe: the case of social work', *Journal of European Social Policy*, 2 (1): 1–15.

Hartmann, B. (1993) 'Population doublespeak', *Women's Global Network for Reproductive Rights Newsletter*, 42: 9–10.

Harvey, D. (1989) *The Condition of Postmodernity*. Oxford: Blackwell.

Hay, C. (1998) 'Globalisation, welfare retrenchment and the "logic of no alternative": why second-best won't do', *Journal of Social Policy*, 24 (4): 525–32.

Hay, C. and Watson, M. (1999) 'Globalisation: "sceptical" notes on the 1999 Reith lectures', *Political Quarterly*, 70 (4): 418–25.

Held, D. (1995) *Democracy and the Global Order: From the Modern State to Cosmopolitan Governance*. Cambridge: Polity.

Helleiner, E. (1996) 'Post-globalization: is the financial liberalization trend likely to be reversed?', in D. Boyer and R. Drache (eds), *States Against Markets: The Limits of Globalization*. London: Routledge.

Henderson, J. (1993) 'Against the economic orthodoxy: on the making of the East Asian miracle', *Economy and Society*, 22 (3): 200–17.

Henson, R. (1996) 'Minimum labour standards and trade agreements: an overview of the debate', *Economic and Political Weekly* (Bombay), April 20–27: 1030–4.

Herod, A. (1997) 'Labor as an agent of globalization and as a global agent', in K.R. Cox (ed.), *Spaces of Globalization: Reasserting the Power of the Local*. London: Guilford.

Hines, C. (2000) *Localization: A Global Manifesto*. London: Earthscan.

Hines, C. and Lang, T. (1996) 'In favour of a new protectionism', in J. Mander and E. Goldsmith (eds), *The Case against the Global Economy and for a Turn Toward the Local*. San Francisco: Sierra Club Books.

Hirst, P. and Thompson, G. (1996) *Globalization in Question: The International Economy and the Possibilities of Governance*. Cambridge: Polity.

Hochschild, A.R. (2000) 'Global care chains and emotional surplus value', in W. Hutton and A. Giddens (eds), *On The Edge: Living with Global Capitalism*. London: Jonathan Cape.

Hoechsmann, M. (1996) 'Revolution goes global: Zapatistas on the Net', *Convergence: Journal of Research into New Media Technologies*, 2 (1): 30–5.

Hoekman, B. and Kostecki, M. (1995) *The Political Economy of the World Trading System: From GATT to WTO*. Oxford: OUP.

Hoggart, K., Buller, H. and Black, R. (1995) *Rural Europe: Identity and Change*. London: Arnold.

Holton, R.J. (1998) *Globalization and the Nation-State*. Basingstoke: Macmillan.

Hort, S.E.O. and Kuhnle, S. (2000) 'The coming of East and South-east Asian welfare states', *Journal of European Social Policy*, 10 (2): 162–84.

Hout, W. (1996) 'Globalization, regionalization and regionalism: a survey of contemporary literature', *Acta Politica*, XXXI: 164–81.

Howard, R.E. (1995) 'Women's rights and the right to development', in J. Peters and A. Wolper (eds), *Women's Rights, Human Rights: International Feminist Perspectives*. London: Routledge.

Howells, J. (1990) 'The internationalisation of R&D and the development of global research networks', *Regional Studies*, 24 (6): 495–512.

Huber, E. (1996) 'Options for social policy in Latin America: neoliberal versus social democratic models', in G. Esping-Andersen (ed.), *Welfare States in Transition: National Adaptations in Global Economies*. London: Sage.

Huber, E. and Stephens, J. (2000) *The Political Economy of Pension Reform: Latin America in Comparative Perspective*. Occasional Paper 7. Geneva: UNRISD.

Hughes, J. (1991) *The Social Charter and the Single European Market*. Nottingham: Spokesman.

Hulme, D. and Edwards, M. (1997) 'NGOs, states and donors: an overview', in D. Hulme and M. Edwards (eds), *NGOs, States and Donors: Too Close for Comfort?* London: Macmillan.

Hymer, S. (1972) 'The multinational corporation and the law of uneven development', in J. Bhagwati (ed.), *Economics and World Order*. New York: The Free Press.

IMF (1996) *Aging Populations and Public Pension Schemes*. Washington, DC.

James, A. (1999) 'The practice of sovereign statehood in contemporary international society', *Political Studies*, 47 (3): 457–73.

Jayaraman, R. and Kanbur, R. (1999) 'International public goods and the case for foreign aid', in I. Kaul, I. Grunberg and M. Stern (eds), *Global Public Goods: International Cooperation in the 21st Century*. Oxford: OUP.

Jefferys, S. (1996) 'France 1995: the backward march of labour halted', *Capital and Class*, 59: 7–21.

Jeffreys, S. (1999) 'Globalizing sexual exploitation: sex tourism and the traffic in women', *Leisure Studies*, 18: 179–96.

Jessop, B. (1994) 'The transition to post-Fordism and the Schumpeterian workfare state', in R. Burrows and R. Loader (eds), *Towards a Post-Fordist Welfare State?* London: Routledge.

Jordan, B. (1996) *A Theory of Poverty and Social Exclusion*. Cambridge: Polity.

Jordan, B. (1998) *The New Politics of Welfare*. London: Sage.

Kahler, M. (1992) 'External influence, conditionality, and the politics of adjustment', in S. Haggard and R.R. Kaufman (eds), *The Politics of Economic Adjustment*. Princeton, NJ: Princeton University Press.

Kapstein, E.B. (1999) 'Distributive justice as an international public good: a historical perspective', in I. Kaul, I. Grunberg and M. Stern (eds), *Global Public Goods: International Cooperation in the 21st Century*. Oxford: OUP.

Kaul, I., Grunberg, I. and Stern, M. (1999) 'Global public goods: concepts, policies and strategies', in I. Kaul, I. Grunberg and M. Stern (eds), *Global Public Goods: International Cooperation in the 21st Century*. Oxford: OUP.

Kay, S. (2000) 'Recent changes in Latin American welfare states: is there social dumping?', *Journal of European Social Policy*, 10 (2): 185–203.

Kayatekin, S.A. and Ruccion, D.F. (1998) 'Global fragments: subjectivity and class politics in discourses of globalization', *Economy and Society*, 27 (1): 74–96.

Keck, M.E. and Sikkink, K. (1998) *Activists Beyond Borders*. Ithaca: Cornell.

Keck, M.E. and Sikkink, K. (1999) 'Transnational advocacy networks in international and regional politics', *International Journal of Social Science*, 159: 89–101.

Keil, R. (1998) 'Globalization makes states: perspectives of local governance in the age of the world city', *Review of International Political Economy*, 5 (4): 616–46.

Kennedy, P. (1993) *Preparing for the Twenty-First Century*. London: Harper Collins.

Khor, M. (1998) 'NGOs in OECD countries protest against MAI', *Third World Resurgence*, 90/91: 25–6.

Kimbrell, A. (1996) 'Biocolonization: the patenting of life and the global market in body parts', in J. Mander and E. Goldsmith (eds), *The Case Against the Global Economy and For a Turn Toward the Local*. San Francisco: Sierra Club Books.

Koivusalo, M. (1999) *World Trade Organisation and Trade-Creep in Health and Social Policies*, GASPP Occasional Papers, no. 4. Helsinki, Finland: STAKES.

Koivusalo, M. and Ollila, E. (1997) *Making a Healthy World: Agencies, Actors and Policies in International Health*. London: Zed.

Korten, D.C. (1995) *When Corporations Rule the World*. London: Earthscan.

Korten, D.C. (1996) 'The Failures of Bretton Woods', in J. Mander and E.

Goldsmith (eds), *The Case Against the Global Economy and For a Turn Toward the Local*. San Francisco: Sierra Club Books.

Kropotkin, P. (1902) *Mutual Aid: A Factor in Evolution*. London.

Labonte, R. (1998) 'Healthy public policy and the world trade organization: a proposal for an international health presence in future world trade/ investment talks', paper to Globalism and Social Policy seminar on World Trade and Social Rights, Sheffield, December.

Lea, J. (1988) *Tourism and Development in the Third World*. London: Routledge.

Lee, E. (1998) *The Asian Financial Crisis: The Challenge for Social Policy*. Geneva: ILO.

Leibfried, S. (2000) 'National welfare states, European integration and globalization: a perspective for the next century', *Social Policy and Administration*, 34 (1): 44–63.

Leibfried, S. and Pierson, P. (eds) (1995) *European Social Policy: Between Fragmentation and Integration*. Washington, DC: the Brookings Institution.

London, B. and Ross, R. (1995) 'Political sociology of foreign direct investment: global capitalism and capital mobility, 1965–1980', *International Journal of Comparative Sociology*, 36 (3/4): 198–218.

Longford, M. (1996) 'NGOs and the rights of the child', in P. Willetts (ed.), *The Conscience of the World: The Influence of Non-Governmental Organisations in the U.N. System*. London: Hurst.

Lopes, C. (1999) 'Are structural adjustment programmes an adequate response to globalisation?', *International Social Science Journal*, 162: 511–19.

Lütz, S. (1998) 'The revival of the nation-state? Stock exchange regulation in an era of globalized financial markets', *Journal of European Public Policy*, 5 (1): 153–68.

Lynch, C. (1998) 'Social movements and the problem of globalization', *Alternatives*, 23: 149–73.

MacPherson, S. and Midgley, J. (1987) *Comparative Social Policy and the Third World*. Sussex: Wheatsheaf.

Madeley, J. (1999) *Big Business, Poor Peoples: The Impact of Transnational Corporations on the World's Poor*. London: Zed.

Majone, G. (1993) 'The European community between social policy and social regulation', *Journal of Common Market Studies*, 31 (2): 154–70.

Mander, J. (1996) 'Facing the rising tide', in J. Mander and E. Goldsmith (eds), *The Case Against the Global Economy and For a Turn Toward the Local*. San Francisco: Sierra Club Books.

Manning, N. and Shaw, I. (1999) 'The transferability of welfare models: a comparison of the Scandinavian and state socialist models in relation to Finland and Estonia', in C. Jones Finer (ed.), *Transnational Social Policy*. Oxford: Blackwell.

Many, Y. (1996) '"Fin de siècle" corruption: change, crisis and shifting values', *International Journal of Social Science*, 149: 309–20.

Markoff, J. (1998) 'Globalization and the future of democracy', paper to XIV World Congress of Sociology, Montreal.

Martin, H.P. and Schumann, H. (1997) *The Global Trap: Globalization and the Assault on Democracy and Prosperity*. London: Zed.

Massey, D. (1984) *Spatial Divisions of Labor*. New York: Methuen.

Matzner, E. (1998) 'The crisis of the welfare state: a game-theoretic interpretation', in H. Cavanna (ed.), *Challenges to the Welfare State: Internal and External Dynamics for Change*. Cheltenham: Edward Elgar.

May, C. (1998) 'States in the International Political Economy – Retreat or Transition?', *Review of International Political Economy*, 5 (1): 157–63.

McClintock, B. (1999) 'The multinational corporation and social justice: experiments in supranational governance', *Review of Social Economy*, LVII (4): 507–22.

McCormick, J. (1995) *The Global Environmental Movement* (2nd edn). Chichester: Wiley.

McDowell, L. (1992) 'Gender divisions in a post-Fordist era: new contradictions or the same old story?', in L. McDowell and R. Pringle (eds), *Defining Women: Social Institutions and Gender Divisions*. Polity Press/Open University.

McLaughlin, E. (1993) 'Hong Kong: a residual welfare regime', in A. Cochrane and J. Clarke (eds), *Comparing Welfare States: Britain in International Context*. London: Sage/Open University.

McMichael, P. and Myhre, D. (1991) 'Global regulation versus the nation state: agro-food systems and the new politics of capital', *Capital and Class*, 43: 83–105.

Meehan, E. (1992) *Citizenship and the European Community*. London: Sage.

Meeker-Lowry, S. (1996) 'Community money: the potential of local currency', in J. Mander and E. Goldsmith (eds), *The Case Against the Global Economy and For a Turn Toward the Local*. San Francisco: Sierra Club Books.

Meiksins Wood, E. (1997) 'Modernity, postmodernity or capitalism?', *Review of International Political Economy*, 4 (3): 539–60.

Michel, A. (1993) 'African women, development and the north–south relationship', in M. Dalla Costa and G. Dalla Costa (eds), *Paying the Price: Women and the Politics of International Economic Strategy*. London: Zed.

Midgley, J. (1997) *Social Welfare in Global Context*. London: Sage.

Midnight Notes (1999) 'Introduction', *One No, Many Yeses*, no. 12. Jamaica Plains: Midnight Notes.

Mies, M. and Shiva, V. (1993) *Ecofeminism*. London: Zed.

Milward, A. (1994) *The European Rescue of the Nation-State*. London: Routledge.

Mishra, R. (1996) 'The welfare of nations', in D. Boyer and R. Drache (eds), *States Against Markets: The Limits of Globalization*. London: Routledge.

Mishra, R. (1999) *Globalization and the Welfare State*. Cheltenham: Edward Elgar.

Mittelman, J.H. (1994) 'The globalization of social conflict', in V. Bornschier and P. Lengyel (eds), *Conflicts and Departures in World Society*. London: Transaction.

Mittelman, J.H. (1995) 'Rethinking the international division of labour in the context of globalisation', *Third World Quarterly*, 16 (2): 273–95.

Mittelman, J.H. (1996) 'How does globalization really work?', in J.H. Mittelman (ed.), *Globalization: Critical Reflections*. London: Lynne Rienner.

Mittelman, J.H. and Johnston, R. (1999) 'The globalisation of organised crime, the courtesan state, and the corruption of civil society', *Global Governance*, 5: 103–26.

Mkandawire, T. and Rodríguez, V. (2000) *Globalization and Social Development after Copenhagen: Premises, Promises and Policies*. Geneva 2000 Occasional paper, no. 10. Geneva: UNRISD.

Moghissi, H. (1999) *Feminism and Islamic Fundamentalism*. London: Zed.

Mohan, G. (1996) 'Globalization and governance: the paradoxes of adjustment in sub-Saharan Africa', in E. Kofman and G. Youngs (eds), *Globalization: Theory and Practice*. London: Pinter.

Moody, K. (1997) *Workers in a Lean World: Unions in the International Economy*. New York: Verso.

Morales-Gómez, D. (1999) *Transnational Social Policies: The New Development Challenges of Globalization*. London: Earthscan.

Moran, J. (1998) 'The dynamics of class politics and national economies in globalisation: the marginalisation of the unacceptable', *Capital and Class*, 66: 53–83.

Moran, M. and Wood, B. (1996) 'The globalization of health care policy?', in P. Gummett (ed.), *Globalization and Public Policy*, Cheltenham: Edward Elgar.

Morris, L. (1997) 'Global migration and the nation-state: the path to a post-national Europe?', *British Journal of Sociology*, 48 (2): 192–209.

Mortensen, J. (ed.) (1992) *The Future of Pensions in the European Community*. London: Centre for European Policy Studies/Brassey's.

Mosely, H.G. (1990) 'The social dimension of European integration', *International Labour Review*, 129 (2): 147–64.

Nader, R. and Wallach, L. (1996) 'GATT, NAFTA and the subversion of the democratic process', in J. Mander and E. Goldsmith (eds), *The Case Against the Global Economy and For a Turn Toward the Local*. San Francisco: Sierra Club Books.

Navarro, V. (1982) 'The crisis of the international capitalist order and its implications for the welfare state', *Critical Social Policy*, 2 (1): 43–61.

Navarro, V. (1998) 'Neoliberalism, "globalisation", unemployment, inequalities, and the welfare state', *International Journal of Health Services*, 28 (4): 607–82.

Nazir, P. (1990) *Local Development in the Global Economy*. Avebury: Aldershot.

Nicolaides, P. (1991) 'Investment policies in an integrated world economy', *The World Economy*, 14 (2): 121–37.

Norberg-Hodge, H. (1996) 'Shifting direction: from global dependence to local interdependence', in J. Mander and E. Goldsmith (eds), *The Case against the Global Economy and For a Turn Toward the Local*. San Francisco: Sierra Club Books.

OECD (1992) *International Direct Investment: Policies and Trends in the 1980s*. Paris: OECD.

OECD (1994) *The OECD Guidelines for Multinational Enterprises*. Paris: OECD.

OECD (1996a) *Globalisation of Industry: Overview and Sector Trends*. Paris: OECD.

OECD (1996b) *Trade, Employment and Labour Standards: A Study of Core Workers' Rights and International Trade*. Paris: OECD.

Ohmae, K. (1995a) *The End of the Nation State: the Rise of Regional Economies*. London: Harper Collins.

Ohmae, K. (1995b) 'Putting global logic first', *Harvard Business Review*, 73 (1): 119–25.

Olwig, K.F. (1999) 'Narratives of the children left behind: home and identity in globalised Caribbean families', *Journal of Ethnic and Migration Studies*, 25 (2): 267–84.

Oman, C. (1989) *New Forms of Investment in Developing Countries' Industries: Mining, Petrochemicals, Automobiles, Textiles, Food*. Paris: OECD.

Otting, A. (1994) 'The International Labour Organisation and its standard-setting activity in the area of social security', *Journal of European Social Policy*, 4 (1): 51–72.

Owoh, K. (1996) 'Fragmenting health care: the World Bank prescription for Africa', *Alternatives*, 21: 211–35.

Paccione, M. (1997) 'Local exchange trading systems as a response to the globalisation of capitalism', *Urban Studies*, 34 (8): 1179–99.

Palan, R., Abbott, J. and Deans, P. (1996) *State Strategies in the Global Political Economy*. London: Pinter.

Pape, W. (1999) 'Socio-cultural differences and international competition law', *European Law Journal*, 5 (4): 438–60.

Patel, P. and Pavitt, K. (1991) 'Large firms in the production of the world's technology: an important case of non-globalisation', *Journal of International Business Studies*, First Quarter: 1–21.

Pauly, L.W. and Reich, S. (1997) 'National structure and multinational corporate behaviour: enduring differences in the age of globalisation', *International Organisation*, 51 (1): 1–30.

Payne, A. (1996) 'The United States and its enterprise for the Americas', in A. Gamble and A. Payne (eds), *Regionalism and World Order*. Basingstoke: Macmillan.

Payne, A. and Gamble, A. (1996) 'Introduction: the political economy of regionalism and world order' in A. Gamble and A. Payne (eds), *Regionalism and World Order*. Basingstoke: Macmillan.

Pearce, R. and Pooni, G.S. (1996) *The Globalisation of R&D in Pharmaceuticals, Chemicals and Biotechnology: Some New Evidence*. Discussion Papers in International Investment and Business Studies, Series B, no. 213, University of Reading, Department of Economics.

Pérez Baltodano, A. (1999) 'Social policy and social order in transnational societies', in D. Morales-Gómez (ed.), *Transnational Social Policies: the New Development Challenges of Globalization*. London: Earthscan.

Perraton, J., Goldblatt, D., Held, D. and McGrew, A. (1997) 'The globalisation of economic activity', *New Political Economy*, 2 (2): 257–77.

Peters, J. and Wolper, A. (eds) (1995) *Women's Rights: Human Rights: International Feminist Perspectives*. London: Routledge.

Pettman, J.J. (1996) 'An international political economy of sex?', in E. Kofman and G. Youngs (eds), *Globalization: Theory and Practice*. London: Pinter.

Petrella, R. (1996) 'Globalization and internationalization: the dynamics of the emerging world order', in R. Boyer and D. Drache (eds), *States Against Markets: The Limits of Globalization*. London: Routledge.

Philip Davis, E. (1995) *Pension Funds: Retirement-Income Security and Capital Markets: An International Perspective*. Oxford: Clarendon.

Phillips, N. and Higgott, R. (1999) 'Global governance and the public domain: collective goods in a "post-Washington consensus" era', Centre for the Study of Globalisation and Regionalisation Working Paper, no. 47/99.

Pierson, P. (1994) *Dismantling the Welfare State? Reagan, Thatcher and the Politics of Welfare Retrenchment in the US and UK*. Cambridge: CUP.

Pierson, P. (1998) 'Irresistible forces, immovable objects: post-industrial welfare states confront permanent austerity', *Journal of European Public Policy*, 5 (4): 539–60.

Pierson, P. and Leibfried, S. (1995) 'The dynamics of social policy development', in S. Leibfried and P. Pierson (eds), *European Social Policy: Between Fragmentation and Integration*. Washington, DC: Brookings Institution.

Pitelis, C. (1991) 'Beyond the nation state? The transnational firm and the nation state', *Capital and Class*, 43: 131–52.

Pooley, S. (1991) 'The state rules, OK? The continuing political economy of nation states', *Capital and Class*, 43: 65–82.

Rajput, P. and Swarup, H.L. (eds) (1994) *Women and Globalisation: Reflections, Options and Strategies*. New Delhi: Ashish.

Ratinoff, L. (1999) 'Social-policy issues at the end of the 20th century', in D. Morales-Gómez (ed.), *Transnational Social Policies: The New Development Challenges of Globalization*. London: Earthscan.

Razavi, S. (1999) 'Seeing poverty through a gender lens', *International Social Science Journal*, 162: 473–81.

Reich, R. (1992) *The Work of Nations*. New York: Random House.

Rhodes, M. (1991) 'The social dimension of the single European market: national versus transnational regulation', *European Journal of Political Research*, 19: 245–80.

Rhodes, M. (1996) 'Globalization and West European welfare states: a critical review of recent debates', *Journal of European Social Policy*, 6 (4): 305–27.

Rhodes, M. (1997) 'The welfare state: internal challenges, external constraints', in M. Rhodes, P. Heywood and V. Wright (eds), *Developments in West European Politics*. London: Macmillan.

Rieger, E. and Leibfried, S. (1998) 'Welfare state limits to globalization', *Politics and Society*, 26 (3): 363–90.

Riker, J.V. (1995) 'From cooptation to cooperation and collaboration in government-NGO relations: toward an enabling policy environment for people-centred development in Asia', in N. Heyzer, J.V. Riker and A.B. Quizon (eds), *Government-NGO Relations in Asia: Prospects and Challenges for People-Centred Development*. Basingstoke: Macmillan.

Ritchie, C. (1996) 'Coordinate? Cooperate? Harmonise? NGO policy and operational coalitions', in T.G. Weiss and L. Gordenker (eds), *NGOs, the UN and Global Governance*. London: Lynne Rienner.

Roberts, J. (1995) *$1000 Billion a Day: Inside the Foreign Exchange Markets*. London: HarperCollins.

Robertson, R. (1992) *Globalization: Social Theory and Global Culture*. London: Sage.

Robinson, W. (1996) 'Globalisation: nine theses on our epoch', *Race and Class*, 38 (2): 13–31.

Robson, P. (1993) 'The new regionalism and developing countries', *Journal of Common Market Studies*, 31 (3): 329–45.

Room, G. (1999) *Social Exclusion, Solidarity and the Challenge of Globalisation*. Working Paper, no. 27, Bath Social Policy Papers, University of Bath.

Rose, H. (1986) 'Women and the restructuring of the welfare state', in E. Oyen (ed.), *Comparing Welfare States and their Future*. Hants: Gower.

Rosenau, J. (1990) *Turbulence in World Politics*. London: Harvester.

Ross, E.B. (1998) *The Malthus Factor: Poverty, Politics and Population in Capitalist Development*. London: Zed.

Ross, G. (1998) 'European integration and globalization', in R. Axtmann (ed.), *Globalization and Europe: Theoretical and Empirical Investigations*. London: Cassell.

Rowbotham, S. and Mitter, S. (eds) (1994) *Dignity and Daily Bread: New Forms of Economic Organising Among Poor Women in the Third World and the First*. London: Routledge.

Ruggie, J.G. (1983) 'International regimes, transactions and change: embedded liberalism in the postwar economic order', in S.D. Krasner (ed.), *International Regimes*. Ithaca, NY: Cornell University Press.

Ruigrok, W. and van Tulder, T. (1995) *The Logic of International Restructuring*. London: Routledge.

Sabel, C., O'Rourke, D. and Fung, A. (2000) 'Ratcheting labor standards: regulation for continuous improvement in the global workplace', 23 February, version 2.0, (http://www.Law.columbia.edu/sabel/papers/ratchPO.html).

Sachs, A. (1994) 'The last commodity: child prostitution in the developing world', *World Watch*, 7 (4): 24–30.

Salazar Parreñas, R. (2000) 'Migrant Filipina domestic workers and the international division of reproductive labor', *Economy and Society*, 14 (4): 560–81.

Samers, M. (1999) '"Globalisation", the geopolitical economy of migration and the "spatial vent"', *Review of International Political Economy*, 6 (2): 166–99.

Sanger, M. (1998) 'MAI: multilateral investment and social rights', paper to International Trade and Investment Agreements, Globalism and Social Policy seminar, Sheffield, December.

Sassen, S. (1984) 'Notes on the incorporation of Third World women into wage labor through immigration and offshore production', *International Migration Review*, 18 (4): 1144–67.

Sassen, S. (1986) *The Mobility of Labor and Capital: A Study in International Investment and Labor*. New York: CUP.

Sassen, S. (1998) *Globalization and Its Discontents*. New York: New Press.

Sauvin, S. (1996) 'International relations, social ecology and the globalization of environmental change', in J. Vogler and M.F. Imber (eds), *The Environment and International Relations*. London: Routledge.

Sayer, A. (1996) 'A review of Post-Fordism: a reader', *Capital and Class*, 59: 151–3.

Scharpf, F. (2000) 'The viability of advanced welfare states in the international economy: vulnerabilities and options', *Journal of European Public Policy*, 7 (2): 190–228.

Schoenberger, E. (1988) 'Multinational corporations and the new international division of labor: a critical appraisal', *International Regional Science Review*, 11 (2): 105–19.

Scholte, J.A. (2000) *Globalization: A Critical Introduction*. Basingstoke: Macmillan.

Scipes, K. (1992) 'Understanding the new labour movements in the "Third World": the emergence of social movement unionism', *Critical Sociology*, 19 (2): 81–101.

Sengenberger, W. and Wilkinson, F. (1995) 'Globalization and labour standards', in J. Mitchie and J. Grieve Smith (eds), *Managing the Global Economy*. Oxford: OUP.

Shaw, L. (1996) *Social Clauses*. London: Catholic Institute for International Relations.

Shiva, V. (1994) 'Conflicts of global ecology: environmental activism in a period of global reach', *Alternatives*, 19: 195–207.

Shiva, V. (1995) 'Social and environmental clauses: a political diversion', *Third World Resurgence*, 59: 2–7.

Shiva, V. (1997) 'How free is free India?', *Resurgence*, 183: 12–17.

Sklair, L. (1997) 'Social movements for global capitalism: the transnational capitalist class in action', *Review of International Political Economy*, 4 (3): 514–38.

Sklair, L. (1998a) 'Competing conceptions of globalisation', paper to XIV World Congress of Sociology, Montreal.

Sklair, L. (1998b) 'Globalisation and the corporations: the case of the California Global 500', *International Journal of Urban and Rural Research*, 22 (2): 195–215.

Smart, C. (1992) 'Disruptive bodies and unruly sex: the regulation of reproduction and sexuality in the nineteenth century', in C. Smart (ed.) *Regulating Womanhood: Historical Essays on Marriage, Motherhood and Sexuality*. London: Routledge.

Smillie, I. (1993) 'Changing partners: northern NGOs, northern governments', in I. Smillie and H. Helmich (eds), *Non-Governmental Organisations and Governments: Stakeholders for Development*. Paris: OECD Development Centre.

Smillie, I. (1995) *The Alms Bazaar: Altriusm Under Fire – Non-Profit Organizations and International Development*. London: Intermediate Technology Publications.

Smith, J. (1997) 'Characteristics of the modern transnational social movement sector', in J. Smith, C. Chatfield and R. Pagnucco (eds), *Transnational Social Movements and Global Politics: Solidarity Beyond the State*. New York: Syracuse University Press.

Smith, J., Pagnucco, R. and Chatfield, C. (1997) 'Social movements and world politics: a theoretical framework', in J. Smith, C. Chatfield and R. Pagnucco (eds), *Transnational Social Movements and Global Politics: Solidarity Beyond the State*. New York: Syracuse University Press.

Smith, M.P. (1995) 'The disappearance of world cities and the globalisation of local politics', in P.L. Knox and P.J. Taylor (eds), *World Cities in a World-system*. Cambridge: CUP.

Snyder, F. (1999) 'Governing economic globalisation: global legal pluralism and European law', *European Law Journal*, 5 (4): 334–74.

Sørensen, G. (1999) 'Sovereignty: change and continuity in a fundamental institution', *Political Studies*, 47 (3): 590–604.

Spybey, T. (1996) *Globalization and World Society*. Cambridge: Polity.

Srebeny-Mohammadi, A. (1997) 'The many faces of cultural imperialism', in P. Golding and P. Harris (eds), *Beyond Cultural Imperialism: Globalization, Communication and the New International Order*. London: Sage.

Stalker, P. (2000) *Workers Without Frontiers: The Impact of Globalization on International Migration*. Geneva: ILO.

Stallings, B. (1992) 'International influence on economic policy: debt, stabilization, and structural reform', in S. Haggard and R.R. Kaufman (eds), *The Politics of Economic Adjustment*. Princeton, NJ: Princeton University Press.

Standing, G. (1989) 'Global feminization through flexible labour', *World Development*, 17 (7): 1077–95.

Standing, G. (1996) 'Social protection in Central and Eastern Europe: a tale of slipping anchors and torn safety nets', in G. Esping-Andersen (ed.), *Welfare States in Transition: National Adaptations in Global Economies*. London: Sage.

Standing, G. (1999) *Global Labour Flexibility: Seeking Distributive Justice*. London: Macmillan.

Steven, R. (1990) *Japan's New Imperialism*. Basingstoke: Macmillan.

Stewart, M. (1994) *The Age of Interdependence: Economic Policy in a Shrinking World*. Cambridge: MIT Press.

Stitcher, S. and Parpart, J.L. (eds) (1990) *Women, Employment and the Family in the International Division of Labour*. Basingstoke: Macmillan.

Strange, S. (1986) *Casino Capitalism*. Oxford: Blackwell.

Strange, S. (1996) *The Retreat of the State: The Diffusion of Power in the World Economy*. Cambridge: CUP.

Stryker, R. (1998) 'Globalization and the Welfare State', *International Journal of Sociology and Social Policy*, 18 (2/3/4): 1–49.

Stubbs, P. (1998) 'Non governmental organisations and global social policy: towards a socio-cultural framework', in B. Deacon, M. Koivusalo and P. Stubbs (eds), *Aspects of Global Social Policy Analysis*. Helsinki: National Research and Development Centre for Welfare and Health.

Sum, N.L. (1996) 'The NICs and competing strategies of East Asian regionalism', in A. Gamble and A. Payne (eds), *Regionalism and World Order*. Basingstoke: Macmillan.

Swank, D. (1998) 'Funding the welfare state: globalization and the taxation of business in advanced market economies', *Political Studies*, XLVI: 671–92.

Swyngedouw, E. (1997) 'Neither global nor local: "glocalization" and the politics of scale', in K.R. Cox (ed.), *Spaces of Globlization: Reasserting the Power of the Local*. London: Guilford.

Sykes, R. and Alcock, P. (eds) (1998) *Developments in European Social Policy*. Bristol: Policy Press.

Tadiar, N.X.M. (1993) 'Sexual economies in the Asia-Pacific community', in A. Dirlik (ed.), *What's in a Rim? Critical Perspectives on the Pacific Region Idea*. Boulder, Colorado: Westview.

Tarrow, S. (1995) 'The Europeanization of conflict: reflections from a social movement perspective', *West European Politics*, 18 (2): 223–51.

Taylor-Gooby, P. (1997) 'In defence of second-best theory: state, class and capital in social policy', *Journal of Social Policy*, 26 (2): 171–92.

Teeple, G. (1995) *Globalization and the Decline of Social Reform*. Toronto: Garamond.

Townsend, P. (1993) *The International Analysis of Poverty*. Hemel Hempstead: Harvester Wheatsheaf.

Townsend, P. (1995) *The Rise of International Social Policy*. Bristol: Policy Press.

Townsend, P. and Donkor, K. (1996) *Global Restructuring and Social Policy: The Need to Establish an International Welfare State*. Bristol: Policy Press.

Tremewan, C. (1998) 'Welfare and governance: public housing under Singapore's party-state', in R. Goodman, G. White and H. Kwon (eds), *The East Asian Welfare Model: Welfare Orientalism and the State*. London: Routledge.

Tripp, C. (1995) 'Regional organizations in the Arab Middle East', in L. Fawcett and A. Hurrell (eds), *Regionalism in World Politics: Regional Organization and International Order*. Oxford: OUP.

UNCTAD (1994) *World Investment Report*. Geneva, United Nations Centre for Trade and Development.

UNDP (various years) *Human Development Report*. New York: UN.

UNESCAP (1988) *Transnational Corporations and Environmental Management in Selected Asian and Pacific Developing Countries*. Bangkok: UNESCAP.

UNRISD (1995) *States of Disarray: The Social Effects of Globalisation*. Geneva: UNRISD.

UNRISD (2000) *Visible Hands: Taking Responsibility for Social Development*. Geneva: UNRISD.

Vander Stichele, M. and Pennartz, P. (1996) *Making it Our Business – European NGO Campaigns on Transnational Corporations*. London: Catholic Institute for International Relations.

Verhulst, S. (1999) 'Diasporic and transnational communication: technologies, policies and regulation', *The Public Javnost*, 6 (1): 29–36.

Vivian, J. (1995) 'How safe are social safety nets? Adjustment and social sector restructuring in developing countries', *The European Journal of Development Research*, 7 (1): 1–25.

Wade, R. (1996) 'Globalization and its limits: reports of the death of the national economy are greatly exaggerated', in S. Berger and R. Dore (eds), *National Diversity and Global Capitalism*. Ithaca: Cornell University Press.

Walton, J. (1987) 'Urban protest and the global political economy: the IMF riots', in M.P. Smith and J.R. Fagin (eds), *The Capitalist City*. Oxford: Blackwell.

Wapner, P. (1995) 'Politics beyond the state: environmental activism and world civic politics', *World Politics*, 47: 311–40.

Ward, K. (1990) *Women Workers and Global Restructuring*. Cornell University: ILR Press.

Warde, I. (1994) 'La dérive des nouveaux produits financiers', *Le Monde Diplomatique*, pp. 15–16.

Waterman, P. (1998) *Globalization, Social Movements and the New Internationalisms*. London: Mansell.

Watson, A. (1992) *The Evolution of International Society*. London: Routledge.

Weiss, L. (1997) 'Globalization and the myth of the powerless state', *New Left Review*, 225: 3–27.

Weiss, L. (1999) 'Managed openness: beyond neoliberal globalism', *New Left Review*, 238: 126–40.

Whalley, D. (1992) 'CUFSTA and NAFTA: is WHFTA far behind?', *Journal of Common Market Studies*, 30 (2): 125–41.

Wilding, P. (1997) 'Globalization, regionalism and social policy', *Social Policy and Administration*, 31 (4): 410–28.

Wilkinson, R. and Hughes, S. (2000) 'Labor standards and global governance: examining the dimensions of institutional engagement', *Global Governance*, 6 (2): 259–77.

Willetts, P. (1996) 'Consultative status for NGOs at the UN', in P. Willetts (ed.), *The Conscience of the World: The Influence of Non-Governmental Organisations in the U.N. System*. London: Hurst.

Williams, F. (1989) *Social Policy: A Critical Introduction*. Cambridge: Polity.

Williams, F. (1994) 'Social relations, welfare and the post-Fordism debate', in R. Burrows and B. Loader (eds), *Towards a Post-Fordist Welfare State?* London: Routledge.

Williams, M. and Ford, L. (1999) 'The World Trade Organisation, social movements and global environmental management', *Environmental Politics*, 8 (1): 268–90.

Wincott, D. (1994) 'Is the treaty of Maastricht an adequate "constitution" for the European Union?', *Public Administration*, 72, Winter: 573–90.

Wolff, J. (1991) 'The global and the specific: reconciling theories of culture', in A.D. King (ed.), *Culture, Globalisation and the World-System: Contemporary Conditions for the Representation of Identity*. Basingstoke: Macmillan.

Wong, L. (1998) 'Social policy reform in China: any role for international organisations?', paper to GASPP seminar, Global Governance and Social Policy, 28–30 May, Kellokoski, Finland.

World Bank (1993) *The East Asian Miracle: Economic Growth and Public Policy*. Washington, DC: OUP.

World Bank (1997a) *World Development Report 1997: The State in a Changing World.* Washington, DC: OUP.

World Bank (1997b) *Old Age Security: Pension Reform in China.* Washington, DC: OUP.

World Bank (2000) *World Development Report 1999/2000: Entering the 21st Century.* World Bank: OUP.

(WTO) World Trade Organisation (1998a) *Education Services.* Background Note by the Secretariat, Council for Trade in Services. S/C/W/49.

(WTO) World Trade Organisation (1998b) *Health and Social Services.* Background Note by the Secretariat, Council for Trade in Services. S/C/W/50.

Wyatt-Walter, A. (1995) 'Regionalism, globalization, and world economic order', in L. Fawcett and A. Hurrell (eds), *Regionalism in World Politics: Regional Organization and International Order.* Oxford: OUP.

Wyckoff, A. (1993) 'Extension of networks of production across borders', *STI Review,* no. 13, Paris.

Yaghmaian, B. (1998) 'Globalization and the state: the political economy of global accumulation and its emerging mode of regulation', *Science and Society,* 62 (2): 241–65.

Yeates, N. (1999) 'Social politics and policy in an era of globalisation: critical reflections', *Social Policy and Administration,* 33 (4): 372–93.

Index